Trail Magic:
And the Art of Soft Pedaling

Trail Magic:
and the Art of Soft Pedaling

Illustrated and written by

Scott Thigpen

Edited by Kate Cleveland

Contributing Editors:
Kim Cross, Chris Freeman, Stacey Gordon

First Printing: 2014

ISBN 978-1-312-51731-

Scott Thigpen
HHB 1401 University Blvd
Birmingham, AL 35233

www.softpedaling.com

ISBN 978-1-312-51731-8

Dedication

To my wife, I never would have been able to do any of this
without you.

In loving memory of Heidi Peterson and Ray Porter.

Table of Contents

Acknowledgements

The events in this book happened because of some very important people.

First and foremost, many thanks to Faris Malki.

Faris runs and owns a chain of four bicycle stores in Birmingham known as Cahaba Cycles. Faris sponsored me during all of my training for the race. Without Faris and his awesome staff, I wouldn't have had any gear or bike to make it across the country. In addition, his mother, Barbara, and father, Kal, treated me like family. I have nothing but gratitude for their love and help.

The helping hands at Cahaba Cycles were also crucial: Zach, Pat, John, Brian and Mike. Especially Zach because we worked so closely and meticulously, crafting an awesome steed—my bicycle.

Tracy McKay was my coach for the race. As someone who completed the Ride Across America (RAAM) and set amazing records across the great state of Alabama, I was honored to have him train me for the Divide. He was one helluva coach leading up to Banff.

Kelli Jennings of Apex Nutrition introduced me to the staple of my diet, the green smoothie. That's such a simplified sentence, it doesn't even begin to describe the help she gave me. She helped me lose 55 lbs. and taught me what each and every thing does that I put in my mouth. Knowledge is power. Knowledge from an enthusiastic and awesome nutritionist is like unlocking the keys to the universe.

She literally wrote the book on this—you can purchase http://www.apexnutritionllc.com/fuelrightblog. It has everything in it that I used to lose the weight and fuel correctly.

Mollie Taylor who did everything behind the scenes like live updating my blog while I was gone, editing everything I published online and kept me laughing.

Last and certainly not least, my wife Kate, who put up with two years of training and all the craziness that ensued: the ups and downs, the tears and laughter, the frustration and happiness. I love you baby. Thank you for sticking with me during the two long years of training and for having my back during the race.

A few other folks that should be mentioned—angels who donated generously to make this dream come true: Zach, Stacey and Mike Davis, Pat Casey, Mike Garner, Jeff Rozycki, Tom Seest, Jen and Steve Nichols, Sunny and Owen Workman, Mom and Dad, Bert and Mary Carol Hitchcock, Amelia Baldwin, Grace Ragland, April and Brandon Penn, Darrell Hobson, Chris Freeman, Beth Pierpoint and my second moms Diane and Ginni of Mulberry Gap in Ellijay, Georgia. You guys really shocked me with your generous donations and I cannot thank you enough.

Other people who gave of their time, finances and effort are Anna Lloyd, Stacey Gordon, Melissa Daniel, Andy Amick, Billy Ritch, Ben Chuang, Mitch Moses, Corbin Camp, Anna Hamel, Allison Lowery, Harold Woodman, Mark Thigpen, Robert Evans, Charles Moore, Monty Morris, Phillip & Katie McGinnis, Mary McWhirter, Tim Cotton, Pete Foret, Véronique Vanblaere, Chris Loy, Lynn Winchester, Kim C, Hugh Harvey, Brynne MacCann, John Kenney, Bruce Dickman, Michael Jeffreys, Randall Naccari, Douglas & Charlotte Daughhetee, Meredith McLaughlin, Thea Hubbard, Ben Welnak, Linda Reimann, Carmen Bates, Karen Tallon, Andrea and Casey Fannin, Robert Brunson., Tuan Diep, Jimmy Brewer, Marianne Lins, Jan Jenkins, Gina Hamel, Thea and Daniel Gilbert, Cody Humphrey, Nathan Hodge, Langston Hereford and Beary McBearington for not eating me!

I had to streamline the book thus some people I had the pleasure riding with got cut out of the story. You are no less important to me and I enjoyed riding and racing with you, I just had to make edits to make the book work well as a whole. I still have the paragraphs saved on a previous draft and if you want to see them, feel free to contact me.

These awesome people that I got the pleasure to ride with were: Dave Rooney, Jeff Mullen, Karlos Bernart, Peter Halle, Ezra Mullen, Eric Foster, Peter Maindonald, Hal Russell, Sara Dallman, Steve Martine, Thomas Borst, Andrew Stuntz, Brett Simpson, Brian Steele, Chris Tompkins, Mirko Haeker, Max Morris, Greg Barrett, Fred Arden, Richard Costello and Michael Gruenert.

Inevitably I have forgotten someone so let me stress how much I apologize for doing that. My memory is sharp, but it's not that sharp to remember 160+ people from the race! So if I left you off the list, let's just say your name is "Kevin."

Thank you so much Kevin, it was awesome riding with you.

Foreword

The last time Scott Thigpen had been on a bicycle, he was a 12-year-old kid with a love of Star Wars and Disney. Twenty-five years later, he was sedentary and rapidly gaining weight. Hello Couch, meet Potato. It was time for a change, for both his body and his mind. Determined to start moving again, Scott climbed on a bicycle one summer afternoon and started pedaling. By the end of the driveway, he was gasping for breath.

A year later, Scott was still trying to stay upright on a mountain bike when he watched <u>Ride The Divide</u>, a movie about an event so daunting, so exhilarating, so tough that few attempt it. But Scott couldn't stop thinking about it. The Tour Divide, a nearly 3000-mile mountain bike race along the spine of the Continental Divide, was his new dream.

Known as one of the toughest races in the world, the Tour Divide is an unsupported off-road event. If your tire is flat, you fix it. If you run out of water, you must find more. If you're caught in the middle of nowhere, exhausted and blurry-eyed? Find a spot to nap amidst nature and try not to bother the Grizzlies.

Starting from zero, Scott trained for two years while maintaining a busy family life, a freelance career illustrating for the Wall Street Journal and The Atlanta Journal Constitution, and a teaching gig at the University of Alabama at Birmingham. Scott was preparing for the ride of his life.

In June of 2013, he climbed on that bicycle again, this time to race against 167 other people from all over the world on a trek that would take him from Canada to Mexico in 22 days.

Captured through Scott's vivid words and wondrous illustrations, this is the tale of one man's quest to break free of the typical life and conquer his wildest dream.

- Amy Bickers

Preface

Thank you for picking up this book and reading my story. This is not a story about mountain biking, being exceptionally fit, winning awards, or getting accolades. This is a story about achievement and what anyone can do about anything they want to do, if they stick to it.

The pages to follow are a couple of years of my life and how one event changed everything for me. I hope you enjoy.

Oh, and it also should be noted I've never written a book before, so I apologize if this isn't on par with Harry Potter. I'm just a

mountain biker with a graphic designer day job, it's a miracle I can string two sentences together sometimes.

This book is around a year and a half of my life, after work with a lot of volunteer help however much credit goes to my wife who helped tremendously with getting it together especially in the 11th hour.

If you find an error in the book or would just like to say hello, I can be found at these places:

Facebook: https://www.facebook.com/sthig

Twitter: https://twitter.com/sthig

My blog I kept for two years while training for the race:

http://www.Driven2Divide.com

There is an interactive story that goes along with this book that includes art, video and pictures from the divide. To access this, please follow this link:

http://www.softpedaling.com/interactive

Introduction

Somewhere in Montana…

Flames licked the trees above me as I attempted to wrap my bandana around my mouth to avoid inhaling the smoke. It was a struggle to get the cloth secure around my mouth and nose since my hands were numb from trudging through the freezing temps over the mountain pass known as Richmond Peak on the Tour Divide Route. At the base of the mountain it'd been warm, but up here on the ridge it was a frozen nightmare with the trees ablaze where lightning had struck one and there was now a forest fire. My GPS was blinking "low battery" and I'd not had any food for the past 4 hours since I had to ditch all of it because of the dense population of Grizzlies that lived in the area and I didn't want to risk attracting one.

When I took a step to the left my foot slipped and kicked some snow off the mountain. I looked down to watch the snow fall on top of the tips of the trees that I was above, or at least what I could see as since my helmet light was dying as well. With my heart beating out of my chest, my hands numb, my stomach growling, light dimming and my GPS dying, I took one tender step forward to keep myself balanced on the side of Richmond Peak's narrow trail, trying not to slip off the side of the mountain and that's when I felt a squish.

August 2012, The North Georgia Mountains

"Bear crap…" I said, "bear crap every damned step of the way here, Diane," my eyes wild as I told Diane and Ginni, the ladies who run Mulberry Gap Retreat, a mountain-biker's haven in Ellijay, Georgia. I sat at a wooden picnic table in the guest barn while they made me a breakfast big enough to fuel last 150 or so miles of the Trans North Georgia Adventure, a

350 mile race from the South Carolina border to the Alabama border across the Blue Ridge Mountains. It was my big training ride for the Tour Divide and what I considered its "meaner little sister" with its 56,000 feet of climbing, a fourth of the Divide's elevation.

Ryan Sigsby, a fellow racer, was also at Mulberry Gap. He had been there for a few hours already and was resting as well. Diane and Ginni brought us over a huge plate of eggs and pancakes and said "Here you go boys, eat up. You won't finish this race if you don't eat."

As we gobbled our breakfast in silence, I poured syrup all over my pancakes and continued to devour them. Ryan looked up at me and said, "So, you think the Divide could be any worse than this?"

Trail Magic and the Art of Soft Pedaling

The Tour Divide

Trail Magic

— A term coined by Appalachian Trail thru-hikers to describe unexpected assistance from strangers, often appearing right at the greatest moment of need, in the form of food, shelter, or encouragement.

The Tour Divide. A 2,700-mile race from Banff, Canada to the south border of New Mexico, this is an unsanctioned and unsupported race...

I had become seduced by it and couldn't get it out of my brain. For two years I trained tirelessly and studied up on it as best as possible. I had no idea what I was getting myself into but suffice it to say that even as prepared as I was, I wasn't prepared enough. The Tour Divide Race was an absolute monster, but a beautiful monster. The route is alive, breathing and waiting to break you as you wind down the tail of the dragon. The Tour Divide is both beautiful and menacing, and each year several knights go into the beast's lair to see if they will come out victorious. This is my story of staring down the monster.

The decision to do this race was not instant. I was inspired by a movie filmed back in 2009 called "Ride the Divide," a documentary about the Tour Divide Race. I remember seeing it and thinking, Wow what a cool thing! I called my wife at work.

"Hey honey, I want you to watch this movie with me—it's really awesome!"

Later, Kate and I watched it together. The film showcased several racers going down country roads and talking to friendly backwoods people. The snow, the outdoors, the openness all seemed so wonderful to me. The music, the characters—*the life*—was enthralling. I loved it so much I watched it again by myself, then yet another time with our local mountain bike chapter, the Birmingham Urban Mountain Pedalers (BUMP).

I began dreaming about the race, about spending weeks out on the Continental Divide camping under the stars, cooking by the fire, meeting unique and awesome racers and being one with nature. At first it was just a pipe dream. Then one day, it wasn't.

I'd been an adjunct professor at the University of Alabama at Birmingham (UAB), where I was teaching a class that let out at 8:30 pm. Being an adjunct professor is not the most glamorous job. The maintenance staff had it better than me as at least they had full time benefits and retirement. Usually near the end of the semester I was completely burned out.

One night I left work and didn't text Kate to let her know I was leaving. I always text Kate when I'm getting ready to go home, especially after evening classes. But I was such in a fog I forgot. I decided to take an alternate route home and just drove around in silence for a while. I didn't get home until 10 pm. When I walked in Kate was livid, wondering where I had been. I couldn't even remember.

"You need some direction!" she said sternly.

I looked at her and said, "I think you're right."

If I tell Kate I will do something, I usually aim to do it so I did some research on how to organize your life. I found a book called Getting Things Done by David Allen, which was about organizing your life. In the first few chapters, David talks about setting a goal. While reading the book, I had the movie "Ride the Divide" on in the background for a fourth time. What if I made that my goal!? I thought about it and said to myself, "I could make that my goal!" And I did. I would spend the next two years preparing for one of the most life-altering things I'd ever done.

June 9, 2013-Atlanta

"Sorry, I didn't mean to bark, I'm really stressed out." My family and I were in the airport hotel in Atlanta and I was flying out the next day to Banff, Canada. I was nervous, sleep-deprived, and had come up with every excuse to quit the Tour Divide Race (TDR) before I even started it.

Kate suggested we go to the pool and let the kids swim while we hung out We eventually joined the tween kids, Ethan and Emma in the pool, throwing a ball and enjoying the warm water. I thought of just how luxurious this was and I couldn't believe I was willingly going to throw myself into a month's worth of minimalistic bike racing that would have me touching three countries. Every time I thought about it, I'd get nauseated.

The next morning, red-eyed and nervous, I rose from a sleepless night, went down for breakfast. Everyone could feel the 800-pound gorilla in the room—the fact that I'd be leaving for a month. My 24 months of 20-hour training weeks for the Tour Divide had left our entire family fatigued. Kate called it my midlife crisis, the bike standing in for the red corvette while the race became my hot mistress.

After choking down breakfast, I grabbed coffee at the airport, which only amped my nerves. As I entered the security line, Ethan, my 12-year-old stepson, started to cry. I told him I'd be back as soon as possible. Kate started to tear up, too, and I gave her a big hug. Emma, my pragmatic stepdaughter was stoic, but sweet. I'd never been away from my family for an entire month before. As I entered into the maze of the security line, my family receded until all I could see were sad little silhouettes.

As I stood in line, trying to swallow the lump in my throat, I thought about how I could lighten the mood. That's when I noticed the guy behind me, an elderly man with a big nose, who looked like one of those grumpy old men who says things like, "You smell like crap, life." I grabbed my phone and texted Kate.

See that guy behind me? I just farted on him.

My family roared with laughter and I went through the terminal.

August 2012—Ellijay, Georgia

I looked at my watch. All 30 of us racers had been waiting too long. I was a wreck waiting at Mulberry Gap for the last racer to show up so we could get shuttled to the South Carolina border to start the race known the Trans North Georgia Adventure (TNGA).

"Okay so the last guy should be here any minute now," said our shuttle driver, Matt as we all waited.

I hate being late for anything. My grandmother used to say if you were 10 minutes early, that was almost 11 minutes late. I'm early for everything, and being held up drives me crazy. I wanted to get to the race start on the Georgia-South Carolina border so we could eat, sleep, and start racing our way to Alabama.

Finally, the last racer pulled up in his car, got out, and apologetically chuckled.

"Man, sorry guys! I got held up getting here, my bad!"

His name was Scott McConnell. I wanted to wring his neck.

June 9, 2013—The Harstell Jackson Atlanta Airport

"We're sorry to inform you folks, but the plane has been delayed in another state by a few hours," a nasally voice said on the airport intercom.

My blood boiled. I knew this would cause me to miss the shuttle from Calgary to Banff and I was going to have to make sleeping arrangements at the airport, which would ultimately mean a bench. I sat and rocked back and forth in my seat on the tarmac. I felt the wheels of the plane start to slowly roll and then finally the airplane took off and I was heading north.

O Canada

When we landed at 1 a.m., and the Calgary airport was empty and dark. "Reckon anything is open?" I asked a guy walking next to me.

"No, nope," he said without breaking stride. So much for friendly Canadians.

I was looking for a bench to sleep on when I heard a familiar "clickity clickity clickity" sound, the hub of a bike wheel turning. Behind me was a guy with a bike set up to race the Tour Divide. Excitedly I turned and yelled…

August 2012: Day 2 of the TNGA

"RIDER!"

It was 3 or 4 a.m. Somewhere in the woods outside Helen, Georgia. I was lost, traveling the wrong way into Helen, trying to regroup. The lady yelling was another racer, Ruth Cunningham, who races many of the Eastern endurance races—in the right direction. She was tough, fast, and devoid of nonsense.

"What are you doing!? You're going the wrong way!"

I explained to her that I was turned around and "out of sorts."

It had been a long night.

I had been riding with a guy named Chris and his brother-in-law. We were making great time, but then his brother-in-law bonked. It's an awful state every racer tries to avoid, when you run out of fuel and your body hits a wall, along with your mind, leading to fatigue, excessive grumpiness, and irrational decisions.

The in-laws decided to set up camp in the middle of the night on a dirt road at the crossroads of Backwoods and Nowhere, where you didn't have to be bonking to imagine might be home to monsters, zombies, oversized bears, and banjo-playing locals. Stopping seemed like a bad idea to me. I figured I could cover more ground at night because I was still wide-awake. Which is one of the lies you tell yourself when you're too scared to sleep on a dirt road in the dark hills of Georgia not far from where Deliverance was filmed.

As I continued through the night, bats flew straight at my lights, whizzing past my ears. Unlike the bats I'd seen in Alabama, these had the wingspans of Pterodactyls.

I continued to ride through the night with headphones, listening to upbeat pop music such as Britney Spears, Hanson and B.O.B. to keep my mood happy. Somewhere between Nowheresville and Youwillprobablydiehereville, my headlamp went dead. I had one tiny backup light, which I held with my teeth as I attempted to find my way on single-track and dirt roads. I was cold, nervous, lost, and just wanted to find a hotel to regroup.

And that's about when I ran into Ruth, who informed me in less than soothing tones that I was headed the wrong way.

After listening to my story, Ruth shrugged.

"Wanna climb the next pass with me and we can just camp at the top?" she offered.

I knew about this next pass—Hog's Pen, an infamous climb that brings cyclists to their knees—and also knew it was in bear country.

"It sounds great, but I've got to go double back and do the part I missed," I said. "Plus I just want to reset and get things in order."

We parted ways and went on.

June 10th, 4:00 a.m.—Banff, Canada

Banff got a little warmer when I saw the fellow rider in the dark airport.

"Hey! You're a Tour Divide rider!" I said excitedly.

"Yep. And you?"

His name was Jeff. I introduced myself.

"Oooh, the guy that blogs about his adventures," he said. "Howya doing?"

I told him I was looking for a bench to sleep on.

"Oh I'm just going to ride on into Banff tonight, want to join?"

Banff was about 70 to 80 miles away.

I went back to bench hunting. As I strolled through the empty airport, I saw some lights go off in a spot with a bench. I rolled my jacket up like a pillow, stretched out on the bench and settled in to sleep.

Which lasted around five minutes.

First it was the whirring of a vacuum. Then the occasional person laughing or chatting. Just as I felt myself drifting off, the baggage claim machines started to run tests.

Wearily I thought about getting up went to Tim Horton's for something high octane. That's when eyes got heavy and I dozed for a moment.

What seemed to only be seconds later, I stirred. I opened one eye and tried to shake the cobwebs out of my head.

It felt like I was somewhere between severely drunk and the hangover that follows a beer binge. I rolled my head to the left and saw a guy sitting next to me. He was tall, skinny, and holding a bike helmet. My bloodshot eyes burned.

"Tour Divide?"

"Yes," he said with an accent I couldn't quite place. "And you?"

His name was Alex Harris, and he was from Johannesburg, South Africa.

"So are you ready for this race?" I asked.

He'd never done anything of this length, but had done some fairly tough races in South Africa and felt confident he'd do okay on the 2013 Tour Divide Race (in which he would place third overall). Almost instantly another man showed up. Yair Ahmias, 63, was from Tel Aviv, Israel, and appeared to be in excellent shape. I was so excited to meet people from different countries. Even in my sleep-deprived state I tried to be enthusiastic asking bunches of questions of what like the culture and lifestyles are like in their respective countries.

I stood up to stretch, and my body reminded me I'd had no sleep. I saw a portly old man stroll to the area where tickets can be purchased for the shuttle to Banff.

"One ticket please," I said.

"You look like hell, man," the old man responded.

I told him my story of sleepless woe.

"Hey, the shuttle doesn't leave for another 3 hours," he said. "We have a coach room here behind me with a couch and a blanket, you want to just crash in there?"

I couldn't have gotten in there quickly enough. I closed the door, turned off the lights and within minutes I was sound asleep on the couch. It was my first bit of trail magic on the race.

In a vivid dream state, I dreamt about missing the bus and missing the race. Strangely, I knew I was dreaming.

Oh god... Have I overslept? I'm still in a deep sleep. Scott, wake up, WAKE UP, W A K E U P !

I woke up abruptly. Where was I? What was I doing? Where the hell was Kate?

I frantically scooted around for a bit and then I realized I was still in the coach room waiting for the shuttle. I felt like I'd been asleep for hours, I poked my head out and the portly man was sitting there.

"How long has it been? Have I missed the shuttle?"

"Nope! You've been in there for 30 minutes. I'll wake you up when it's time to leave." Relieved I went back to sleep.

October 8th, 2009—Birmingham, Alabama

The alarm went off at 3:45 a.m. Kate was still sound asleep as I got up, grabbed my workout clothes, and was off to spin class. I'd been working on getting up earlier and earlier as I came to enjoy the stillness of the morning and the sight of sun coming up.

While I loved going to spin class, the drive there was always stressful. I had to beat not one but two trains that blocked the crossings and chug along at a snail's pace, always when I needed to be somewhere. To top it off, my bladder would let me know NOW is the time it needed attention as I frantically sipped more coffee, so by the time I got to spin, my heart rate was already through the roof and I was good and warmed up.

I always picked a bike in the back so I could clock-watch.

"We're just going to open up the legs, get your heart rate up to around 65% of max at the end of this song," the instructor said. "You have five minutes."

I'd known Stacey Davis for about four or five months after joining the mountain bike community. She said if I joined her spin class it would help me with my biking, especially with how new I was to the sport. I was overweight by about 50 pounds and could barely ride a bike, but spin class seemed to make riding a bit easier with each class. I soon got addicted to them and went every week...despite the trains and my ill-timed bladder.

Stacey and I became very close friends and I always looked forward to chatting after each spin class. We'd talk about bikes, exercise, and life. She'd mentioned she was interested in doing a race called the Leadville 100 one day.

"So what is that? Some kind of ride through the woods or something?"

She said it was a mountain bike century, a 100-mile race across some of Colorado's highest altitudes. I told her that I wanted to do the Tour Divide.

"Oh Scott," she said. "You need to start with something smaller—you don't even have the base for that."

"What's a base?" I asked.

"My point exactly. Why don't you choose a smaller race like the Big Frog or maybe even the Cohutta 100?"

June 10 a.m.—Calgary Airport

There was a knock at the door.

"Sir, we're about to leave for Banff, are you ready?"

"Yep, I'm ready!"

"Didjya get any sleep?"

I smiled and said, "Well a few winks here and there, enough to dream for a moment."

I walked outside the airport and the cold wind surrounded me. Alex and Yair were climbing aboard and I followed them.

"No bike?" the driver said.

"No bike. It's on its way."

As we pulled out of the airport and started going through Calgary, it didn't seem as pretty or as "magical" as I expected. I dozed. I awoke when I felt a nudge from Alex.

"Hey Scott...check it out."

There is no picture, rendering, or illustration that could describe what I saw through the window. In shades of purple, blue and grey, the snow-covered mountains extended into the clouds. I lost my breath for a moment, then whipped out my phone and started snapping, knowing that none of my photos would do justice to the sight.

The lobby of the YWCA in Banff was littered with bikes and riders waiting to check in. Behind the desk was a wiry, generously pierced teenager with a tattoo on his wrist that said: FUK U.

"Name." he muttered, not bothering to raise his spiky head.

"Scott Thigpen."

"Don't see it."

"I registered over a year ago, I have the confirmation email right here."

He looked around, pressed a few buttons then went back and got the manager. The manager, who couldn't have been more than 20, took 20 minutes to come out of her office. She looked as put-out as the first kid about having to find my reservation.

"See?" She said to the spiky-hair kid. "Right here: Thigpen."

The kid looked at me with apathy.

"Here you go, here's a key and here's the Wi-Fi passcode for the day. You're downstairs."I walked downstairs with my duffle bag and found my dorm room. I knew I'd be sharing it with other bikers and hikers in the area but was not prepared for what was next.

As I opened the door to a room with eight bunk beds, I was met with a smell that was the olfactory love child between a locker room and a college bar. I waded through beer cans littering the floor. Tour Divide bikes leaned against bunk beds, and trekking poles lay scattered beside overnight backpacks.

Well, Scott. This is what life is going to be for the next month, better make the best of it.

I found the only open bed, a top bunk that wobbled horribly. Every plug was occupied by charging devices. Clothes exploded all over the bathroom.

Jesus! Who lives like this!?

I showered off and went upstairs hoping for some fresh air. There was a little cafe in the YWCA. Behind the register, a manager was showing a new hire the ropes of the job. I walked up and grabbed an apple and ordered a beer.

"Is that all, sir?"

I blinked. That accent definitely wasn't Canadian.

"Um, yeah. You're not from here are you?"

"No I'm from Australia."

"Oh, why are you in Canada?"

"Oh it sounded like a good idea. That's $9.75 please."

I blinked again.

"For an apple and a beer!?"

"Yep."

While eating my overpriced lunch, I watched Tour Divide riders milling about with their bikes. Some looked intense, while others were relaxed, laughing and chatting. I wished I'd had my bike but it was still in Utah making its way up to Canada on the back of a friend's car.

"You're Scott...right?" someone said as I was finishing off my nine-dollar beer.

"Yes, yeah that's me. Who are you?"

"I'm Sean! We met on the internet, remember?"

I didn't remember; I am horrible with names. In fact, I told everyone whom I had met on the Internet before the Tour Divide that I was really bad with names and would just refer to everyone as "Kevin." I thought for a moment and then said it finally had hit me, and now I remembered.

Sean had bright blue eyes, and was tall, young and thin. Dressed in jeans a long-sleeve shirt; he was pretty chilled out compared to how uptight I was.

"So did they stick you in a crap hole with a bunch of bros as well?" I asked.

"Huh? What are you talking about?"

"You know, the living conditions for the next few days. I had to climb over a mountain of clothes, beer cans, and god-knows-what-else just to get to my bunk."

"No, no it's just me in a nice room by myself. There's three other beds in there, that's all."

I was instantly jealous.

"Man, you lucked out. I bet I don't get one ounce of sleep for the next few days, not a good way to start out the race."

Sean thought for a moment.

"Well why don't you ask to trade rooms and just stay in mine?"

"No, no no," I said. "That wouldn't be fair to someone else who had the room booked." But then I reconsidered. You know, this is a race, and I need to be at my best...and the early bird does get the worm...

So I went to the front desk and said, "Can I switch rooms with him?"

The young punk grimaced and let out a long sigh while pressing some buttons on the computer.

"Sure, yeah, whatever..."

I abandoned the bro-hole and moved into Sean's room. It was clean, had one bike in it, and smelled of, well, nothing. It also had a nice window, which offered both a view and a pleasant breeze. I stretched out on the bottom bunk and fell into a deep, guilt-free sleep.

That night I dreamt about what it'd be like on the Divide race and how it'd be great to be up against my racing buddy Scott McConnell keeping each other's morale up and bantering all the way to finish line.

August 2012: 20 miles left on the TNGA

"Man, it's good to hear you make a joke again" Scott McConnell said. "I thought I'd lost you there for a moment."

Scott had indeed lost me there for a moment, which began about the time I realized my phone had fallen out of my bag and was somewhere, miles back, on the trail. I knew instantly how it had happened: During a quick break, I had discovered phone service in the middle of the woods. Excited, I texted Kate to tell her I was okay and nearing the end of the race.

A few hours later, when my phone was gone, I realized that when I put my phone back in my bag, I'd forgotten to zip up the pouch, and when we started down the rocky terrain it bounced out. I handled it by becoming grumpy, pitiful, withdrawn, and snappy with Scott.

After a spell I regained my composure and my sense of humor, but it was largely due to Scott's never ending happy disposition that cheered me up. By the end of the TNGA, I had gained a lifelong friend. We'd worked so well together to keep each other going and had come in middle-of-the-pack for the 2012 race across Georgia.

"Man I hope this happens on the Tour Divide, you and me getting to race together," I said.

"Definitely!" Scott said with a laugh. "You're great to ride with!"

10 a.m. June 11, 2013: Banff

I was in my bunk bed reading when the door swung open and it was Scott McConnell. I jumped up and yelled *"Scott! Man, so good to see you again"* I ran up, gave him a giant (manly) hug. "Glad you are here!" My nerves ebbed a little knowing I'd have a racing buddy for at least a leg or two.

That night many other Tour Divide riders started checking into the YWCA. There was a giant common room where the racers would gather and chat. Veterans were there beating their chest telling horror stories of just how tough it was last year and how they braved it all with three broken legs, half eaten by a bear, and still managed to get fifth place overall. One guy, Max was particularly chatty about his venture last year, talking about all the horrible things he endured. "Well why are you back?" I asked.

He remarked that he wanted to do it again and be faster, quicker and also document his trip.

Sean came in and announced, "Hey have you heard about Billy Rice? He's trekking his way up through Montana, and he'll be in Canada before you know it! Check out this video he just posted."

A crowd of people ran over to Sean and watched the video on his phone. I'd heard about this Billy guy starting in New Mexico and riding his bike up to Canada, only to turn around and go back down to New Mexico.*Sheesh, and I thought I was nuts!*

After the Billy Rice Fan Club stopped swarming around Sean's phone, I watched the video. It was Billy talking about how sleep deprived and tired he was. He was crossing some creek and looked happily fatigued. I was a little intimidated and figured he must be some kind of mutant athlete.

Watching the video, though, gave me the great idea to document my trip as well. While I like photography, I'm a little gun shy about filming myself. But I thought the people back home would like to follow along, and it'd be a way that Kate at least could see me...even as dorky as I'd look.

During all the bravado talk by the veterans, a couple of kids walked in wearing matching Whiskey shirts. (Whiskey is a brand of bicycle fork.)

Fans? I wondered maybe they worked for Whiskey and wanted to cheer everyone on. The girl was very tall, slender with cropped hair and glasses. The guy next to her was noticeably shorter than her, with a swipe of hair that fell in his face. They spoke to a few people, walked around the room introducing themselves, and then came up to me. There was a near 20-year difference between us; they could have been my kids.

"Hey, I'm Taylor and this is Kristen, see you at the starting line?"

"You're racing?"

"Well yeah, we didn't fly up from Columbus, Ohio for nothing."

Apri 15, 2013: Birmingham

"How many miles so far?"

I was nearing my 12th straight hour on the indoor trainer when the message popped up.

"I'm almost at 200, Paul," I typed back.

"Holy cow! Man, I'm going to buy you a pizza and have it delivered to you right now!"

Paul, from Utah, was also training up for the race, and we had been in touch for a few months online. My coach, Tracy McKay, had me scheduled for a 400-mile week. Since I still had to work, I opted for the trainer, as that seemed the fastest way possible. Paul was completely baffled at this, and had been requesting updates ali day long . He wasn't alone. Who pulls a 200-mile ride straight locked into a trainer with no breaks? People who are nuts, that's who.

SCOTT! WAY TO GO! WE'RE ALL CHEERING YOU ON! texted Gina Hamel, a dear friend of mine.

When I finished the 200-mile trainer beast of a ride, Gina and her sister Anna both wrote accolades cheering me on as I about collapsed on the couch. The Hamel sisters would be my best cheerleaders during the entire race.

"So how are you getting your bike to Canada?" Paul inquired.

I had really not thought about it much.

"I don't know, if I ship it, it could get delayed in customs, and if I bring it on the plane, it could get damaged."

I thought about it for a moment.

"Hey, you're driving up to Canada, can I ship my bike to you and have you bring it up there?"

"Sure, man."

He said he would not be up until two days before the race but that was fine. I wasn't really keen on shipping my bike, which is worth more than my car, to a complete stranger, but Paul seemed to be a reputable guy (and he was). I had my bike packed up and shipped to him by my local bike shop sponsor, Cahaba Cycles, about 2 weeks before the race. You would have thought my heart had been ripped from my chest.

4 p.m. June 12th: Banff

Two days before the race I sat outside waiting on Paul to arrive. It seemed like an eternity watching the sun go down but finally late that afternoon he pulled up and I saw the my bike box strapped on top of his SUV. I meticulously pulled out each piece, making sure not to damage the parts. Everything seemed to be intact, so I started assembling. Paul helped and we caught up a bit while I put the bike together. Then, when I placed the rear wheel on the frame, it wiggled loosely.

"Uh oh…" I said.

"What?" Paul said.

"Well this is not good, the hub, it's all wobbly, it's making the back tire wobble all together."

What could have caused the wobble? That little piece of metal was worth more than what I could make in forty thousand years. And it was supposed to be indestructible. Taylor walked over and looked at it.

"Hey, didn't you race the Cohutta 100 this year?"

The Cohutta is a 100-mile endurance race that starts at the Ocoee River Welcome Center in Tennessee and follows single-track and dirt roads into Georgia and back with about 14,000 feet of elevation. I had tried to tackle the Cohutta in 2012, but foolishly got eaten alive attempting it. After getting disqualified for failing to make a mid-race cutoff time, I vowed to come back and race it the following year. Scott McConnell and I met up and camped for the 2013 race, and even though we were at the trailhead, we both nearly slept through it. When we woke up, we were met with dismal, cold rain.

Which of course meant: cold mud.

April 24th, 2013: The Cohutta 100

The ice-cold rain spattered my helmet and my jacket. I watched the beads of water roll off and soak into my kit, instantly making me colder.

"I want to thank you for coming out to this very cold and wet Cohutta 100. We hope you have a good time. But be warned, that single track is going to be muddy!"

I was back to tackle the Cohutta 100. It was the only race in which I'd been disqualified for failing to make the time cutoff. To help make sure that I finished the race as well as the Tour Divide, I would need a reliable monster of a bike.

Faris Malki, owner of Cahaba Cycles, generously sponsored me with an all-steel singlespeed Niner bike built up by Zach Davis, my main wrench. It was shiny, red, and so beautiful I was nervous about getting it dirty. But bikes are made for being dirty, not pretty, and I figured 100 miles of extremely rough terrain was enough to break it in.

The 2013 Cohutta 100 delivered a lot of rain, mud, and cold. The bike took a fair beating over the course of the day, but held up well. I didn't realize how much mud crept into the back hub, destroying the bearings inside and causing a nagging wobble.

June 12th: 7pm Banff

The air was cool in Banff but I was hot under the collar about The Wobble.

"Sean, can you look at this?"

Sean, a mechanic, disassembled the hub,

"It seems to be okay man, I think it's just going to wobble."

"Well, not much I can do." I said.

There's a magical moment in every cyclist's life and that magic occurs every time he gets on a bike. The way the brain stabilizes to keep the body's balance on the bike, the first turn of the pedal, the "click-click-click" of the drivetrain in motion—it's one of the best feelings in the world.

I hopped on my bike and instantly felt the joy of being able to ride again. I had so much nervous energy that I rode out into downtown Banff and hammered around the postcard town, zig-zagging through the streets and darting off on a trail. I zoned out, noting the waning sun and feeling the cool breeze. I loved this bike.

I powered up a long, winding trail, and it was a wonderful. My legs needed this. I got to the top and listened to the howling wind while overlooking Banff. It was beautiful, I was going to race the Tour Divide, and I was going to finish it. This was the start, this was me preparing to make it to Mexico!

Mexico… I looked to the south and thought, *Wow, that's really far.*

I rode back down the hill, hit the trail, and whipped around the corners before heading back to the dorm. It was getting very dark now and I had one more day in Canada before the race started. Preoccupied, I nearly took out an elk that was standing right in front of me. It didn't move. I didn't move.

Steady there old man, let me just get your picture.

It darted off before I could draw my phone. Twice my size, this thing could have easily made quick work of me.

The next morning I went out to the local cafe connected to the YWCA and had breakfast with Scott McConnell and a few other Tour Divide racers. We talked about past races, thoughts on what we were going to do, and basically connected by telling stories. As I looked over our group huddled together chatting over coffee I started to think, *You know, there are no black racers here.*

I was born without a filter between my brain and mouth. So right as that thought occurred I heard myself saying, "*You know, you never see any black racers here.*"

That's when Prentiss Campbell walked up on his bike.

Prentiss was from New York City. He has his own urban style, which included low-top Converse Chuck Taylors, which would serve not only as casual wear, but bike racing shoes. Don't laugh—he had already done the Tour Divide, and last year and it had taken him around 30 days to finish, a pretty good time if you're sporting one gear on a bicycle. This year he was back to beat it.

I bombarded him with questions, seeking tips and advice. Prentiss was also being pulled in a few different directions from other vets who wanted his attention. So I quit pestering him for now. I started to walk off when someone called my name.

"Hey Scott, It's Kevin!"

I turned around and saw Kevin Campagna, a rookie like me, waving. I'd met Kevin on Facebook and had gotten to know him. He had served the USA in the Middle East and was keenly interested in starting a group that focused on cycling and PTSD. He asked if I wanted to go ride around to loosen up our legs. I agreed, and off along the pretty paved trails we went.

Surprisingly quiet for a Texan, Kevin was thin, with a perfectly groomed beard, and extremely pleasant to ride with. Paul and a few other folks joined our leisurely tour of Banff. We rode into the outskirts of Banff, enjoying the scenery, and as riders peeled off it was just Kevin and me.

"You want to go see what the start of the race looks like?" he said.

"Sure, man. Let's go look."

We rode towards the race official race start, a hotel that looked like a castle, at the top of a very steep, winding road. The thin air felt like it was strangling me. My heart was beating out of my chest, and every big gasp of air sent only a trickle of oxygen to my lungs.

Oh crap! This is bad, I'm dying here. God, I hope Kevin doesn't see this or he'll think I won't be able to handle any of the Tour Divide's elevation.

I turned around to see Kevin in the same misery.

"Are you struggling with this thin air too?" I asked.

He gasped: "Yes!"

We continued to take it easy up the hill and rounded the corner to the start of the trail.

It was so quiet we could hear the crisp leaves flickering. The trailhead was like the mouth of a dragon laid open, and I was willing to ride right into it. I kicked my pedal and rode over a small dirt mount, diving into the mouth of the Divide.

It was a pleasant drop into the trail, a large gravely road with thick forests on either side of as it cut into the backwoods of Canada. It was beautiful. As Kevin and I rode deeper into the trails we saw another biker coming back out. It was Ryan Sigsby

"Well hey man, how are you? Haven't seen you since the TNGA," said Ryan.

Ryan smiled and said how excited he was to be here. He also had another type of smile on his face, and it took a moment, but suddenly I realized why the grin. As we all rode back to the start of the trailhead we saw his pregnant wife.

"Oh wow, congrats man! Better pedal fast eh?" I said.

Ryan laughed. "Not until October!"

Before long, it was time for the pre-race meeting held by Crazy Larry.

Crazy Larry Melnik was the self-appointed race director of the Tour Divide. Which is funny, because the Tour Divide is not a sanctioned race but an underground event, completely unofficial, and yet organized. Crazy Larry directed it anyway, and had told us of a "mandatory" meeting in bar in downtown Banff.

Around one hundred and sixty racers were getting food and beer and waiting on Larry's arrival.

"That's not the guy from the movie!?" said a racer.

"No no, that's LITTLE Larry from the movie," said another.

"I wonder if we'll see him," remarked a third.

Not to be confused with Crazy Larry, Lil' Larry was an iconic figure in the movie *Ride the Divide.* A stout, toothless logger with a funny laugh, he could have been mistaken for a Hobbit from J.R.R Tolkien's Lord of the Rings, or possibly a dwarf. His cameo in the movie made me think *Aww, I wanna meet this fella one day!*

"DUDE!" said one guy. "Did you not hear about Lil' Larry from Ride the Divide? You know he was that logger right? He was logging on a national forest and the swat team, like, jumped down some ropes from a helicopter, came down and burned his house to the ground and then he got smoke damage in his lungs and died of cancer. Dude—the movie killed him!"

I don't know how accurate that story is, but suffice to say I found out that Crazy Larry was a local Banff native and Lil Larry was a Montana hillbilly who is indeed deceased, though the story of his demise is one that needs some fact-checking.

Crazy Larry started talking about what to do if you encounter a bear, a mountain lion, or a hillbilly. He called Matthew Lee, the originator of the Tour Divide Race, and held his phone to the microphone as Matt wished us well. He gave everyone directions as to where to be, when we'd be leaving, and some other basic info. And he reminded us never to quit.

June 14, Before Dawn

On the morning of the race, I took the last decent shower I'd have for weeks and put on the clothes I would wear for a solid month. My brand-new bike kit smelled wonderful. With my racing shoes, arm warmers, and leg warmers, I felt like a superhero suited up to take on the foes of the day.

The sun was out and it was bitter cold as I hopped on my bike and coasted down to McDonalds. There was a line a mile long there of racers getting their last warm meal for a long time. I ordered a few breakfast burritos and connected my phone to the Internet only to get a text from Kate.

Hey baby, I know you don't want to hear this since you're about to start the Tour Divide, but your Spot isn't working nor registering on the system.

My "Spot" was a satellite-tracking device that would beam up my location as I moved across the Divide. I'd used it on the TNGA as well to test it out. It is the most frustrating, disastrous pieces of technology I've ever used.

August 2012: Day 1 of the TNGA

Somewhere in the Georgia Mountains I looked down at my Spot Tracker, which was blinking.

"Red lights are bad on this contraption, aren't they Chris?"

Chris Loy, a tall wiry racer, stopped pedaling and looked.

"Yeah your Spot is supposed to blink all green to show it's getting reception to the satellite. You're not getting tracked."

"Crap—this is my first ever long distance race, and I bet my wife is freaking out!"

"Well you have batteries, right?

"Sure I do, let me just pop them in… wait, it's still not working."

"You need lithium batteries in it to work."

I had none. Chris and I pedaled on through the north Georgia mountains for hours when I finally got to a place with cell service which, when my phone connected I had a very calm but nerve-wracked voice message from my wife. Her voice was calm, calm like a bomb before it exploded.

"Hellllooooo, I'm sure you know by now your spot isn't working. It's showing you at the start of the race not moving. Could you please kindly turn it on???"

For the rest of the TNGA I looked for lithium batteries at every convenience store and Dollar General, trying to make it connect and trying to communicate to Kate that I wasn't dead. I vowed that when I was on the Divide Race I would carry 8 trillion lithium batteries. And here it was moments before the race start, and once again it was happening.

6 a.m. June 14th: Banff

I yelled a few choice words and ran out to my bike to see what was going on. It was blinking green. Another text came through from Kate.

Ah, there you are. I see you now. *GO BABY GO!*

I went back to my breakfast burritos.

"It's time!" someone said, at last. Tour Divide riders poured out of McDonalds to join up with more than 160 riders in front of the YMCA.

"OKAY LISTEN UP!" Crazy Larry yelled. "WE'RE GONNA GET A GROUP PICTURE AND THEN THE RACE WILL BEGIN!"

Crazy Larry went on for what seemed to be hours taking group photos of us, making us yell, cheer and do other outgoing things I've never particularly enjoyed doing. So we cheered, we chanted, we threw our hands in the air.

"OKAY SO NOW WE'LL BIKE TO THE START!"

I thought this WAS the start. But no, we had to bike to the trailhead, the mouth of the divide. Everyone sort of stood around, confused. Crazy Larry came up to us one last time and started saying his well wishes to everyone, and then he went into a few stories of how he got out of some situations while on the Divide race.

I just wanted him to say, "GO!"

Scott McConnell said, "Hey I'm going to get up with the leaders. See you soon?"

"Sure man, see you soon." I said.

Finally Larry started the countdown.

"FIVE!"

I thought about all the training I'd done up to this point and couldn't believe I was here.

"FOUR!"

I should quit, give up—I'll never make this race.

"THREE!"

Oh god, this is the dumbest thing I think I'd ever done in my life.

"TWO!"

Did I forget anything back at the hotel, where's my wallet? Do I have my wallet!

"ONE!"

Wait, Larry, don't say Go just yet, I...

"GO!!!!"

ALBERTA

Day 1: 8 a.m. The Mouth of the Dragon

Everything went quiet except for the clicks of shoes connecting with pedals. I could feel my heart beating in my throat, and I thought I might throw up. I watched racers dive into the mouth of the Divide. The knights were going to slay the monster that was awaiting them. Waiting to damage their steed, break their minds and their bones. The dragon was real—it breathed, it shape-shifted, it was beautiful and evil. It was the Tour Divide and I rode straight into its lair.

Wow man, am I really doing this? Damn!
It was a comfortable pace, and yet I was passing people.
"Hello Scott!" a familiar British accent said.
It was Mauro, the British singlespeeder and he'd caught up with me.
"Fancy seeing you here!" I responded. "Hey man, it's great, yes?"
"Yeah, I love it!"
He started to talk more, and I heard a grinding sound his bike. One of his bags had caught his tire and he had to hop off his bike to fix it.
"You okay!?" I hollered as I rode off.
"Yes! I'll catch you soon Mr. Thigpen!"
After what seemed like hours, signs of others started to appear. People were crowded all over a climb, wielding cameras. I remember seeing a video of this where Tour Divide racers would try to make the climb with people rooting them on. Some did, others didn't. It was a very tough, but short, climb. I started into it and my legs screamed, I continued to ignore my legs' pain and kept going up. I hit the apex and landed onto flat land.
"HELL YEAH!" I screamed and kept on riding.
The Canadian terrain is absolutely beautiful with its majestic skies, and mountains that make skyscrapers look wimpy. The sun, however was not cooperating. It started to duck between some nasty dark clouds.

26

I heard the whirring of a wheel behind me and pulling through.

"Hi again," she said.

It was Kristen, the girl in the "Whiskey 7" shirt.

"Hi," I said back.

We both rode in silence for a while, listening to fat tires roll over the gravel. I'm uneasy around strangers at first and feel the need to talk because I don't want to seem anti-social, when essentially that what I want to be, especially when I'm on a bike. Generally when I'm training or exercising, I do best if I can live inside my head. I made awkward chitchat for a while. Eventually I rode on and caught up with my Banff roommate, Sean.

We walked our bikes through rocky spots and plunged into forests, moving from single track trail to wide open dirt roads. As the road widened, cyclists started to open up their legs and really kick in the speed.

Kristen caught us and said politely, "You guys have a good ride!" before flipping down her sunglasses, placing her hands on the aero bars and shooting off like a bolt of lightning. Sean followed suit. If you've never heard of aero bars, imagine a pair of bullhorns mounted on the handlebars of a bike. Most often used by triathletes seeking the greatest aerodynamics and efficiency, they require a fair amount of balance, which is not something I possess. Especially on a dirt road. I decided it was time to give my brand-new aero bars a try.

As I sped down a steep hill, now locked into a precarious position, my bike started to lean to one side. I overcorrected, turning the wheel too hard, causing my bike to jackknife and flip. I flew off my bike, somersaulting on the ground, and caught sight of my bike and all its precious cargo flipping down the trail. As I shook it off, a fellow single speederer zoomed past me in aero.

How the hell are they doing this!?

I decided I was not one for this position on a steep downhill and resumed pedaling upright and safely, wind drag be damned!

Minutes before we left Banff, racers got an email from Matthew Lee stating that there was a mandatory reroute off a trail due to "heavy grizzly activity." I've always been pretty nervous about bears because they are large, you can't escape them, and if they're feeling moody they can do things like rip your arms off. When we got to the reroute, I peered down the trail and didn't see any bears. It looked like a nice trail but I stayed on the road instead. This lead to a nice surprise: a convenience store located in the middle of nowhere. There were tons of racers hanging out, eating ice cream, chatting and talking about the day's events so far.

I bumped into Sean, Scott, and a few other people and asked them how their ride was going. They seemed to be in good spirits, but none such as Sean, who had found ketchup-flavored potato chips.

"Only in Canada, man" he said. "You wanna try one?"

It tasted, shockingly, like a marriage of ketchup and fried potato. I wanted to hurl.

To rid my mouth of the horrid chemical ketchup taste, I got some ice cream and chocolates, and then rode out with Sean and a few others.

"Hey Scott, our first mountain pass over the Divide is coming up. This is going to be exciting! Our first part of the Continental Divide."

I didn't know what to expect when we got to the top. Everyone ended up pushing their bikes up the insanely steep climbs. When we got up there, we all rested. I looked over and saw the series of mountains that was the Continental Divide. I kind of sat there and then smirked, because they looked like, well, mountains. I guess I was expecting magical ponies and rainbows, or something, and the reality was underwhelming. It was beautiful, and I was happy for the chance to see it, but I was just hoping for something more I suppose.

We made it to a ridge on the Continental Divide and it finally leveled off, something I was sure I'd never see again in my life. As my body started to relax and give way a bit I looked ahead and saw a sea of bikers powering along the rolling ridgeline. I spotted Scott McConnell way ahead. As I stood up on my pedals for a punch of power and speed, I felt my adductors, the small muscles in the thighs, seize up.

"No, nooooo not this early in the race!" I yelped as the pain seared through my quads.

As I felt my leg turning to stone, I threw my bike down and stretched as my coach Tracy had instructed me for such an occasion.

Later, as I continued to pedal along the ridge, Eric, a guy from New Zealand caught up to me.

"The downhill is coming up, right?" I said. We'd been climbing for some time and I was very tired.

"Sure, mate," he said.

But was not downhill. It was "Tour Divide downhill," which meant a lot of uphill in the down.

"Greeaaat," I smirked, and rode on.

The clouds were dark blue, grey, and threatening to pound us with rain, thunder and lightning. As we reached the apex of the climb I was back off my bike pushing. I wanted to save some energy because I wanted to get really far on the first day. That's when I spotted in the mud the imprint of an enormous, giant bear paw. I stopped for a moment and put my hand in the paw print. I have big hands—like, enormously big hands—and even with my outstretched fingers my hand fit snug within it.

Christ...

I'd never seen a bear before, let alone a grizzly in the wild. I didn't want to.

The terrain would change from extremely hilly to a nice pleasant flat. Fellow racers would pass me; I'd pass them, and so on, and so on. I looked down at my GPS and noted I was not too terribly far from a town—just about 20 or 25 miles! —When the screen of my GPS saw the splat of a raindrop.

The rain now spattered my glasses, helmet, and bike. I knew that rain was inevitable, but on Day One, really?

Oh well, this is the Tour Divide, I said to myself and kept going. The splatter became a steady stream.

A grizzly looking fellow a little older than me pulled up and said, "You look like you're struggling there a bit."

"I'm just adjusting to the rain, starting to get cold."

"Well you know we have a long, long ways to go."

We rode in silence and I finally said, "I'm Scott, by the way."

"Name's Rob Orr," he muttered and we resumed the silent pedaling.

It seemed as if hours went by riding with my silent partner. We started to hit a paved road and I heard Rob clicking his gears. Then his tires made a *whoomp-whoomp-whoomp* sound as they girth of them rotated over the asphalt. He leaned into his bike and was gone. Again, back to solitary riding.

I decided to get out the rain gear. I hate stopping, because stopping means more time off the bike, more time wasted not getting to the next destination. For a near 3,000-mile bike ride, you might think you could take your time, but no. Minutes add up. So I limited my off-bike time as much as possible. By now, the rain was coursing down and in the few minutes it took me to get my rain gear on, I started to freeze up.

Damn it!

I get so cold quickly and I don't deal well with it. I saw that a town called Elkford was coming up.

Maybe they have some stores where I can get some supplies.

"Hey, you're that Rohloff guy," I said as I caught up with someone just a few miles before Elkford.

"Huh? Oh, yes, yes," the guy said quietly.

A Rohloff is a brand of hub that goes on the back of a bike, with internal gears that switch in and out. Many Tour Divide riders have them. I have always wanted one, but at a starting price of $1,200? No thank you.

"I'm Scott."

"I'm Ty," he said quietly, and we kept riding in silence.

I would wager that like me, many riders are rather introverted. I mean, you have to be to take on such an intense race that requires such self-sufficiency and solitude. We exchanged a few words and then through the rain, cold and bitterness we popped onto a road which led to houses then led to a country store littered with Tour Divide bikes all around it. We both hopped off our bikes and went inside, dripping wet.

"Dude, I'm just not gonna stop eating."

The speaker was tall, wiry, blonde, and had attempted the Divide last year, but due to a knee issue, he had to drop out. His name was Eric Foster, and he was definitely not an introvert.

"Dude, I remember last year being here, like all the racers were here. I got out before most of them so I could get a jump-start to the next town. Dude, you pushing on?"

I was still processing everything he was saying. I just nodded.

"Dude, you're going to love this race, dude. I'm going to finish it and be up at the front as long as my knee stays together."

"That's great man." I said, smiled, and then wandered into the restaurant.

Outside the sky was grey and the rained pounded on. Inside, Tour Divide racers were packed into the tiny country store restaurant, jockeying for a seat to rest their bones. The walls were dark brown, illuminated only by the fluorescent lights of the glass refrigerators filled with grab-and-go sandwiches. I got lucky and found a seat next to Prentiss, Ty, and Taylor and Kristen, aka The Kids.

I couldn't stop shivering. As I peeled off each layer, water dripped from each garment. We all sat and talked about the day so far and what lay ahead. Prentiss said that Sparwood was a nice stopping point for most riders however some would push on. He said that after Sparwood it was called the "Bear Interstate." I thought about how far I'd push for the evening and figured Sparwood would be a nice stopping point to camp.

Ah, camping. The thing I'd been looking forward to the most on the Tour Divide. Raised in the Cub Scouts, Webelos, Boy Scouts, I got my Eagle Scout and was a member of the "Order of the Arrow," the not-so-secret fraternity of the Boy Scouts. From a very young age until around the time I graduated high school, I generally could be found in a tent sometime during the summer (and even winter) months. For the race, I'd purchased a bivy sack, a one-person cocoon that was a cross between a tent and a sleeping bag. I was excited to camp, but not so much in Grizzly country.

I ate my sandwich, some cookies, and sucked down a sugary soda. Back home I usually live on green smoothies. So going from home-prepared meals to processed food was a recipe for gas and acid reflux.

As everyone started to pull on their gear and rain ponchos, the rain ebbed. After a quarter of a mile it went away and the sun peeked out, warming everything up. It was hard not to think of the weather as a villain purposely trying to make our lives a living hell. I kept my rain gear on, just in case. But with a full belly and miles to go, this wasn't smart. We soon hit a huge climb that went on forever, which meant I warmed up like an oven. An oven cooking undigested food. Fun times.

Despite the warning signs, my legs felt unnaturally strong and I was climbing fine for a while when all of the sudden—WOOSH! —A semi truck passed me going at least 100 miles per hour. I don't like riding on the road with cars on a good day. With a full belly, cold legs, and a climb making me teeter left and right on the road— treacherous combination. WOOSH!

Kristen pulled up next to me.

"It always takes me a bit to warm up to climbs," she said, but as she continued to grind up the mountain, she got faster and faster. Then going by both of us was Taylor, also riding a single speed. I sat and marveled at his climbing prowess with only one gear. He seemed to not even be fazed by the steep climb, and disappeared around a corner. Kristen, now in full Wonder Woman mode, powered up the mountain as well. I tried sticking with them, expending precious energy to keep up with two people half my age. With each pedal stroke I got slower. My breath became labored and sweat poured out of me, turning my rain gear into a sauna. I finally had to give in, get off my bike, and start pushing.

I felt sorry for myself. I couldn't climb like them. I had trained for two years to be able to move at a speedy and steady pace, and yet here I was on day one of the Tour Divide, and already sucking wind. I didn't want to give into the negativity, so I turned on my iPod. I don't know why, but Kennedy's "We go to the moon" speech came on, so instead of music, I listened to the second son of an Irishman's speech. The words Kennedy uttered instantly changed my mood and thoughts:

But why, some say, the moon? Why choose this as our goal? And they may well ask why climb the highest mountain? Why, 35 years ago, fly the Atlantic? Why does Rice play Texas? We choose to go to the moon. We choose to go to the moon in this decade and do the other things, not because they are easy, but because they are hard.

It set me on fire. I shed my rain gear, told my legs to shut up, and climbed the rest of that damned mountain. When I got to the top, I double pumped my fist in the air and screamed HELL YEAH! before diving down a dirt road into the back forests of Canada.

I felt unstoppable.

Until I noticed that the sun was setting on a forest full of bears. Why am I so scared of bears? I don't know. I just had it in my mind that bears wait until dark to pounce on their prey. Especially cyclists. I kept my eyes peeled around every corner. The road became rocks, and then the rocks became something nearly unrideable, which forced me into full-on bike-lugging mode. I tenderly padded over a series of giant loose rocks, paying special attention to not slip, as the fall was pretty far down.

The terrain went down and my spirits went up, because legs were spent. The last bit of the sun was peeking through the woods. I zoned out, looking at the beautiful scenery, checking my GPS periodically to make sure I was on the right track. Going quickly down the side of a mountain, I glanced once at my GPS and then flicked my eyes back up, when I did I saw a giant, large, black animal coming straight at me.

Or, rather, I was coming straight at it.

I slammed on my brakes, skidding to one side and almost losing my balance.

OH HOLY HELL! I screamed in terror. This was it. I was going to get mauled by a bear on day one of the Tour Divide. I could hear the eulogy:

Scott Thigpen was an ambitious guy, trying to take on a monstrous race when all the signs warned against doing it. He was stubborn and gave a valiant effort but didn't even make it one day before being mauled by a bear.

I'd heard a few years back that a Tour Divide rider hit a bear and fell off a cliff. (Somehow, he didn't die.) I didn't want this to be my fate, especially on Day 1. When I looked up, I realized it wasn't a bear, but a cow.

Standing aimlessly in the road, it stared at me blankly, chewing its cud.

"SCREW YOU, COW!"

(Ok, so I used other words but my mom is going to read this book.)

"GET THE HELL OUTTA THE WAY! GO ON! MOVE! MOOOOOVE!"

But of course it wouldn't move. It just stood there. I pushed my bike around the cow and back on to the dirt road. The sun was setting, but since it was June in Canada, I was able to go for long strides without turning on my lights.

I went by fields with prancing elk, but no bears. The fields turned to houses, and the houses turned into the outskirts of Sparwood. It was late, around 10 or so. I didn't know where everyone was camping. "

I'll just keep looking.

Then I saw a hotel sign. With glowing orange letters: VACANCY.

"NO!" I said out loud "No hotels."

I kept pedaling and saw a sign for camping.

Finally.

"SCOTT!" I heard someone yell. "YO SCOTT, HEY!"

There were Scott McConnell, Ryan Sigsby, and Kevin Campagna.

"HEY!" I yelled back and rode over to them. They were standing in front of a burger joint.

"We got here about 20 minutes ago and they were closed," Ryan said, "but then they felt bad for us and gave us all these burgers!"

He held a sack filled with burgers. The smell of the buns, meat, and cheese traveled from the bag and swirled in my nose, sending my senses into overload of desire.

"You want some?" he said. "I can't eat anymore!"

I ate one burger in two bites and grabbed another. I had not had any real food for the entire day. It was yet another bit of Trail Magic.

"We're thinking about getting a hotel for the night and skipping the camping," Scott said. "We're all nasty and wringing wet. We want showers."

I caved. Camping, schmamping. I love showers. We all piled into a room at a hotel where a few other racers were staying. After my shower, I called into MTBCast.com to narrate my podcast. Then I called Kate.

"Baby you are just flying!" she said. "You are so far ahead of everyone else! Great job!" I told her it was a tough, but epic day. We said our I love yous. And I went back into the room, where we faced the uncomfortable dude math: two beds and four guys.

We were too tired to care. I slid into bed next to Scott.

"Hey, I need to warn you about something my wife tells me I do in my sleep," Scott said right before I fell asleep. "I kick."

BRITISH COLUMBIA

Day 2: Yes, he kicks

Despite the hotel bed, I didn't sleep well. In fact, I awoke every hour on the hour and then drifted back into a dream-charged sleep. Most of the dreams involved falling; right before I hit the ground, I'd wake up. Then I would struggle to fall back asleep because my bike's back hub was wobbling pretty badly, and that's all I could think about.

By the time I settled into a good rhythm of sleep, and wasn't getting karate kicked by Ralph Macchio over there, the alarm went off around 4 a.m. Ryan wanted to get a jump on the day and get ahead of the other racers. As we startled abruptly out of sleep, I considered throwing Ryan out of the window of our hotel. But Ryan is a fairly likeable guy, so I refrained this one time from doing so.

Everyone started scrambling and getting out the door. I didn't like this because I wanted to take a minute to inspect my bike. I rolled out of bed, quickly stuffed my sleeping clothes in a crevice in my bike, and put on my cycling kit. It was damp, but not sopping, and didn't smell too terribly bad. We quietly rolled our bikes through the hotel halls and moved them downstairs. As we did we saw several other racers coming out of their rooms heading to take on day two as well. So much for our little "Get ahead of everyone else" plan. I reconsidered throwing Ryan out the window.

Ryan, Scott, Kevin and I cleaned our bikes and pedaled over the gas station across the street for breakfast. Nutritional pickings were slim. I opted for packaged pastries, peanut M&M's, a brownie, some nuts and a few Gatorades. There was coffee, but nothing to mix it with. I would rather drink acid than black coffee. These days I actually put butter or coconut oil (or both) in my coffee. Don't laugh at my buttery coffee; try it. It's even smoother than half and half.

"Where's the cream and sugar?"

She wrinkled her nose and said, "Well people around here work for a living and bring their own cream and sugar."

"Uh, okay. At home, in America, they give you cream and sugar with your coffee at every gas station for FREE—LIKE YOUR HEALTH CARE!"

(Okay I really didn't say that, but I wanted to. Canadian Sparwood store clerk lady, if you are reading my book—you should know I almost said this to you!)

Trying to choke down tar-grade black coffee, I said, "Hey where's Scott?"

Ryan looked around. "You know I don't know, he was just here. I guess he got a start on the day. You ready?"

I wasn't, but I said yes. I threw out the coffee and when it hit the ground, I swear it dissolved the asphalt. I looked up to where we were going and for the miles I could see, it was all smooth and paved. While no one was looking, I did a small victory dance. We rode off towards America, land of the free cream and sugar.

I was trying to stay with Kevin and Ryan only to realize that on the flats, my singlespeed was no match for their gears. When the street leveled out I'd hear "click, click, click" and watch the derailleurs shift on their bikes and before they disappeared down the road. I would try to pedal faster to keep up, but soon realized that was a waste of energy, and it wasn't even 6 a.m. Eventually I was alone. I like alone; it means I get to go inside my head and daydream, think about random things and "zone out."

The paved road started to go up, which I didn't mind as I enjoy a good climb. In the distance I saw a cyclist. I finally caught up to a guy named Matt Slater from Ohio. Matt was no stranger to endurance cycling, and had hung out with previous celebrated racers like Jay Petervary and Jill Homer. As we continued to pedal, I started to get ahead of him. Not to be impolite, I told him good day and continued riding solo. I knew the Divide Route would soon turn to rougher terrain, so I tried to soak up the crisp air and smooth pavement.

Up ahead and I saw Ryan and Kevin riding back towards me.

"Wrong way. Wrong way," said Ryan, pragmatically.

My GPS showed us going in the right direction.

"Says here that we're fine."

"No, here on the map it says we are to take a dirt road, not the road."

We looked around and saw nothing. Kevin pointed down below the road to a gully.

"I think I see tire tracks. Yep, those are tire tracks."

I looked at what appeared to be a dirt road next to the nice paved road.

"The paved road looks just as good," I protested.

"I don't want to get disqualified, but do what you want."

We all backtracked, lugging our extremely heavy bikes over the railing, and scooted down the hill to the muddy fire road. The group surged ahead of me and I crept through the muck only to dump back out on a paved road not even a half-mile from where we originally were. Kevin, Ryan and Sean dropped me once again, and I was on my own for several hours happily enjoying the pace and some Pop tunes pumping through my earphones.

There are a few people who do the Divide with no music. These people I refer to as mutants. I love music and am intrinsically tied to it, especially rap music. Much to my parents dismay, I discovered "Yo, MTV Raps" as a kid and my heroes of music became The Fat Boys, Run DMC, LL Cool J and Public Enemy. These classic rappers now got me through British Columbia, their rhythmic beats and quick rhymes like a metronome for my brain, distracting it from my suffering legs.

The route finally started to trend down, a nice winding ride that snaked to the bottom of the next mountain. I whipped around a corner and saw two cyclists with their bikes flipped upside down. It was the kids, Kristen and Taylor.

"Y'all okay?" I said.

"Eh…" said Taylor "Kristen's got a busted spoke. Trying to fix it."

I bid them farewell and kept pedaling to see that my nice smooth journey of a road stop and the dirt road begin. As I rolled into the road I found Kevin, Sean, and Ryan taking a break and eating. I followed suit, only to have them finish and pedal off, leaving me. For once I was kind of tired of being alone, so I wolfed down a candy bar and did my best to catch up with them. The dirt road was muddy and rutted, so maneuvering was rough. As we rode together, I put my music in to climb, slow and steady, up the mountain.

From time to time Kevin would say a few words to me, and I just nodded, because I couldn't take my hands off the handlebars and didn't want to seem like I was ignoring him. He would talk, and occasionally I'd laugh to show I was engaged, but I couldn't hear him over my music. One time I laughed and said "yeah, that's funny" and Kevin sort of frowned. He probably told a story about how he rescued fifteen children from the top floor of a burning building, but was unable to rescue the pets.

I was pretty impressed that I could hang with all of them; generally single speeders don't have a problem on climbs—it's the flat roads. After several more hours we'd made it to the top of a mountain. We stopped for a moment and a cyclist powered by us and didn't say anything I took note he was another single speeder. Currently on day two by my calculations, I was in second place while Scott McConnell was somewhere up ahead in first. Now I was in third.

Wow… I said to myself. *Never thought I'd stay up front like this.*

I've always been a little touchy about going downhill. I'd once lost control going downhill and cracked my collarbone. Not two years later, I cracked my other collarbone doing the same thing. When I take off my shirt and look in the mirror I have a crooked shoulder line, like Lurch from the Addams Family. It's awesome. Sometimes when I sleep at night, I can't lie on either side because there's too much pain through either shoulder. So I'm rather timid about flying downhill now.

I watched Ryan and Kevin tear away as they disappeared down the mountain.. They turned into tiny marks in front of me and then eventually the security blanket of communing with people disappeared and I adjusted to the solitude.

Hours later I rolled up on Ryan, Kevin, and Sean resting. They'd picked up two new people, a crazy looking kid with wild hair and a scruffy beard. His name was Joseph and I'd have been impressed if he was even 18. The other guy was around my age, had a goatee with some silver in it, small eyes, and an interesting accent I couldn't place. His name was Eddie. I'd speak to Eddie and he'd ignore me. I figured he was some hoity toity racer that didn't have time to talk to us no-namers. In fact he ignored me twice when I'd try to chat with him. I try not to pass judgment on people, but folks who have their nose shot straight up in the air do send me over the edge.

As we pedaled away, everyone took off except Kevin.

"I'm Just going to take this next section slow, it says we're going to get wet."

I didn't know what that meant. There wasn't a dark cloud and not a drop of water anywhere... well, except until we crested a mountain and I looked down. With patches of snow here and there, the trail was a stream of water flowing down the side of a mountain that seemed to never end on the steep descent. I applied my brakes and squeaked down it hoping to not crash over the slick rocks. I followed Kevin and we splashed down the side of the mountain all the way to what seemed like a small river with the other riders on the other side of it. Kevin stopped to put on his waterproof socks, I already had mine on.

"Come on guys! You can do it!" screamed Joseph. "Ride it hard!"

I gingerly stepped through the water, looking for rocks to balance on as I walked my bike through the roaring waters, not able to really see where to put my foot next. The last thing I wanted was for my bike to tumble over with all my warm dry clothes in it. I continued to totter through the crossing and finally made it to the other side. My waterproof socks were anything but. However, it was still relatively warm and I was mostly dry.

Predictably, everyone left, me powering down the hills then back up the mountain. I took my time and looked at the views instead of burying my head in my handlebars. Snow became more abundant and the climbs were long, but easy enough. I got to a summit and there was snow everywhere, with the freshest air I'd ever brought into my lungs. It was cold, crisp, and pure. I felt alive.

I pedaled a little longer only to once again run into the group finishing off snacks and getting ready to leave while I'd just sat down to rest.

"We'll wait a minute for you, Scott," Ryan said.

"Thanks but if you guys want to go, go."

They waited as I put on a heavier jacket, and wolfed down my 6th candy bar for the day. The descent was steep, fast, and furious with amazing landscapes and patches of snow everywhere. I wished I were not in a race setting so I could stop and take more pictures, but it was late afternoon and I could smell the United States—and I wanted to be in my own country if, only to surpass that mental hurdle.

We continued to fly down the hill when Ryan, the leader of our pack of Hell's non-combustible-engine Angels slammed on his brakes near the bottom of the mountain.

"IT'S BILLY RICE!" he screamed.

It was indeed the man who was traveling from Mexico and going up to Banff, only to turn around and go back down to Mexico.

" 'Sup guys," Billy said as he rolled to a stop with big grin on his face.

He looked weathered, but in great spirits. I was sort of star-struck to see anyone taking on a near 6,000-mile bike race. He was taller than I'd imagined. His hands looked beat up, but he looked like a million bucks compared to me. I was unsure whether I would make it to Montana.

I wanted to introduce myself, but stepped back as everyone bombarded him with questions and introductions. Billy seemed like such a rock star, but not as much as a rock star as my perceived image of the Prima Donna Eddie who refused to talk to me, who I'd watched ignore other people, too.

Billy grinned a big toothy grin, saying we were in for a big surprise up ahead.

Ryan nodded. "Yeah it's the wall before the entry into the United States, right?"

"Mmm hmmm, you boys enjoy." Billy said he was aiming to make it to Banff before evening. That was more than one hundred miles away, and the sun was now past high noon.

Eddie fell back and said his bike was messing up. Kevin also seemed to be slowing down. I felt smug that my bike was holding together. Then I realized one of my cleats on my shoe was wiggling loose.

Oh god, seriously?

By the time I got off my bike, the screw had wiggled off and was nowhere to be found.

I stopped and fixed my shoe. I looked up and saw Eddie nearby not saying anything. He was wiggling his crank by holding the pedals; it was noticeably loose as if it was going to fall off any moment.

He muttered "I'll walk to Mexico if I have to."

I said, "Well that's the spirit man, but I bet a bike shop is coming up."

He said nothing back. This pissed me off. I was so tired of his *"I'm too good to talk with you"* attitude and I yelled,

"HEY!" looking at him a little angrily.

He looked up and said, "Oh, oh sorry I didn't hear you, you see I'm deaf in one ear and can't really hear well."

All the anger and resentment flooded out of me, in no way was Eddie being rude to anyone, he simply couldn't hear with all the howling winds and sounds of bikes. I felt terrible for judging.

"NO WORRIES MAN. YOU GONNA BE OKAY?" I spoke loudly.

"Yeah, my bike just needs to hold together until we get to Whitefish, Montana."

I thought about Whitefish, which was still two days away and it was through heavy bear country, something I wasn't very keen about.

I got my cleat repaired; Eddie waited on me and we rode off to find the others. We finally did find everyone breaking before a steep incline.

"So this is the wall, eh? Doesn't look so bad." I said courageously.

"This isn't the wall. That's still 20 miles down the road." Ryan muttered.

I cringed and away we went making the ascent up. Some rode it, others (like me) pushed. We had the wonderful aroma and visual appearance of bear scat from one end to the other on the road and it was like maneuvering through land mines.

"What the hell is wrong with these damned bears! Do they not know bear hygiene or something!?" I yelled,

"We're going through the bear highway, this is one of the most densely populated areas of Grizzlies." Eddie said,

I looked around and saw huge tracks everywhere. I kept my eyes peeled looking for bears, partially in fear and partially in curiosity. Nothing, but their presence was there and that was enough for me. While I never saw one, not even the outline of one, I could feel them. I could feel them staring down at me ... or maybe it was just me.

When I was a kid my granddad told me a story where years ago, he had taken my mother, her sister and my grandmother out to a state park. There was a bathroom break and when my Mom and grandmother went into the State Park restroom, a downpour of rain happened. I guess bears don't care for rain either because one bear mosied underneath the roofed restroom area to get out of the downpour as well. When my mom and grandmother came out, mom placed her hand on the railing to walk down the steps, except it wasn't the railing, it was the bear's head. Mom froze in panic and all granddad knew to do was honk the horn startling the bear which allowed mom and grandmother to an Olympian's sprint to the car. Even though I didn't come along for many years after that, I think some of that trauma was genetically passed down to my psyche. While we took a break The Kiwi found us and said, "Ah, coming up is the fun stuff mates!"

I didn't know what he meant, and wasn't thinking straight because I was hot, tired and was ready to be in the USA, we were so close.

Kevin and Joseph caught up to us while Eddie was nowhere in sight. We all stuck together through this dense trail area. Sometimes when I was pushing my bike, my shoe would completely disappear in the mud. The trail was almost not a trail at all. But I was hopeful because it looked like we were heading towards a clearing and then it happened: The Wall. It was not a trail, it was not a steep incline, and it was the side of a mountain with rocks jutted out here and there. It was a wall of a mountain.

"For real?" I said.

"Yep" said Joseph, "This is it, let's get to climbing."

Ryan made his way up the wall struggling, followed by Joseph then Kevin and then finally me. I followed every bit of what Kevin was doing. He'd use his bike as a pickaxe hoisting it onto a rock,

43

squeezing the brakes and then pulling himself up with his arms. At one area his foot slipped and the penalty for error was great here. I watched a few rocks slide from under his foot and with my good arm I caught him to stabilize so he could push up.

"I want to beat you, Kevin," I said. "But in a sprint to the finish, not with you splatted on a bunch of rocks."

He laughed nervously we continued climbing. I looked down beneath me, tiny rocks would slip under my feet and I'd watch them tumble down freely; hit the ground where we were at the bottom and roll down into the stream. I gritted my teeth and continued to use my bike as a pickaxe following Kevin up this wall on a mountain.

Twenty or thirty minutes later we all made it to the top. It was nice and flat and the trail became a dirt road. Everyone stopped and I excitedly said

"America! The USA! We're there guys! WE'RE THERE!"

We all cheered and got super excited that we were going to be in the United States at any moment...except we weren't. Not yet, not even close.

The wall had been a fight and it took a lot of energy, but the Port of Rooseville, Montana was in our grasp and there would be vending machines with sodas, restaurants, beer and all the food we would want. It was there, I could feel it, and we hopped on our bikes and tore off the long dirt road. We ripped around the corner and it sort of pitched up for a second. Hopped on up on adrenaline, I easily made it up the small hill, which turned into another climb. I continued climbing it and it continued to get steeper. I pushed all the energy I had knowing that any minute now the downhill was coming until I went around another hill and saw that we were on another mountain pass. I pulled out my GPS and looked at the elevation profile, I couldn't even see the top. Ryan looked at his map and grimly said

"We've got around 10 more miles of this."

My heart sunk; at most I was doing maybe 1 mile per hour, maybe less. I tried to ride but I had used up all the energy on the wall and excitement thinking I was getting into America. Joseph, Kevin and I slowed to a miserable walking crawl however Ryan continued to ride on. We pushed; we pushed for what seemed like hours. We took a small break at a bend and watched a series of racers power up the hill effortlessly; I still don't know how they were riding 50+ lb. bikes and making it look like it was nothing. We watched the racers zip past us and wearily Joseph, Kevin and I pushed on. We turned to another part of the mountain to be faced with the howling winds; and snow was now collecting and was getting more and more dense as we trudged on. Another turn and another disappointing view of nothing but up. Someone had built a tiny snowman and put a happy face on it with pine straw and rocks.

"Adorable" I muttered, defeated, and kept on walking.

"AMERICA!" Joseph screamed. I looked back and saw his pale face with wild eyes pushing his bike. "WE'RE GONNA GET TO AMERICA!" Then he hacked up a lung.

I followed suit when I tried to take in a big gulp of air only to be met with thin oxygen. I shared in Joseph's breathing and coughing issues.

"Sup guys" I heard someone casually say as the kid Taylor rode up.

He was neither winded nor looked tired.

"Big climb eh?" He said.

"How is he doing this???" I said to myself.

"So where's um… what's her name?" I asked Taylor.

"Kristen? Oh she'll be here soon, she's just slower on some climbs."

"You get that spoke fixed on her bike? She looked like she was favoring a foot, too." I asked.

"Yep. So you know this descent is bad, right? It's very steep downhill, proceed with caution." said Taylor.

I took a breath of what air I could and rode. It was indeed steep, very steep. In fact it was so steep I was afraid of tumbling off my bike at times. My hands were numb and aching from grabbing the brakes to control my speed. After what seemed like hours going downhill I finally saw it, the sign saying America. I started to ride faster only to be passed by Kristen and then I had a pity party.

"I'm so slow, I'm never going to make it. I'm not going to make it to Mexico; this was a stupid thing to do. I should be home with Kate; I can't believe I put her through all this. What a dumb choice to choose SINGLE SPEED! God Scott, you are an IDIOT!"

I continued pedaling muttering negative things to myself looking at my handlebars. I looked up just for a second to make sure I wasn't going to run off the road and I saw several blinking lights, some stores and the gates saying "United States."

MONTANA

My morale changed instantly. I'd made it to America.

"There's a Subway just down the road here," said Kevin. "Follow me."

I assumed Kevin had looked it up on his GPS and it was going to be right around the corner. I quickly found out that Montana's "right around the corner" is more like "Twenty miles of farmland, ten miles of suburbs, another five miles into a town and/or city, a Subway."

Montana was beautiful. I see why they call it the Big Sky state—endless miles of clouds, prairie, and small towns. There was not much energy left in me but I worked to stay with Kevin on the flat roads. He'd said the Subway was *"right down the road"* so I figured *"Any minute now."* I finally gave out trying to keep up with Kevin and he dropped me. The road was sparsely populated with little houses here and there but no town in sight. I looked at my GPS to see where the Subway was: "Subway. Eureka. 25 miles."

I dropped a resounding (and satisfying) line of 12-letter expletives in the middle of the road. At one point I was so angry and yelling so much that I thought I was speaking as two different people. I realized, after I shut up, that there was a goat behind me that would baaah every time I'd drop an expletive that started with the letter F. This goat obviously delighted in cyclists that rode by and dropped a line of verbal bombs not suitable for a Sunday afternoon church revival.

It was late now but the sun had not gone down and there was plenty of daylight left. I continued to ride on long stretches of road until I came to one crossroad. I looked to the left and there was flat farmland as far as I could see. I looked forward and the scenery repeated itself. The GPS said to go to the right. I did, and it was the same scenery except for a small farm; then a few more farms and a house and finally I came upon a gas station when I saw it, the Subway… with at least 20 bikes wrapped around it.

With my stomach now piloting my body, I made a beeline for the doors, rested my bike on other people's bikes and flew in. The line was backed up with racers and there were two Subway "Sandwich Artists" (I love that title that Subway uses for their employees) frantically taking orders. Apparently minutes before the racers showed up, the entire Eureka little league "Lincoln County Lions" baseball team had come through. The employees had not had so much as a minute before all the Tour Divide racers showed up.

Joseph was ahead of me and coughing up a storm. His eyes completely red now, he looked like he was going to die. He ordered a vegetarian sandwich.

"You don't eat meat?" I asked.

"No man, no animals for me."

"You know I respect that and all, but on this race you need proteins."

"Nuts, man!" Joseph said in a weary smile.

Without any thought to calorie restriction, ordered three sandwiches; two for that night and one for breakfast. The "Sandwich Artists" made them up while I urged them to keep gooping on the guacamole. I got my sandwiches and started to devour one. Then it hit me how tired I was and I started to think about camp. I was filthy, muddy, wet with sweat, and completely blitzed. I looked out at my bike leaning on other racer's bikes. The thought of camping sounded like murder.

I walked out to my bike and saw two racers walk around a corner. Connected to the gas station was a hotel: dingy looking, but a hotel nonetheless. I ran over, looking for the office to get a room. No office. I had sandwiches in one hand, my bike in the other, my helmet balanced on my bike and all my wet gear on the seat. I kept frantically walking around in the parking lot looking for the office to check in when my helmet started to slip. I reached to try to grab it with my chin and then my clothes fell off the saddle . I tried to grab them with my hand that was full of sandwiches and the clothes and the sandwiches fell on the parking lot asphalt which had a nice mixture of gasoline, tire residue and cigarette butts. Then my bike fell out of my hand and crashed to the ground too. I was so tired, so exhausted and now completely angry.

When I'm tired and angry generally I try to focus in on one thing to gain control of something as it helps me simmer down. During these moments of trying to gain control, outside forces trying to interrupt me usually are met with a strong emotional reaction by me (I constantly work on this in my daily life).

While I was trying to pick up everything, I heard a gruff voice say "Looks like you forgot your motor on that thing ha ha!"

I looked and several motorcycle gang looking people were rather enjoying my follies and decided to make light of it while I was trying to gain some control over my frustrating situation.

Generally I'm a nice guy, happy-go-lucky and adhere to the "*cup is half full*" attitude. But not tonight and not in the mood I was in. I looked down at my bike on the ground, my sandwiches sitting in god-knows-what and my clothes strewn on the asphalt now collecting the oils from cars, motorcycles and suvs. I looked up at the motorcycle riders and with a lost temper screamed

"Well you can laugh at me OR GIVE ME SOME DAMNED HELP! WHERE'S THE DAMNED OFFICE TO CHECK IN, JERKS!?" (I didn't say jerks; it was more of multiple 12-letter explicatives.)

I couldn't believe the words coming out of my mouth; more so, I couldn't believe I was saying this to a gang of hulking motorcycle riders that probably were rejected from the Hell's Angels because they were too large. One guy stepped off his bike and walked over to me. He was double my size, and quite intimidating. I figured I was about to get decked in the parking lot as he loomed towards me. When he got within "head clobbering distance" he calmly said:

"Hey dude, it's right over they're where you pay for gas."

He then leaned over, picked up my bike and handed it to me. I grabbed my clothes, helmet and sandwiches and ran into get a room. "*One please,*" I said to the checkout clerk. She looked up at me and with an exhalation of smoke from both her nostrils she drew another puff on her cigarette and said:

"Well we're out of bottom rooms but there is still one up top if you wanna lug that big ol' bike of yours up there."

"I'll take it," I snapped, and gave her my debit card not even caring about the price of the room (fortunately it was only $59.99).

I walked out of the room and headed towards the stairs. When I got there, two of the motorcycle men were standing between the stairs and me. I figured I was going to get my body pulverized. Strangely, the opposite happened. One guy reached out and grabbed my bike and said "Here let me help you with that" and the other guy grabbed my wet clothes and carried it up to my room.

"You look tired." one guy said.

"I'm really sorry." I muttered.

"No harm, dude. Rough day?"

"It's been very hard and tiring."

They were on vacation riding across the country and stopped here for the eve. They were possibly the friendliest and nicest Hell's Angels gang I've ever met. I wanted to hug the guy I cussed out and told him that I would never forget his kindness. I went into the room, got in the shower then collapsed in the bed.

I slept. Hard

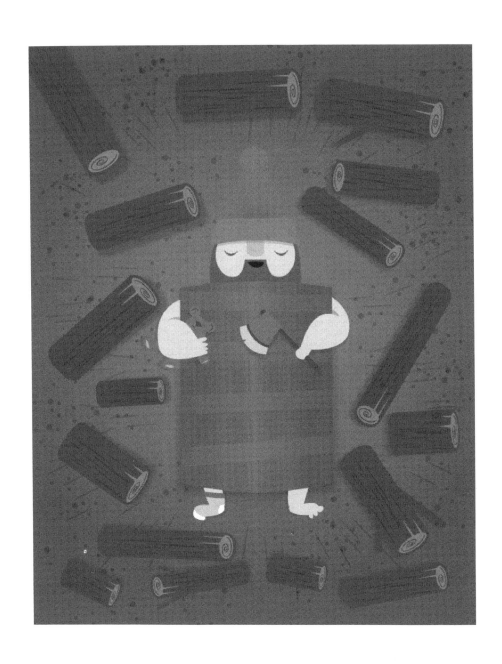

Day 3: Snow Bears

Waking up was not easy. I'd crack open an eye then fall back into a deep sleep. My mind was screaming *"Wake up! Wake up! Wake up!"* But my body was having none of it. Tracy, my coach said that the brain would do everything it can to keep you comfortable. It's my opinion that we, as a society, are sometimes lazy and overweight... because it's comfortable.

Forcing myself out of bed, I realized I was sweating. While it wasn't particularly cold, I'd cranked the heat up way up the night before because I was so cold from all the sweating. Every part of me was wet.

My bike clothes and bike were a sad state of affairs. After two days it looked like they'd been ridden to hell and back. The leg in my bike kit was already starting to unravel and the bike's pristine red and white were now a muted coffee cream and dirt red. Despite the horrid climb over the wall, all the way up some ungodly mountain pass, I felt renewed physically but a little let down because I was sure everyone else had left hours before.

I opened the door to get some fresh air. Immediately a blast of cool, crisp air hit me in the face. I took a long breath and took it into my lungs. It was extremely refreshing. When I looked down off the balcony, I was surprised to see several racers meandering about and gearing up for the day.

Below me Sean, Ryan and Kevin were getting ready. I figured I'd never see them again as they hopped on their bikes and rode off. I went inside and inspected my bike. Given the circumstances, everything seemed intact. However the hub was really wobbly now and my back tire had some major wiggle in it. I wondered if this was going to affect the ride. I stuffed everything in my bags, went inside the gas station, bought a fair amount of candy bars for the day and started my journey towards Whitefish, which apparently boasts a fair amount of grizzlies.

Riding through the town of Eureka, looking to pick up the next segment of the Divide, I saw one cyclist over to the side looking at his bike. It was Ron, the singlespeeder from South Carolina. I smiled, waved and kept going on. Then it hit me, I just passed another single speeder! This moved me up the ranks. I was metaphorically patting myself on the back getting lost in my own thoughts about how good I was doing when I almost ran into Prentiss and another racer, Matt. Both veterans of the race finishing last year, they were heading in the wrong direction.

I stopped and asked, "What are you guys doing! You're going the wrong way!"

Prentiss said they were going back to Eureka and get some food before the long journey to Whitefish. More back patting as I passed another singlespeeder.

I started towards Whitefish alone. For at least 20–22 miles it was all paved road, and it was bliss. The weather was perfect, the sun was out and there was a mild breeze. I had my earphones on, singing loudly to some embarrassingly bad current pop music and was up out of the saddle of my bike dancing along giving cars who drove past me a rather great show.

I zoned out and enjoyed the bliss, in fact I enjoyed myself so much that I rode right past a turn I was supposed to take and continued climbing for a few miles. When I looked down at my GPS I said, "*Oh crap...*"

Looking up, I saw that other riders had missed the turn too. I stopped and waved at them but they didn't see me and continued down the wrong path until they disappeared. I shrugged, stopped, and checked my phone to find I had service. There was a message beeping from Kate and my family. I pressed play on the video to find my stepson had dressed up like a bear and his sister was pretending to be me on the Divide route getting eaten by the bear. After the skit they both yelled "*Happy Father's Day*" and the video ended. Tears flooded out of my eyes as I both laughed and wept somewhere on a dirt road. I tried to regain my composure for a few moments when I heard "Hey!" I whipped around and it was Ron from South Carolina.

Ron had a wonderfully pleasant presence, easy to be around with a giant red beard and wild blue eyes. He was always peppy and talkative and I was happy to see him here, kind of. Dammit, I had such a lead on him too!

I tried to get my composure quickly and said "Well hey man, just rubbing the dust out of my eyes." I knew he wasn't buying it. "And watching this Father's Day video my kids made for me."

He chuckled, talked about his family as well and then I said, "Hey did you know we're on the wrong path? We need to turn around!"

So we stopped, filled out water bottles by a waterfall nearby and headed down the right path.

Riding singlespeed with geared people is hard, but riding singlespeed with a fellow rider who also chooses the one gear is great. We were generally evenly matched, I was a tad faster than him on climbs but he was much more adept going downhill at fast speeds and we were the same on the flats. As we hit one climb I dug my legs into it and powered up it, dropping Ron for some time. At the top, I stopped to look over the side of the mountain. Words, photographs and paintings could not describe what I saw. Endless miles of purple mountains, saturated with beautiful green trees, valleys that extended on for forever and seemed to be miniscule from where I stood way above

It was the annual BUMP N GRIND Race at the end of May put on by the Birmingham Urban Mountain Pedalers (BUMP). Bump N Grind is an infamous race through all of Oak Mountains' trail system that attracts both the pro and the beginner to tackle several forms of racing over the course of two days. That includes a downhill over a rock garden, a flow track, a cross-country race and a mountain bike-ish cyclocross race; it makes for a very fun weekend.

I'd just turned 40 and I was going to be a trail marshal for Bump N Grind making sure the racers were taken care of at my segment.

Before I scooted out to the trail my friend Mickie grabbed my arm. "Hey Scott, I've got a whistle for you to take on your Divide trip."

Mickie was one of the first bikers I'd ever met; she's probably one of the kindest and big-hearted people I know. With a passion for bikes, gadgets and trails, she's always out to support the cycling community.

She pulled out a yellow whistle and said "You can hear this for miles, it'll scare any bear away. I hope it comes in handy."

As Ron and I made the descent I pulled out the yellow whistle and stuck it in my mouth. It was a flat whistle made out of hard plastic and probably one of my most useful pieces of gear I ever had out on the Divide. I had my whistle out because the descent we were taking was on a dirt road with quick turns and I wanted anything on the other side of that turn to hear me coming. So as I'd near a turn I'd lay down on the whistle hoping to scare it away. I saw a fair amount of bear scat and prints but no bears. Thank you yellow whistle, mission accomplished, no bears.

Ron didn't use a whistle but would make noise with his mouth to scare bears away as well. We continued riding down the mountain and it came into a flat, long dirt road with trees that seemed to touch the sky. As we pedaled Ron motioned for me to look to my right, I did and saw a camping spot.

"You see that?" Ron said. "That's where Ollie and Craig spent their first night last year on the Divide." I was on two full days of my race and last year's leaders Ollie Whaley and Craig Stappler had pedaled non-stop until here. I was, to say the least, humbled.

I reached down to get a water bottle and noted it was empty. I reached for my other water bottle and noted it was low. I was not worried at all because every 15 or 20 minutes there was a waterfall with fresh water flowing from it. Even though I sterilized all my water with chlorine tablets, I didn't really need to - it was running straight off a mountain and I was practically at the top. I decided to find what looked like "the best" waterfall to fill my bottles up with. I found one run off with a massive flow. I stopped to fill my bottles and rest my legs a bit. I looked back down the trail and saw a biker. "*Must be Ron,*" I thought, but it wasn't, it was Prentiss and trailing him was Sarah, one of two female racers.

I'd been told about Sarah and how she was an absolute beast and was made of steel nails. As I took a break I watched her power it up the hill effortlessly followed by Prentiss. They zipped up the hill, and then disappeared. After filling my bottles, I followed suit and started to climb up the mountain after Prentiss and Sarah. As I whipped around a corner I noticed the temperature dropping a little bit, but nothing to really write home about. As I continued to climb I noticed some snow in the distance, then some snow closer to my tire. A little more up the climb and a lot more snow now. Then the entire road I was climbing was absolutely white. I continued trying to stay on the bike and push through it spinning up through the blanket of fresh white frozen hell. I was up out of my seat with my head buried in the handlebars. I wasn't looking up; I was just trying to get up the side of a snowy mountain.

"Nice work" I heard a panting breath say as I passed Sarah.

I was surprised; I'd caught her and now was passing her... barely.

"Thanks." I panted and continued to climb until I just completely gave out. I stepped off my bike panting in the snow watching Sarah continue powering it up the mountain of what seemed to take little effort on her part. I walked.

As I continued to walk I noticed some very familiar footprints, it was the bottom of Chuck Taylor shoes and when I looked up and saw Prentiss also breaking (and panting).

"HOWDY!" I yelled several feet back in the snow from him. I spent a little energy trying to catch up with him.

"Hey yourself." Prentiss said with a grin. When I caught up with him, we pushed together. Up above we'd see Sarah off her bike, and then on her bike, then back off her bike until she was hiking in the thick snow.

"It was worse last year, you know" said Prentiss.

We continued trudging through the snow only to be passed by hikers powering up the hill. They smiled, kind of laughed at us and then disappeared.

Prentiss smiled and said, "You've never been up here, have you?"

"No." I said.

"You're about to be in for a surprise."

We rounded a corner where it was flat and Prentiss said "Welcome to Red Meadow Lake."

I stopped, a tear formed in my eye as I took in the sight. On top of the peak of a mountain there was a lake, which was as clear and pure as angel tears. You could see straight down to the bottom, as the only thing that really touches it is snow from the lone peak above us. There were people fishing in it, some people were hiking around it and taking pictures and I just sat awestruck.

"Please get a picture of me!" I asked Prentiss excitedly.

He snapped a few shots of me. I walked slowly to enjoy the lake, the sights and the beauty. It was a mixture of white, green blue. I have never seen anything that pure.

As we continued to walk, the snow got about shin deep and I looked for lines that other bikers had made to maneuver through. Finally, an opening appeared filled with obvious fat mountain bike tires. I decided to try to take it, hopped on my bike and started pedaling.

I said to myself "Hey lookit, I'm biking through snow, I should do that Alaska race because I'm like a Billy goat that can't get knocked off his bi..."

And WHOOMP I slipped, fell and landed in the snow.

Prentiss laughed and said, "You okay?"

I nodded in pain and wearily and started to get up.

I put my hand in the snow to push up and looked just ahead of me. There was a track, an extremely large track. It was a grizzly track - one of many that spanned way behind me and far ahead. I stuck my hand down in it; it was twice the size of my hand. I sat and swallowed for a moment and looked on, then I saw cub prints too, which was just a tad smaller than my hand. "Jeez!" I said to myself and was a little humbled. I looked ahead and saw Prentiss walking along and I thought

"Well maybe they'll eat him first" and kept pushing my bike.

We came to a fork in the road and stopped.

"Which way do you think it is?" I asked Prentiss.

Up until now I'd been relying on people for turns. Right, left and me didn't get along very well.

I can look at a map, it can clearly point left and my brain gets all jumbled up second-guessing "is that my left or the map's left? Maybe it's the north left!"

With my ability to flip flop things and transpose numbers in my head, I get turned around easily. Prentiss looked at the map while I looked at my gps.

We eased down the hill and enjoyed a nice, long and easy downhill until we crossed a bridge, which had three people on it, two women and one man. The man was in a muscle shirt, cowboy hat and had a Fu Manchu mustache. The two women were rather...earthy to put it nicely and they were looking over the bridge. We rolled up slowly and in my friendliest southern accent I could muster I said a resounding "Howdy, y'all!" And they all whipped around quickly and clearly surprised.

The man turned, grabbed the tip of his hat and nodded as if by reflex, the women both turned around and smiled a toothy grin while they drew their pistols two their sides. My southern drawl morphed into a more panicked squeak.

"Uh, hi...." I said nervously.

"Uh... um, what are y'all doing?"

"Fishing!" They said laughing at the realization they had scared us.

I laughed nervously and rode on thinking this gave new meaning to shooting fish in a barrel.

Several hours later I was on the outskirts of Whitefish and I was off in my own little world when I heard "SCOTT!" and looked over to my left seeing Joseph, Eddie and Prentiss. I hopped off the bike lane to where they were: a rather large convenience and grocery store.

"Whoa, look who it is" I heard a familiar voice say; it was Kevin, Sean and Ryan.

"Oh wow! Hey guys! Never thought I'd see y'all again!"

"Big news dude, check it!" Joseph said pointing to a man in a jeep. "He's the mechanic for the bike shop down the road, he said he'd service our bikes!"

This was one of those moments that being in the right place at the right time was on my side, trail magic again? Check!

"So my wheel is wobbling," I said to the man in the jeep.

"Well just come on down, it's a mile from here. There's even a great pizza parlor right next to us!" He said glancing at my bike.

All of us as a group rode out from the grocery store. I watched Ryan, Kevin and Sean ride off to the left to head towards Columbia Falls, Montana and we rode into the downtown Whitefish. We got to the bike shop and they let us in the back. It felt like I was in the mechanic's shop in Cahaba Cycles back home, a musty smell of bike tires, stations with various tools and equipment to keep bikes running and a bunch of friendly and relaxed staff.

"Get some pizza next door, it's good...but first let's take a look at your bike." He said and moved some stuff around on my bike messing with the tire. "Hmm..." the mechanic said like a doctor does when they know something is up.

"That's bad... that hmmm you just made." I said.

"Well, you need to get it fixed, your wheel won't last until New Mexico."

"Well what should I do?"

"Well we're too small here to fix it, make it to Helena and I bet they can figure out something."

Helena was the next major town and it was a long way away. But I thought it was my only hope.

"Can you at least keep me together until then?" I said

"Yes" he responded and proceeded to tinker around on my bike, tightening up as much as he could and getting as much dirt off of everything as possible.

Meanwhile Eddie was buying a new crank set as his had completely fallen apart and the rest of our gang was just resting.

"Soooo… pizza eh?" I said.

"Yes, just next door, you can leave your bikes here."

When I came back in, Ron and Ty had showed up and were getting pizza. Also Matt, who was with Prentiss back in Eureka had showed up but he was in a flannel shirt, a pair of shorts and sneakers. I looked at him oddly because most racers when they are dressed down simply take off their jersey and remove their suspenders. Before I could open my mouth he said, *"I quit"* with an apologetic face.

"I'm done, I'm sick and I don't feel like going on."

I don't know why but this hit me like daggers in the back.

"Why!?" I protested.

"I'm just too sick, too tired and just can't go on."

It really started to freak me out—the first person on the Divide Race I knew that had quit. I felt like I'd been stabbed. I said "man I'm so sorry, I hope you have a safe trip home."

He nodded and said "I will."

"Hey we're ready to go… me and Joseph are leaving. You wanna come? We want to make it to Columbia Falls tonight." Eddie said, nudging my arm.

We hopped on our bikes and started out of Whitefish.

"There's a hotel there, I think," Eddie said.

"I'm trying hard to not stay in those, I've already spent 2 nights in a hotel as is." I growled.

"Well I wonder if there is an RV park or campground or something there."

I decided to try something extremely foolish, which was to pedal my bike and look on my phone at the same time for this RV Park. I pulled it out, balanced myself on my bike and opened up Maps app. It confirmed that there was indeed a RV park just down 20 miles away. I thought to myself *"well isn't technology just grand"* and that's when all of a sudden I lost my balance and wiped out on the road. Eddie and Joseph didn't see the wipeout and kept pedaling. I just laid on the ground in pain as I watched them ride off into the sunset. A car came up next to me.

Day 4: Columbia Falling

"You okay? We saw you fall!" The driver asked, alarmed.

"Yeah, just rang my bell a bit." I said rubbing my head.

"What happened!?"

To save face I said I was just exhausted and fell over and how I'd ridden from Canada to Whitefish not stopping for sleep and this was my giving out point. I think they bought it, I'm not sure. The lesson here is don't use your phone and bike or you'll have to lie.

"Could you tell those two bikers way up there I wiped out and I'll be there shortly?" They nodded and drove on and alerted Eddie and Joseph of my fall. I caught up with them.

"What happened?" Eddie asked.

"Oh, um, my back tire is just so wobbly that it threw me off balance and I fell over." I said sheepishly

Eddie looked back at me puzzled and not really buying my story.

"I was trying to use my phone and bike at the same time, not a good plan." Hanging my head.

We all laughed and I did too, kind of, as my leg was in some major pain from landing on the asphalt.

The ride out of Whitefish was very pleasant, we had a gold and orange sun beaming on us, it was mostly flat and the ride was pretty on backwoods paved roads. I learned that Eddie's son has a disease called the Shwachman-Diamond Syndrome, which is a rare illness that is a bone marrow dysfunction among other debilitating things. He was attempting to raise $100,000 in funds to donate to research for the cause. Joseph was maybe 20 and had been off and on with college, was working at a multinational coffee shop chain and one day just up and left to do the Tour Divide Race. He had no interest in going back to the very popular multinational coffee shop chain when he got back. He owned a plot of land, an Airstream and some chickens. I was envious, I wanted pet chickens too.

We pedaled on the long flat road and eventually saw "Welcome to Columbia Falls." Eddie said, "There's GOT to be a place somewhere to stop for the night, right?" I was sort of half committed to stopping, part of me felt like riding on. Even though I was very tired my body kept saying, "just pedal." We rode through town, I noted a coffee shop, restaurant and the other places there were all closed but maybe would be open tomorrow and I could get a quick meal on the go. Even though it was still daylight, it was really 10pm at night and most places, like all small towns, had closed.

We started to leave Columbia Falls when we saw a hotel and across the street, an RV park. We pulled up to the park and it too was closed already. I peered in the door of the office and saw no one stirring. We rode around the office a few times and then finally decided on taking a bathroom break here and moving on. As I tried to find a private place to do nature's business, I heard a voice say,

"Can I help you?"

A man was standing just outside his office/house. He'd been watching us from a video camera and wanted to make sure we weren't vandals.

"Need a place to camp, anything open?" I asked. He thought a moment and said

"We're closed but I'll go ahead and open up for you guys." He said

Today was just overflowing with Trail Magic.

We went into the office and Joseph screamed "ICE CREAM!" and dove into the freezer looking for the perfect ice cream bar. Eddie and I paid for camping spot and he said "anything else?" I looked around the room and saw everything any camping convenience store would stock - conventional camping equipment, candy bars, soft drinks and canned goods such as sardines and… chicken noodle soup! I went over to the aisle and grabbed two cans, then got a third. I walked by and also grabbed a t-shirt that said "Columbia Falls RV Park."

"I'll take all these and this snazzy shirt," I said and dropped everything on the counter.

"No, wait" I then dashed over to the soft drinks and got two cold Coca-Colas.

We walked outside and the owner walked us to where we'd be camping.

"Now we saw a grizzly roaming around here the other day, so keep your garbage in the bear-safe canisters." The owner said.

"Lovely…" I said and took note of the dumpsters where they had locks on the lids.

The camping area was nice; our area had a nice soft patch of green grass surrounded by an orange fence to sort of wall off the other RV campers and hungry bears. I rolled out my camping gear and set it up; Eddie and Joseph did the same. I finished setting up, and reached over and grabbed a can of Campbell's Chicken Noodle soup. I ripped off the top and didn't even think about a spoon, I just downed the entire thing, and then I grabbed another and did the same thing followed by swallowing a can of Coke in two gulps. "I'll save the other coke and soup for breakfast" I said with a smile to Joseph and Eddie who sleepily laughed.

I grabbed my shorts that I used for sleeping and my newly acquired t-shirt and made my way to the communal showers. The shirt was ironically funny as it had a picture of an RV Camper, some wolves howling and of course said "COLUMBIA FALLS RV PARK" on it. I loved it.

As I started peeling off my bike kit (which now was starting to stink badly) I stopped and looked at myself. My beard had grown out and was unruly with more streaks of grey in it than I'd like. There were pronounced laugh lines on either side of my nose that extended down past the edges of my mouth. My body didn't look like I'd thought it would on the Divide. I had these images that I'd look like some muscular Greek god from all the biking I had done. Instead I looked like a haggard old hobo however my legs did look rather toned. My belly was bigger than I thought it'd be. Perhaps it was just the bloating. I got in the shower and turned on the hot water letting it hit my beat up body. It felt wonderful as the steam rose up. I just stood there under it, not wanting to move at all.

Two things I hated on the Divide were the moments before falling asleep and the moment of awakening. The moments of falling asleep had my brain so ransacked that I was only going to get maybe three hours of sound REM sleep only to hear the chimes of watch alarms and phones at 3:45 and 4:00 to get a start on the day. I would get particularly nervous if I didn't get to sleep until midnight because

I knew I might only get 2 hours if that. It was near midnight at the RV Campsite in Columbia Falls and I was still wide awake.

The buzzer went off at 3:45. I didn't want to get up. I wanted to lay in this nice comfy patch of grass forever and be happy. I was warm, I didn't want to get on my bike but hey, coffee would maybe get me up.

"There's a diner 30 miles away. We could get there before 10, you know." Said Eddie.

"Okay," I said.

Hours passed by and finally we saw cars pulling into and out of what we hoped was Echo Lake Cafe, and it was. We rolled up and it was a well kept restaurant, almost new looking in fact. We walked in and I made a beeline to the outlets to charge up my phone and batteries, a practice I found to become common anytime there was a stop and an electrical outlet. Eddie and Joseph did the same and then we sat down looking at the menu

"You're part of the race, right?" Said the waitress.

"Yes ma'am, and prepare to make several trips back here with lots of food!"

"Okay" She said chuckling. "So what would you boys like to start out with today?"

I looked over and looked up one of the biggest breakfasts I could find. There seemed to be one with everything... fruit, potatoes, sausage, eggs, pancakes and yogurt. "That one" I said. She took Eddie's and Joseph's orders and then walked off. Eddie took out the map and was reviewing what was to come.

"Looks like there's a lodge, then the dreaded Richmond Peak, then Seely Lake. Gonna be a big day!" Eddie said. I remember hearing something about something that someone said about this Richmond Peak, but I couldn't remember clearly what it was about. Was it in Jill Homer's book about the Tour Divide and how she said it was so hard? Maybe it was Paul Howard's book? I couldn't remember, I'd just heard Richmond Peak was bad. Or was it? I don't know, I couldn't remember.

The food came out; and it was a feast if not an orgy of food. I shoveled as much food in my mouth as I could. Sufficiently full with more carbs and coffee than my body could hold, we stood up and I

66

felt the sluggishness of carbs making their way through my body slowing me down. I knew I'd have to push through that. We also ordered egg and sausage burritos to go. When she brought the doggy bag out and handed it to me, it was heavy; like it must have weighed at least 3lbs. You know who wasn't going hungry today? This guy,

this guy wasn't going hungry.

As I was winding down the huge downhill I found myself starting to really buckle under the grease and undigested food just hanging around in my stomach. I felt green and I'm sure I looked it too. I continued to pedal and then involuntarily heaved.

"No Scott, you can't throw this food up. You need it!" I said to myself and then shoved down the heaving again. I continued to ride for a long time dealing with the sickness that was swirling in my stomach, then it hit me. I wanted to quit. My brain started to play tricks on me telling me I'd gotten giardia, some bad infection from

undercooked eggs or was generally dying of every cancer imaginable at this very moment.

I started to bargain with myself.

"Okay, well… if this continues for more than one hour, I'll quit."

I continued riding and one hour passed. The terrain was still a dirt road with no signs of life anywhere and I was still dealing with the upset tummy and undigested food and because of the position I was in on the bike, it wasn't digesting anytime soon.

"Just 30 more minutes and if it's not ebbed, you're quitting Scott!"

I reached down to get a sip of water, but the bottle was empty. The sun was out and beating down on me, it was hot and it was miserable with the eggs still sitting there, the mentally 800lb egg burrito in my backpack and the general fatigue that was coming on me.

Fortunately I heard the sound of running water and I stopped my bike and went over to the stream. There was moss all around it and I took off my shoes, sat on the cool spongy grass and put my feet in the water while sterilizing my bottles. The water cooled my body and settled my stomach a bit.

"Oh god this is great"

I rested for a while almost falling into a sleep. The last remnants of the greasy breakfast digested and ebbed and I could feel myself coming back to life. I took one good sip of cold, cold mountain water and then refilled one more time for good measure. I continued on and at a more pleasant pace.

I saw a small bridge with a sizeable creek running under it. I threw my bike down and zipped under the bridge to drink some cold water and rest. I was now back to being hungry so I ate from a candy bar and stuck my feet in the cold creek water. I heard the gang of cyclists finally show up. "HEY!" I yelled as they rode by and they all saw what I was doing and also came down under the bridge to cool off and stick their feet in the water. Joseph had bought large can of coconut water and passed it around for everyone to drink. I took a giant gulp and that's when I heard Eddie scream

"NO!!!! STOP!!!!! NO NO NO AAAAAH!"

We all leapt up because we thought a bear, zombie or something, was eating Eddie. When we came from under a bridge a giant suv was trying to make it's way around all the downed bikes in the road, Eddie was trying to prevent this... one of the bikes directly in the SUV's blind spot was mine so I ran towards it trying to stop the drivers.

In Alabama, we cyclists are not a liked animal at all. It's gotten downright ugly between me and motorists before when a motorists thinks it's their God-given right to blow you off the road just because you're going slow. I'm used to people wanting to pick fights with you because you're on two non-motorized wheels and I was pretty sure I was about to be in an altercation with an SUV driver as it rolled to a halt and it's door flung open as I grabbed my bike. I braced for the worst.

The man got out, he was a thin, wiry with a pronounced grey beard. He had brilliant blue eyes, a fisherman's cap on and a pair of khaki shorts, white socks, low cut hiking shoes and a Hawaiian shirt.

"I'm sorry, I didn't see your bike there," He said apologetically.

"Huh?" I said tensed up, out of breathe and was expecting to get chewed out.

He repeated himself

"Sorry about that, didn't see your bike. Is it okay?"

"Well... yeah, uh thanks! I'm sorry too!"

"No, no, was my fault, shouldn't have tried to weave around the bikes. You look tired, do you want some soda?"

Ah soda, a cake in a can is what I call it. I said "yes sir I do" and he walked around back while the other passengers exited the vehicle now surrounded by cyclists. Trail magic appears again.

"What are you boys doing" the wife of the man said. We explained the race and she said, "Oh that just sounds so exciting! Are you boys hungry!?" Before we could even say "yes" she pulled out a cooler full of bars, fresh fruit and more sodas! "Have all you want! We were just hiking and were going back home, this is all we have left." I tried to be modest and only get a few things but the lady said "oh, take more... you've got a long ways until your next town." So I took as much as I could, I stuffed as many bars, fruit and sodas as I could on my bike. I thanked everyone in the SUV profusely and started to ride out. The other racers lingered and stayed for a while to continue chatting with the hikers, I wanted to get a move on and make it to the next town.

The hikers had said to be aware of bears because this area was thick with them. It was around 4 or 5pm now and there was still full sunlight. I continued a long and hard climb until finally my legs gave out and I threw my arm over the handlebars and rested my head on the arm.

"You don't look so good there" I heard a familiar voice say. It was Rob Orr; the grizzly cyclist I'd temporarily rode with outside of Banff.

"I'm just so tired," I said. "Surely that town will be here soon, right?"

"You got hours, boy."

I sat there for a while and thought about how hellish "hours" sounded and decided to just bite the bullet and go.

I rode for what seemed an eternity, finally experiencing some hot weather as well. I saw a sign for a lodge that was just a few miles ahead. As I rode towards the lodge I saw a series of campground areas but no Tour Divide riders. When I got to the lodge I saw a couple of bikes and immediately when I rolled to a stop the bottom of the sky fell out and started to rain and pour. I grabbed some necessary things off my bike and ran inside.

The lodge was rustic, very upscale and had every kind of dead animal stuffed and nailed to the wall that you could imagine. There was a family eating dinner and a bride and groom checking out the place as a possible spot to get married in. There was a beautiful lake and a very rustic looking bar. I walked up to the bar and sat down all my stuff. A lady in a long black dress and blonde hair walked out.

"Hi, can I help you? You're with the race, right?" The waitress said.

"Yeah, could I have a water and a beer please?"

"Sure" She said pouring me a Pabst Blue Ribbon.

"Would you like to order something?"

"Yes and I may want to stay the night, too." I said once again going against my vow to camp more than stay in a room.

By now I didn't care anymore if I camped or not, in fact I had resigned to the fact that staying in hotels and lodges made me stronger in the morning, screw this camping crap!

She handed me the menu and I looked it over. There was steak, salmon, tuna and lamb on there with descriptions and no prices. I knew what that meant, it meant if you had to ask, you couldn't afford it.

"Sooo, room and lodging is…?" I said with a leading question.

"185 for the night but that includes dinner."

"Well how much is dinner?"

She said something to the tune of 50-60 dollars and I thought about all the money I'd blown through just to make it through here.

"Could I pay a little bit just to sit down and rest for about 2 hours while I charge my phone and gadgets then I'll take off?"

"I'll have to ask the manager, one second."

As she walked off one racer came down from upstairs. Apparently he was staying here at the lodge, he was tall, thin and had a quiet disposition.

"Hey there" he said with an instantly recognizable German accent.

"You're Scott Thigpen, I read your blog. I'm Mirko."

"Hi Mirko, you staying here tonight?" I responded.

"Yes, my knee is acting up and I need to rest it."

I had considered asking him to let me sleep on the floor for a fraction of the price, but I decided against it. Mirko was very pleasant, in fact I met a number of German racers while out there and they were all so unbelievably polite and nice. My interaction with German culture is very little and I know hardly anything about anything German however all I have to base things on now is just how polite their cyclists are and that they made a cool movie called "Run Lola Run." Mirko went for the dinner that was included in his lodging fee. I was starving and suddenly realized I had that egg burrito sitting in my backpack, the egg burrito I'd purchased about 12 hours ago. I thought about it and thought about how it's probably gone bad but then I started rationalizing. *"How bad could cooked eggs and sausage have gone in an aluminum wrapper? Right? RIGHT?"* I grabbed my backpack and casually sauntered into the restroom.

In what was an act of depravity I ate my extremely large egg and sausage burrito in the lodge guest restroom. At least it was a nice restroom, which was clean, but it still bugged me out that I ate in the same place you poop. I looked at myself in the mirror while I ate, my beard was now tangled, unruly and had bits of egg in it. My eyes looked heavy and I had a sunburn where the heat of the day had cooked me. I finished wolfing down the burrito and it was bliss and I honestly couldn't have cared less if it had gone bad and was going to kill me. I went out to the lodge and found one of the nice leather couches and dozed for a few moments.

I couldn't really afford to stay there at the lodge, but I also didn't want to bike out and camp in the middle of no where because it was bear country and my bike was a walking meat wagon with all the beef jerky and food stuffed in it. I considered my options, finally gave in and decided to go ahead and do it however every red flag in my brain was waving saying "NO!" I remember a guy named Rob Roberts that had done the Tour Divide previously and was following my progress. I messaged him and said, *"How bad is Richmond Peak?"* He said it wasn't overly bad but that there were some sketchy spots, and if they were just too sketchy, for me to just walk. I told him I was nervous and his response was:

"Bears are scared of big dudes with southern accents singing at the top of their lungs. I'll share my song with you....

"Go home bear

Leave me alone Mr. bear

just passin' through

want no trouble bear

move along now bear

just passin' through

Go home bear"

I rolled my eyes at his poor attempt at humorous songs, half smiled and went out to my bike. The rain had stopped and I took everything out of my bike, repacked and took a deep breath. I put one foot on the pedal and hoisted off to Richmond Peak.

There are some dumb, really dumb things I've done in life, but none have been as stupid as trying to take Richmond Peak, Montana in the middle of the night, alone. The day was waning and I started in on the climb. It was a long climb but nothing I couldn't handle. My legs had been in superman mode for the past few days and I was still going strong. I gritted my teeth and kept pedaling on the fire road. Eventually the fire road turned into a trail and all I could see were the remaining purples of the Montana sky, then the moon and shadows. I started to get a little nervous so I put in my iPod and listened to some poppy music. I'd accidentally grabbed one of the kid's playlists when copying over mine so what I'd hoped to be what I call "working man's music" like Johnny Cash, Hank Williams III (not Hank or Hank Jr), Eminem, Nitty Gritty Dirt Band and Atmosphere ended up being Ke$ha, Hannah Montana (not Miley Cyrus), One Direction and a bunch of other bubble gum music songs. Fortunately the bubble gum music songs are happy enough to take the edge off a very dark, scary hike through bear infested woods. I kept my eyes peeled for anything but wanted nothing more than to find the light of another biker so I would know I was in some company.

The trail turned back into a road and it was now pitch black dark. I started to break down a little bit because I was convinced by now that every grizzly bear in America was hot on my trail. I continued to ride and finally the climb partially started to flatten out. I wiped my forehead thinking I was done however when I checked the elevation profile, I realized I'd only just begun what was going to be a long, long night. As I started into the first descent it was all pitch black dark by now. I grabbed a bite to eat and started downhill, that's when a series of orange eyes all lit up in my lights. I skidded to a halt and started to breathe heavily. At least 8 pairs of orange eyes stared back at me and didn't move. I was stunned and frozen in my tracks. I tried to sing the song that Rob Roberts has mentioned.

"*Misst.... Missster bear... don't eat... oh god*" With a surge of adrenaline, I screamed "*GET THE HELL OUT OF THE ROAD OR I*

SWEAR TO GOD I'LL THROW THIS DAMNED BIKE DOWN YOUR THROAT!"

To my surprise the orange eyes all darted off and now somewhat relieved, I realized they were all elk. I grabbed my very loud whistle, stuck it in my mouth and with a new found adrenaline I poured downhill blowing my whistle as loud as possible to scare off any wildlife that would be lingering in the dirt road.

The next climb was worse, but only to be matched by the worseness of the climb thereafter. I was sweaty, tired and just didn't know how much more I had left in me but there was no way in hell I was sleeping in these woods, I could feel everything staring at me, waiting for me to let my guard down. The road leveled off for a moment then did a switchback where I saw a man-made sign jabbed into the ground. As I made my way around it I looked at the sign. It was warning that this was heavy grizzly activity, not to go ahead alone and to make sure your food was packed in airtight containers. Well I was alone, I had beef jerky stuffed from one end to the other on my bike as well as M&M's, snickers, a slice of cake and Sour Patch Kids all shoved into what was definitely not an airtight container.

I sat there and thought about going back down to the lodge, but I'd spent hours just getting to this point. I looked to see when the next town was and it was going to be easily another 3-4 hours to get there. I tried my best not to panic and kept looking back for any lights of a fellow biker foolishly taking this climb like I was. No one.

I ate a bunch of my food and threw out the rest that wasn't sealed. It really killed me to do that but I really had no choice.

"Enjoy these peanuts and candy, Yogi... You suck."

I hopped on my bike and started the slow and grueling climb. I kept the bubble gum music going however a feeling of dread just came over me. I stopped, looked back and felt like something was following me, but nothing was. I collected my thoughts and continued to climb. I stopped again and looked back, I swear I thought something was following me. My lights peered through the fog and cold behind me, as I looked, nothing.

I continued to pedal and between my nerves the drop in temperature; I was a cold nervous wreck. A few more bubble gum songs by pop singer, Ke$ha came on and I started to sing along;

happy music makes for a happy Scott. Then I saw it. There was movement in the corner beam of my light, I saw it move, this was it. It was going to be a Grizzly and I was about to become a snack. My adrenaline spiked along with my heart rate and I started to breathe heavier and heavier. I yelled "COME ON BEAR! DO YOUR WORST!" And bit down on my whistle and blew. The movement tore out from the bushes and darted out in front of me. I started to scream again however the frightened rabbit I'd scared to death probably was in worse turmoil than me as it scurried across the road and down the mountain. I sat there and felt waves of relief and anxiety flow out of my body. "Damned rabbits" I said and by this time I'd used up so much energy that I couldn't pedal anymore and I had to start pushing. An hour went by or so as I'd push, stop, freeze up from the cold and then continue to try to ride only to push, stop and freeze up again. Rabbits would dart in front of me and while I was much more relaxed, I was still keenly aware there were bears in the area.

I looked down at my watch. It was two in the morning and I was tired, really nerve wracked, cold and scared. I would have done anything to find a fellow rider while cresting Richmond Peak and that's when I noticed it, two lights ahead of me up on the peak of the mountain. Finally, it was two bikers and I blew my whistle hard and started screaming at them. I saw their lights flicker and move but not really towards me. But I was sure they heard me.

I picked up the pace and blew my whistle again, again the lights flickered back and forth, and then one disappeared and appeared around another tree. "HEY! HEY HEY!" I screamed but nothing. I pedaled faster, and then faster trying to catch them. I wanted so bad to see another human, someone to talk to and feel safe in numbers. Nothing. Their lights, which were an odd orange instead of the bright white that most bikers had on their bikes, just sat and flickered back and forth. As I got closer the lights look like the eyes of an angry Tiki God or something, something like an Angry Bear Tiki God. I started to get a little nervous that maybe they weren't bikers but some raging backwoods hillbillies bent on taking out bikers up on Richmond Peak in the middle of the night. I started to get scared and slowed down my pace.

The road ended and turned into a trail that steeply went up, the trail got narrower and narrower then I heard "crunch." I looked down and my shoes were in a foot of snow. I decided to move to the left to get out of the snow, but there was no left. My foot found no ground, it was straight down and when I looked all I could see were the tips of trees. I looked over at the other mountains, sheet lightning would hit and I'd see the sea of mountainous nothing with me surrounded by darkness. I trudged through the snow hoping I wouldn't slip off the mountain. I looked up and noticed I was closer to the two other bikers with their lights, but it wasn't lights after all - it was fire. Two trees were on fire and it was now spreading down the mountain towards the trail I was heading towards.

I frantically picked up the pace and walked faster through the snow occasionally slipping and making it to surer ground. Smoke surrounded my nose and eyes. I started coughing and grabbed my bandana wrapping it around my nose and mouth. My eyes watered with the billows of smoke and in a panic I said "screw it" and hopped on my bike powering through the snow, with a few flare ups of fire to my right where the forest had started to burn (I later found out that lightning had struck two trees and caught them on fire). I flew down the snowy trail trying to get through the smoke, see which way to go and not cough up a lung at the same time.

"*GO GO GO!*" I yelled and hammered it down hitting limbs, briars, slipping in the snow and trying to keep upright. The upright part didn't work out very well and I bit it pretty hard one time. I got up and took a long breath full of smoke and coughed uncontrollably again while flames licked up here and there around me, I was a nervous wreck. I grabbed my bike and continued hammering as hard as I could zip through the cold night and going down. The smoke started to ebb, the trail started to clear out, there were no bears and I was going faster than I'd ever gone at night on a single-track trail. I was covered in sweat from panic, fear and fatigue. The snow started to fade and then it happened, I hit a fire road that was all the way down. "HELL. YES!" I screamed and let off the brakes flying down the road at speeds I'd never take usually, especially at night. I didn't know what shape I was in, I didn't know what shape my bike was in, I didn't care, I just wanted off that damned mountain.

Twenty minutes or so went by and a new issue, cold, replaced relief. It was still in the 30's and the sweat that covered me was now chilling me to the bone. I started to shake and had nothing else I could put on because I had everything I possibly owned, on. To make matters worse I experienced a new sensation, one that would appear many times to the very end of the Tour Divide.

This new sensation was when my front wheel hit the miles of divots or washboard terrain that was made into the dirt roads by cars, bulldozers, rain and erosion. As I whipped around a corner and hit the washboard part of the road my teeth and bones were instantly sent into a violent vibration and rattling.

"*WHAT THE HELL WAS THAT!*" I screamed as I vibrated through the divots.

Then I hit another long patch of vibrations and I was constantly working to pick better lines through all the washboard roads. It became tedious, and then it became an act of patience, which lent itself to almost losing my temper. I was shaking uncontrollably from the cold and sweat and also kept getting surprised by the washboard roads. I kept riding and was desperately looking at my GPS seeing how close Seely Lake was. It showed five more miles, then four and a half, and then I saw lights in the distance. To put the icing on the cake my lights started to dim and flash low batteries followed by my GPS flashing low batteries. Three miles, the lights grew bigger. I hit another round of washboards jarring every bone in my body. I hit a fork in the road and saw a sign that said "Seely Lake," I hammered it. The lights got bigger and signs of life started to pop up on the dirt road; neighborhoods then the city, which had a hotel. I zipped under the awning, taking note of all the Tour Divide bikes there and knocked on the door, which was closed, no response. I went to a window and it said, "buzz for service." I pressed my fingers on the buzzer and 4 minutes went by with no response. I was freezing now and shaking uncontrollably.

"Yes…" A sleepy lady said.

"Do you have any rooms available?" I said with my teeth chattering.

"No…" she said. "We have a sister hotel a few miles down the road you can stay. It's 85.00"

"85!?" I said shivering "Do you have a cheaper room? I don't need anything special!"

"No…" She said angrily and hung up the phone.

I started to tear up and panic more. I wanted to just be warm, I was filthy wringing wet and panicked getting colder and colder. It didn't take long to realize I was sleeping in a hotel and was very thankful of the people who kindly pitched in during my fundraiser to help finance these rooms with a heater in them.

I beeped the hotel clerk again and she, in an exasperated tone answered with "yes…" I told her I'd take the room. She let me in the lobby; it was somewhat warm but I was still shaking.

"You boys are nuts, you know."

"I know."

"Lotsa people give up here in Seely Lake."

I had thought about giving up a little bit but couldn't bear the thought of not finishing.

"I'm not quitting, I just need to be warm." I said.

She gave me my key; I went outside and raided the snack machine getting some cokes, candy bars and Cheetos. I stuffed my bag full and could feel the cold surrounding me with my wet clothes. I drove my feet down into my pedals and for one and a half miles or so; I went as hard as I could to generate heat. When I made it to the hotel I flew into the room, threw off all my clothes and ran into the bathroom. I turned the water on as hot as it'd go and until it was near full. I jumped into the water and even though it was piping hot, I could not stop shaking.

I laid in the water for some time letting the heat massage my body. I looked down at my legs; the muscles were as tight and pronounced as I'd ever seen them. If I were entering a leg contest, this would have been my one chance as muscular as they were. I leaned my head back and let the water hit the back of my neck, and exhausted, I fell asleep in the tub.

Day 5: Rootin' Tootin' Saloonin'

I'm not sure how long I was asleep but when I came to my entire body was completely waterlogged, especially my feet and hands, the water was cold and I was immediately shaking again. I stood up and let the shower hit me with full heat again. Once I somewhat warmed up I went into the bedroom and turned the heater on full blast and stood in front of it drying off. While the heater started to warm up my frozen body, I looked over all my bike clothes strung everywhere from where I'd thrown them off. Filthy, wet, smelly and me with the thought of putting them back on for another long ride tomorrow just sounded awful. I grabbed them all, threw them in the bathtub and let them soak while I fell asleep in the bed. I didn't set an alarm, I didn't care what time I woke up, and I was going to sleep in as long as I wanted.

I fell into a deep sleep, harder than I'd ever slept before that I could recall. I didn't dream, everything was just blank. If I'd been a machine you could say my batteries were completely shut down and not even the charger was working. I was completely worn out.

Hours passed but in my mind, I was only asleep for minutes. Eventually I woke up and wearily stretched. I didn't hurry out of bed; in fact I made it a point to not move very fast. I went into the bathroom and looked at my clothes soaking in the tub, all the water was brown from the dirt, grime and sweat from them. I grabbed them and draped them over the shower rack, turned on the timed heater in the bathroom and walked outside in my shorts and Columbia Falls RV t-shirt. It was warm, peaceful and I enjoyed the sun beaming down on me. Today was a new day.

As I rode off into the woods, I was dealing with a lot of depression for this leg of the race. I'd taken a fair beating the night before and it was still eating at me. Regardless, the ride out of Seely Lake was absolutely beautiful, even with the "Warning, Grizzly Bears" signs every 500 yards. Occasionally I'd see a jeep or a truck drive by on the beat up fire roads. At least the climbs were mild. Sometimes they got bad but then they'd always ebb a bit. There was a beautiful stretch that ran by a flowing river for some time. I saw a few beavers playing in the water, some deer and vast amounts of birds; it was generally a lovely, heavenly forest.

For all of nature's beauty, I was pretty depressed and not really happy to be on a bike, I wanted to be home and I wanted to be done with this race. I really struggled with these negative thoughts for hours trying to fight off the temptation to give in and be done. As I continued biking for a large portion of the afternoon I watched the terrain change from hilly to flat, then to giant open "Montana Big Sky" plains. The scenery seemed to have stretched on for a while and the dirt roads were not so bad to be on.

I saw a sign that said, "Welcome to Ovando!" Then another sign that said "A great place" only to be followed by another sign that said "You'll love it here." These all seemed to be a welcome for me as I was tired and hungry. As I biked I saw a tiny figure appear coming towards me on the dirt road. As I got closer it was a young girl in flip-flops, pigtails and riding a run-of-the-mill kids' bike.

"Hey mister, you're one of those racers, right?" She said.

"Yep. Hey, so this town coming up, any food there?"

"Yes, there's a saloon there."

"A saloon!?"

"Yes sir, Trixi's Saloon or you can eat at the Stray Bullet Cafe."

I thought I'd entered into a western movie or something.

"Can you take me there?"

"Yes! Sure!" She said excitedly knowing that she was going to help someone.

And I followed her along as she hammered her little bike in front of mine. I could tell she loved doing this; I followed her along making sure she always got to stay ahead of me. She said, "There you go" and pointed to the mighty town of Ovando, Montana.

Ovando is 9 miles wide, it has around 5 buildings and that's it. That's all of Ovando, period; a post office, a saloon, a general goods store and an outfitters shop. I rode my bike up to it, hopped off and leaned my bike against the wooden fence of the porch. The door opened up to the outdoor shop.

"You Scott Thigpen?" A lady said coming out of a store called the Black Angler. Confused I said, "Yes?" I said bewildered.

"Been trackin' you for the past hour or so. Welcome to Ovando, name's Kathy Schoendoerfer, go get you some food in there, it's delicious."

I walked in the Saloon/Cafe and sat down. There were a few folks in there eating a late lunch. The waitress who was no more than 15 years old came over to my table where I sat alone. "What can I get you sir?" She said nervously; apparently this was one of her first days. I said, "I want a water, a chocolate milk and…" I looked over and saw they had beer, in fact they had beer called "Moose Drool" and I said "One of those Moose Drools too!" She brought the three drinks over and I downed the water, the chocolate milk and nursed the beer. I looked over the menu and they had every type of cafe food you could imagine. I opted for a salad and asked them to put extra leafy greens in it along with chicken. I sat there tapping on my beer making the bubbles in it pop off the side of the glass and float up to the top. I felt alone.

The salad came out, it was enormous, with boiled eggs and chicken in it and loaded with spinach. I sat and munched on it and then I heard the door open again, the bell jingled and I heard my name called "SCOTT THIGPEN!"

I looked back and it was Joseph, Eddie, Ty and a new guy named Jeff. My jaw fell open, my mood instantly changed and I ran over to give Eddie and Joseph a giant hug. "I'm SO GLAD TO SEE YOU!" We laughed; we all got another beer (now my third one) and sat and ate, ordered more food and enjoyed being merry and happy. Afterwards we went over to the outfitter store, The Blackfoot Angler and bought supplies for the road. Apparently the Tour Divide is a big deal for them so they have lots of things stocked for racers such as bike nutrition, tires, tubes, pumps and anything else you could imagine. I talked to the friendly lady Kathy and she told me about bears.

"Hadn't been a person killed by a bear here for 30 years and the only reason one guy died is because he thought it'd be a bright idea to kill an elk then dispatch it right there at the camp. Big ol bear came in with her two full-grown cubs and ate the elk and then the man. Message here, Scott? Don't dispatch your kill at camp. You'll be fine on your bike."

I smiled and walked outside. Joseph and Eddie were horsing around on their bikes as well as Ty and Jeff. With now three Moose Drools in me I got on my bike and started horsing around. We started popping wheelies on our 50lb tour divide bikes and then it hit me that I needed to ride as I was just lingering too much.

"Hey guys, you ready to roll?" I asked everyone.

"Yes, in a minute." Joseph said.

They lingered for several minutes and I got antsy and so I finally said,

"Hey guys, I'm going to soft pedal and keep my legs moving. See y'all in a bit?"

Joseph said sure and I lightly hit the pedals, heading towards the prairies.

I soft-pedaled.

The ride out from Ovando was absolutely pleasurable. Flat, plains, a cool breeze, a bit of wind, a little bit of more wind, some more wind, a little stronger wind and then when I went around a corner and I saw a massively large storm heading towards me and I was riding into it like a game of chicken.

Bears have always scared me, but only in a half-joking manner… lightning however is an entirely different animal for me. Unbiased and unruly, the electricity generated from storm clouds can put you down in a half of a heartbeat. As I rode into the storm I saw several small animals scurrying for cover. Rats, pheasants, turkeys, deer and elk were bouncing left and right running and ducking for cover while I was riding straight into it. It sort of begs the question that us humans are the top of the food chain with the dumb stunt I was doing. I went across a bridge and lightning struck closer than I'd like. I jumped and rode faster to catch a minivan stopped watching the storm.

"Hey!" I said as I rode up, hoping they'd take pity on me and let me sit in the car while the storm passed.

The man rolled down the window, he had his family in there, a wife and two boys.

"Hey I'm in a bike race and I need to make it across that plain there, that storm, you guys get twisters?

"Nope, no twisters. Just storms."

He never gestured to let me sit in the car as the rain started to pour. I'm sure I looked like some wooly thug and I wouldn't let me sit in my car either. So I said, well hey I'm going to go sit under the bridge for a moment.

I pulled my bike under the bridge and watched the bulk of the storm pass. Lightning struck left and right and I sat and cringed. One strike got particularly close and it sent me into a panic. In an act of stupidity I ran out from under the bridge, hopped on the bike and in the lightning, wind and rain I hammered it! I rode past the family in the minivan and powered it on through the prairie and plains. "Don't die, don't die, don't die!" I screamed and flew down the road as fast as my one gear would let me; adrenaline carried me for the mile or mile and a half through the plain. Lightning would strike close and I'd scream in panic. I kept on the gas and even though my adrenaline was in production, my body's ability to produce power and speed was starting to wane quickly. I rode through a small farm and the wind picked up tremendously.

As I rode through the farm area I saw doors and windows flapping with horses and donkeys calmly but deliberately making their way inside the barn doors to get out of the rain, I had half thought about joining them when without a moment's notice the lightning stopped, the wind died and the sun came out. The storm had immediately blown past me and was making its way back to Ovando. I stopped and looked to see if I could see Joseph, Eddie, Ty or Jeff… nobody. Before me was nothing but sunny skies and peace. I rode on through the gates of the farm area and into an open prairie. All around me were painted horses calmly eating in a field. I rode by them admiring the majestic and calm nature of the horses. There were three horses in the road and I decided to get up close to them and get a picture. I slowed down and hopped off my bike, whipping out my phone to snap a few shots. As I did the horses nervously pranced away and I heard the snort and neigh of a horse behind me.

I looked behind me and at full speed a larger horse, who was apparently the protector of horses, was barreling at me at full speed. "Okay okay, I get it, I'm leaving," I said and I hopped on my bike and calmly biked away, the hoof stomps got louder and now the horse was in full pursuit of me. "OH CRAP!" I screamed (But I didn't say crap) and dug into the pedals once again asking my body to perform unnatural speeds on a very tired and spent cardiovascular system. I biked hearing the stomps of hooves catching up to me. The horse neighed a warning sound and I felt like I was Ichabod Crane being pursued by the headless horseman. I pedaled as hard and as fast as I could and finally the prairie dumped into a trail and the horse ran off, satisfied that it had protected its herd.

After a few climbs the terrain was pleasant with lush hills of nothing but grass and beauty. The sun was out and the rolling green landscape seemed to go on for forever. As I pedaled along, I'd pass a few ranchers in their trucks, and they'd smile and wave. Then I went down one hill and came up on another one and suddenly I was nearly knocked down by a wall of wind.

I don't know how fast the winds were blowing, but it was the strongest headwind I've ever had to face in my life. I had to dig my feet into the pedals to even move and that was going somewhat downhill. Then the splat of rain hit my helmet. "Aw damn, again?" I said as the rain came down in sheets on top of me. At least there was no lightning this time and I continued to pedal catching up to another cyclist. "Helluva weather huh?" I yelled. "Ugh, yeah this sucks!" And we braved the wind trying to ride through the hellish terrain, which finally dumped out, into a paved road, which became the town of Lincoln.

As I rode into the town the wind and rain stopped, I saw a RV campground that welcomed tent campers too. It was 15 dollars, had a communal shower that seemed to be in working order as well as a communal bathroom. I rode around and saw a series of hotels and lodges, all showing cheap prices but I was sick of paying for lodging and wanted to use my camping equipment I'd paid a zillion bucks for. I went back to the RV Campground and started to get my stuff out. It started drizzling again and the area I was going to set up in was already a damp sponge and was beginning to become a swimming pool.

"HEY!" recognizing the familiar voice of Joseph. "Hey man! Come room with us!" They were riding in and had called ahead about lodging.

"No man, I'm tired of paying high prices for lodging." I replied.

"Dude, we're all getting a room together… all separate beds and it's 12 dollars each for us, it's got a sauna."

I thought about a shower, the sauna and a nice warm bed. I caved in and joined in. We all got there, got our room and stripped down and put on our non-biking clothes. After that we hopped on our bikes and headed into town and found a restaurant - the only restaurant - called The Moose Joose. We all piled in, and we were the only ones there. They had a bar, a warm area and an all-you-can-eat pasta buffet. The waiter came up to our table; he had most of his teeth, was dressed in flannel and had bright blue eyes. "You boys want the buffet?" He said and we all replied in unison "yes." I ordered another Moose Drool beer as well as everyone else and we ran to the buffet.

My nutritionist Kelli said for me to eat light during the day and then pile in the calories when I'd stopped riding for the night. I ate. I ate so much that I about popped. In fact I ate so much that it appeared I had a food baby poking out of my stomach. Our waiter was probably the most overly friendly person in the world, so much so that we thought maybe he was going to hunt us down and kill us in our sleep (that was our little joke, he was a perfectly nice guy). We sat and talked about the day, the storm, huckleberry pass and getting into Lincoln.

"Soft pedaling huh, Scott?" Joseph said with a smirk. "You dropped us like a bad habit."

"I rode slowly for a long time soft pedaling, where were you guys!?" I said defensively.

They said they saw the storm and decided to wait it out while I foolishly rode through it.

We went back to the motel and stripped down to nothing, grabbed all of our towels and all sat inside the sauna. I'm someone that's rather uncomfortable with being around anyone in a bathing suit because there's already too much skin too close to me but being in a sauna with 5-6 naked men that I barely knew was a new level of discomfort.

I nervously tried to make small talk and get to know everyone. Jeff was from California and apparently was having trouble with his neck, Ty ran a bike shop and had been a bike model too, Joseph and Eddie I already knew about but we decided to chat a bit about their lives leading up to this and how it'd been for them.

After the sauna I talked to Kate on the phone and told her about Ovando, the moose beer and the man sauna. There was a long pause on the phone and she finally responded back with "Are you in a race or on vacation? Regardless, have fun in your Bromansion."

Day 6: The Bromansion

The next morning's climb was brutal but I made it to the top of the Continental Divide crossing once and admired the view; it was beautiful. I wished nothing more than my wife to be there with me. She loves to bike and does it for pure enjoyment, and I knew she would enjoy this scenery. What she loves more, way more than beautiful scenery is terribly fast and dangerous downhill. Kate is rather the thrill seeker and would easily jump out of a plane where I like to cautiously take it easy and safe. As I started the descent I did indeed have a blast but did so at a very controlled pace. I just didn't want to bite it. As I went down a portion of the mountain I looked out to see rolling hills of lush green grass, farms, prairies and beauty that would occasionally bring a tear to my eye. I rounded a corner and as I hit the straightaway something black darted in front of me. It was huge, scared me to death and I slammed on the brakes almost flying off the bike. When I stopped and panted I got a lick in the face from an extremely large Labrador retriever. As I sat there panting I put my hand on its head. I didn't know whether to twist it off or pet it I was so surprised.

Two women walked up and yelled "Awww, Baxter! You back off now!"

"No no, it's okay, he just scared me to death. I thought he was a bear!"

"That's why we have him, to scare off bears!" The women chuckled enjoying their hike for the day.

I asked them if I was close to a town and they said that Helena was not too terribly far away but I still had miles to go. I bid them farewell, patted Baxter on the head one more time and rode off.

I dipped down a hill only to be hit with another hard gust of wind. I wrapped around a corner to be hit with an even worse gust of headwind. I pedaled hard, and the roaring wind sound picked up and grew stronger. I thought about Erik and what he must have gone through last year dealing with this; it was rather miserable. I hit some flat farmland and was now in a deadlock with the wind. It blowing towards me and I was pushing against it. I stood up out of my seat, on a flat surface and pushed as hard as I could.

"NOT GONNA DO IT, WIND!" I screamed and took a turn, and immediately the wind died off and I resumed a pleasant climb in the middle of a prairie and a farmland. An hour or so passed and I finally reached a road. I knew it; I was near Helena, and I was starving. I rode up to the top of a hill, crested it and saw a spray painted sign that said "Tacos, Emiliano's." I dashed across the busy road and into the tiny taco stand.

"Buenos Dias my friend!" Emiliano said.

"Buenos Dias, como estas?" I responded in very bad Spanish.

"Bien, et tu?"

"Mas a manos. Esta es cansado." I said probably not doing the Spanish language any justice.

"?Tienes hambre?" he asked.

"Si, horrible!"

"Well what do you want my friend!?" He laughed.

I looked over the menu, there were bacon wrapped hot dogs.

"I'll take tres caliente perros por favor!"

"You got it!" Laughed Emiliano. "Why are you dressed so funny?"

I explained to him the race, he'd not heard of it and asked if more racers were coming, I told him around 100 more.

"How can I get them to come here?" He said excitedly.

"Maybe put up a sign that says 'Tour Divide Riders, eat here?'" I suggested while I watched the wheels turn in his head.

He had the radio going and I heard "Warning Helena Montana, looks like hail and flash floods are heading your way. " I felt safe inside this little taco stand and didn't even think of budging while Emiliano made my bacon wrapped hot dogs. He brought them out to me, two greasy dogs wrapped in bacon wrapped in a bun with onions, peppers and much grease dripping all over them. They were bliss, I ate them almost instantly. I called my wife and between smacks I said:

"Baby…"

::smack smack smack::

"baby… I'm eating"

::smack smack gulp::

"I'm eating bacon wrapped hot dogs, my god… I'm leaving you for these dogs."

She concurred that she would also leave me for bacon wrapped dogs. I told her about my bike sort of falling apart and how I was going to make it to the Helena bike shop to get it fixed. I slurped down my coke and headed into town with intent to make it to the Great Divide Cyclery nestled in the heart of downtown Helena. As I pushed off and headed into town I felt my helmet get hit by something, then something again and again and again. Hail and lots of it. It came down and pelted my arms, my helmet, my eyes and my legs. Giant welts started to form on my body as the hail violently came down. Cars would ride by me and I'd see the sympathetic looks of people in their vehicles as I continued to get beat up by hail. Finally after I'd had enough of it, I saw a place called "Mattress Madness" and I rode underneath the awning waiting out the hailstorm. A man poked his head out.

"Son, you okay?" He said looking at me crazily.

"Well I'm wet and freezing."

"Come on in, boy."

I walked in and it was warm, and there were mattresses everywhere. The man and two of his employees came out and looked at me like I was an alien.

"Son, what are you doing?" The elderly man asked.

Shaking, I told him about the race. He said "Come on in here" and gestured to another show room. I walked into it, and there was a bearskin hanging on the wall and everywhere in the room there were furnaces. "We just don't sell mattresses, son, we sell furnaces too! Go on and turn a few on for him!" He gestured to one of his employees

"I'm… I'm not… I'm not imposing right?" I said with my teeth chattering.

"Naw boy, you look miserable. You just pop a squat in front of one them furnaces and warm yourself up for a spell."

I thanked him profusely and curled up in a little ball in front of one furnace while another warmed my back. It was bliss and I didn't want to move. Outside I watched the hail just violently pound down while I dried out. I looked down at my watch; it was 5:55 and the bike shop closed at 6pm. I started to get nervous and so I walked out into the hail.

"Boy, what are you doing!"? The boss said

"I've got to get to the bike shop at 6pm, it has to be serviced." I said nervously.

"What bike shop? Oh the one downtown? You ain't gonna make it!"

"I've got to try!" I said now with a heightened state of existence.

I ran out to my bike, dug into the pedals and through the busy traffic and hail, I made a valiant effort to the bike shop.

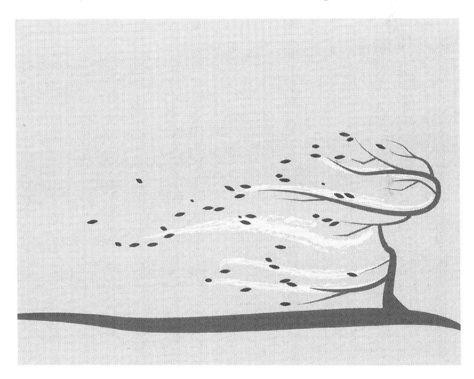

4:30pm, 2013 The Cohutta 100 Mountain Bike Race

"How much time do I have to make the cutoff?" I screamed at the volunteer.

"It's gonna be tight, you've got exactly 2 hours before cutoff. You better pedal hard."

The Cohutta 100 is a mountain bike race that spans from Georgia to Tennessee and then back. It's grueling, it's hard and the year before I'd been disqualified for missing the cut off times. This year I aimed for that to not happen. I remember racing as hard as I could push it and grinding it trying to make it to the final cut off. I looked down at my watch showing the minutes counting down until I would be disqualified. I made it with just minutes to spare and remember the feeling of victory making it passed cutoff and finally, once and for all, finishing the Cohutta 100. Making cutoff in harsh conditions of the Cohutta 100 meant I could do anything if I put my mind to it.

5:57

The hail had stopped and I booked it as fast as possible to the Helena Bike shop. I was lost, which way do I turn!

5:58

Going down the busy city streets I hopped a curb and promptly landed in a puddle splashing me and all my gear.

5:59.

OH GOD ALL OF THESE BUILDINGS LOOK THE SAME!

6:00

Is that it? That's it. That's the bike shop!

"PLEASE DON'T CLOSE PLEASE DON'T CLOSE!" I ran in yelling.

"Dude, don't worry, we're here for you crazy Tour Divide Racers, just go next door and they'll fix you up." The clerk said calmly.

I walked my bike over next door where there were a few Divide riders getting their bikes looked at. I walked in and the technician guy said "What's up with your bike?"

"My bike hub is all wobbly," I said.

"Well roll it in over here, you thirsty? You want a beer?"

"Uh, yeah?"

He motioned me to come behind the counter and back there they had a fridge with a handle built into it that had a keg connected to it inside.

"Pour away, man." He gestured.

And I did. I downed the beer immediately and poured another, which I also downed. My body was screaming for calories and hops and yeast was just fine and dandy with me. My bike disappeared and I made a few phone calls while they doctored on it. As I was checking for messages "The Bromansion" group appeared which consisted of Ty, Eddie, Jeff and Joseph. While I was on the phone Joseph mouthed "HOW DID YOU GET AHEAD OF US?" and made my arm go around in a pedaling motion. I heard Joseph go back to the group and laughed saying "He said soft pedaling."

We went to a bar in downtown Helena. We sat around, talked about the day over more cold beer. We laughed, we were having a really good time, almost too good of a time by my standards. In my mind the Tour Divide was supposed to be about roughing it and staying in dirty clothes in your tent dealing with the howling wind. But I was comfortable, dry and warm and was enjoying it. I didn't want to munch on a twig for dinner, I wanted this burger. I didn't want to crawl in my tent; I wanted a nice warm bed. "I hear the Lamplighter hotel is cool." Everyone perked up and we all spilled out of the bar and headed towards the hotel. When we got there, Kristen and Taylor were there as well. They came over and hung out for a while. It felt like a frat party with people laughing, enjoying life. I texted Kate a picture of us at the bar and the only response I got was "The Bromansion."

Six guys and one girl all were enjoying a great time. While we sat around, Kristen moved to get to a chair and grunted. I looked down and her foot was heavily bandaged and she could barely put any pressure on it.

"What happened??" I said surprised.

"Tendonitis. I spent a day in the hospital because of it." She responded flatly.

She did not give one look for sympathy votes nor did she give off the "look how tough I am" vibe either, it was just matter of fact, her leg hurt and this was the way to solve it. I would have quit.

The laughter started to ebb and I went into one room to get ready for bed. Jeff came in and took the other bed. Jeff was from the West Coast and other than his neck killing him, he was enjoying the race. When everyone slipped off into slumber I set my alarm for 3:45am. While I loved everyone in the group, I needed to get away and get serious. I enjoyed the laughing, the fun times but I felt like I needed to make up some ground. Tomorrow would be the day I pulled away and would stay on my own for the rest of the Divide.

Day 7: Hell In Ya'

Descending into the valley off the mountain I noted my bike computer said it had dipped below freezing. My body started to freeze up as the wind hit me since I was descending so quickly. My teeth started to chatter and I could feel my skin turning blue underneath all the wet and freezing clothes I had on. I passed through a valley where the sun broke through the trees; I tried to use it as a time to warm up by slowing down... nothing. I continued riding and whipping around dirt roads that would have otherwise been a wonderfully pleasant ride but I was in agony with the cold surrounding my body.

The road pitched back up and I was into another nasty climb, which meant more sweat and... something hit my face. Then another thing hit my face. I looked up into the sky... snow, and not just a little bit. There was tons of it. At least it wasn't really sticking but it did get me wetter and wetter. Needless to say I was less than happy about this. I whipped out my iPhone and made a funny video then continued to trudge on up the mountain. The terrain got worse until it was near full on rock climbing and the climbs got more brutal. There was a small creek crossing where the snow was melting and drizzling down the mountain. I stepped in it by accident having my foot sink down into the mud. I stopped and got a stick then wrote "THIS IS HELL" in it for bikers to know my frustration.

As I continued to push up, the snow got worse and I was slipping and sliding. I decided if I couldn't beat it, I'd join it so I found a Christmas playlist on my iPod and enjoyed some old fashioned Yuletide carols as I continued to the top; anything to keep positive. When I got to the ridge of the mountain it was indeed breathtaking. To be at the top where only a few trees extended higher than you with snow coming down all around was both something to behold and something I never hope to go through again. I continued pushing my bike until it was completely flat and then I started pedaling through the snow enjoying the beauty that surrounded me as I listened to Jingle Bell Rock in the month of June.

Up on the cold mountain above Helena and towards Butte, I finished the ridge and enjoyed the view and the snow. I started to go down what was an extremely rocky section; in fact there was no trail, just rocks. I had to check three or four times to make sure this was the right way down because once I was down these rocks, there was no going back up, at least for me. Without thinking I picked a line and bounced down the rocks with little to no trouble. The terrain did finally get rough enough that I had to back off my bike and edge down the mountain to not completely bite it but I was really happy I'd made it this far.

Lots of people thought I was nuts for riding a singlespeed across the Divide, and maybe I was. I get called eccentric all the time and nowadays I just embrace that term. Never did I wish I had gears until this flat road into Butte, Montana. It was absolute hell as I trudged at a whopping 10-12 miles per hour fighting the wind and having my legs scream because there was absolutely no break in pedaling nor any elevation to at least warrant getting out of my seat. I hated it, I hated life and I certainly hated this damned race. I said a few choice words and kept pedaling. Eventually the wind stopped and I started to see a descent, a rather big descent going down and down fast. I looked to my left and saw the huge city of Butte, Montana. I'd arrived; it was hell but I'd arrived. I flew down the now paved road into the city, excited to get my parts to my bike and keep going. I went zipping in and out of roads to get to The Outdoorsman run by Tour De France winner, Levi Leipheimer's brother, Rob. I rode into the shop and immediately Rob runs out, grabs my bike and says, "Rest area is over there with candy bars and sodas, we'll get started on your bike." Like a pit crew they immediately disassembled my bike and started cleaning it. Within minutes they had the bike back together.

"You're good to go!" Rob said.

"You fixed the hub already!? That back wheel was really wobbly!"

"Oh…" Rob said quietly. "Oh you're that Scott guy, um, I've got some not-so-good news for you. Your part won't be here until FedEx delivers it tomorrow around 10:30 or 11:00."

My heart sunk; that was a half a day's riding that I'd miss just sitting around waiting for that part.

"Oh god…" I said trying not to be upset.

"You want a room? We have a hotel connected to this shop, we have a Tour Divide discount."

I knew the "Bromansion" crew was coming in so I decided to go ahead and get a room. Sadly I sulked over to the front desk of the hotel and got a room, I went upstairs, threw all my clothes off, put on my Columbia Falls RV shirt and shorts. Then I went down stairs just hoping a miracle happened and they had fixed my bike while I was up there.

"Nothing?" I said.

"No we can't fix it without the part, sorry," said Rob. "We'll hop on it as soon as it comes tomorrow."

I sat there trying my best not to get upset.

That night as I started to slip off into slumber a new thing hit me, acid reflux. Another fraternity party greasy pizza consumption by the Bromansion in Room 109 in Butte was making it's way back up my throat and it was killing me. I grabbed the hotel key and tiptoed down to the lobby to get a soda to help ease the acid reflux. As I was getting a Sprite I heard a British accent say,

"Ah ha! I caught you man!"

"Huh? Wha? Oh hey Mauro!"

It was Mauro, the single speeder that had the bike that was geared the exact same way mine was. He'd just gotten in and was freezing and hungry. I told him I thought there were some places open around the corner and he dashed off to get some food. I got my Sprite and started to walk back to the room. A weary Tour Divide rider walked in the door and stated firmly "I quit.", then sat down in the lobby. I thought "I could quit here you know, no one would fault me for a broken down bike and a series of troubles, right?" I walked back to my room downing the Sprite, then went and laid back down letting fatigue overtake me and falling off into a slumber.

Day 8: A Wolf In Fleecer Clothing

That morning I remember hearing the stirring of people, then a yawn and then the swishing off movement as everyone started to get out of bed. I rose up and watched everyone start getting their bikes ready.

"You could sleep in and leave at 10:45 with me, you know." I said hopefully.

"You know we have to ride, man. Right?" Said Joseph. "But I'm sure you'll soft pedal really fast and catch us."

"I know." Trying to smile.

Ty looked over and saw that Jeff was still in bed motionless.

"Jeff…" Ty said. "Jeff it's time, let's go."

Jeff murmured something.

"What?" said Ty.

And Jeff murmured again only to be asked by Ty again saying "what?" again.

"You heard me… I QUIT," yelled Jeff.

The whole place went silent and everyone stopped getting ready.

"Dude, whatever, get out of bed and stop playing", Ty said brushing off Jeff's angered statement.

"I'm not playing, I'm done. I can't do anymore of this," said Jeff.

Eddie and Joseph stepped in trying to motivate him but it was no use, Jeff was throwing in the towel. Everyone tried one more valiant effort of motivating Jeff but they couldn't even get a "maybe" out of him.

Saddened, we all parted ways, the group headed towards the next part of the route and I walked downstairs hopeful my part for my bike had showed up.

"No part?" I said to Rob hopeful.

"No part."

I sat and tried to mitigate the anxiety, an hour passed and no delivery. Another hour passed and more Tour Divide riders came in then zipped right back out. It was now 11:30 and I was about to come unglued. "If it doesn't get here in 15 more minutes, it's not coming today." I about blew a gasket. One day was bad, two days would have cinched it for me and I would have quit. Mauro walked in and we spoke again. He said he'd be happy to hang around a few minutes to see if my part came in or not so we went across the street to the pharmacy, picked up some Sour Patch Kids and Cheetos then started to check out. As we did the manager came over and stopped us. "Hey you're part of that crazy race, right?" We nodded and Mauro said something to him alerting him to his origin of country, Britain. Fascinated, the guy drilled him with questions about being over here and what he thought about it. I kept peeking out the door hoping to see a FedEx truck. Nothing.

When we walked back, I finally saw it, a FedEx truck heading our way. My heart leapt up in my chest and I sat elated only to be completely let down as the truck rode right past the bike shop. I was crushed.

Noon. No FedEx truck. I walked into the back of the shop.

"Just give me my damn bike and I'll just deal with the risk of a wobbly hub, Rob."

"Now listen, if you ride out of here and your bike breaks down in the woods somewhere, this will have been all for naught." Rob said pragmatically.

I wanted to protest and that's when I heard the roar of a truck come to a stop in front of the store. It was the FedEx truck. A wave of relief came over me and I ran towards the door snatching the package from him and running back to where Rob was practically shoving the package in his hands. He and his technician worked quickly to take the wheel apart, put in the necessary parts and reassemble it. Like a NASCAR pit crew they worked quickly and methodically. He shoved the wheel back on, attached everything and put the bike rubber side down and said "GO MAN GO!" I grabbed the bike and ran it out the shop, put my feet into the pedals and I was off. Or at least I thought I was off, something was making an awfully bad noise in the back and it wasn't riding correctly at all. Then I heard from behind me

"Whoa! Whoa! Whoa! Stop!!!" It was Rob running after me.

I stopped, turned around and looked.

"We left out a part, come back." He said out of breath.

I spent a ton of energy building up to go and now it was completely deflated. I walked back to the shop and Rob took the wheel apart again, reassembled NOW with the missing part then said, "Okay, you're good to go, I promise." He said wiping the sweat off his forehead.

"I can't say I'll miss Butte, but it's a beautiful place. Thank you." I said and I finally rode out of Butte.

I'd ridden about 2 miles out of town when all of the sudden the bottom completely fell out of the sky. Torrential rain came down and soaked me to the bone. I stopped to put on my rain gear but it was already too late, at least it was leading up into a climb and I could be a little warm. I whipped around the corner on a paved road and saw another biker also putting on his rain gear. I passed by and looked, I blinked and then said:

"J.D.! How are you man!?"

I'd met J.D. online a year before the Divide took place. He'd attempted it last year and due to some injuries he was unable to finish it. We kept up through the Internet for sometime with me drilling him about everything he could remember about the Divide and him asking about what I thought about this or that piece of gear.

Due to the rainy conditions we did not chit chat for very long and hopped on our bikes settling into a climb. I like climbing, I like it better than going downhill so once I get good and settled into a climb I sort of lose the sense of what's around me and hyper focus on my pedal strokes. Because of this, I'm able to keep a fairly good pace up a long climb but the flipside is that I zone out and become unaware of anything else. Here I dropped J.D. and never really realized it. When I yelled behind me "Helluva rain, eh?" I heard nothing. When I took a moment to look back I realized he was gone and I was by myself again, that was until I saw a speck way ahead of me. It was Mauro and I was catching him on a climb.

"Heeeey man, now I've caught you!" I said with a smile. Mauro looked back and laughed, "You must have gotten your bike fixed quickly eh?" I told him that they did get on top of it and as soon as the bike was ready to roll, so was I. We rode together for a spell and then the Divide turned off the road and onto yet another dirt road. It was beautiful; you could see rows of mountains for infinity. We took some pictures and then J.D. and another guy named Daniel showed up.

100

Daniel was a lawyer by trade and insanely funny. His quick wit blew mine out the water and there wasn't one thing I could snap out of my mouth without him coming up with an equally snappier retort.

We rode together for what seemed forever, the sun was out and the warmth and the beauty of the scenery was absolute heaven. Daniel and JD were having lunch, so I proceeded to dig through my bag to see what I had to eat; it wasn't much. I guess I'd not really paid attention to what I was eating and how much I had left. I had part of a candy bar, some Sour Patch Kids and that was about it. Funny thing about not having a lot of food in your system, it's like a man bitten by a wolf and a full moon rising, you get irritable and change.

Fortunately the "Hunger moon" was not upon me yet and I was eating my half candy bar, popping a few Sour Patch Kids and trying to match wits with Daniel's sharp mouth. Daniel talked about that he had brought a fishing rod along with them (a collapsible one) and had already caught a fish. J.D. talked about how he liked to spelunk and had actually been in my "Alabamian Neck-o-the-woods" area diving down into caves.

While this group was not the "Bromansion" group I had been with, it was fine and I enjoyed their company. We rode on, Daniel would jump in front of JD on the dusty road, slam on his back brake and spray dirt all over him, and I picked up the pace and caught up to Daniel and JD.

"I think there's a town not far from here in Wisdom, Montana" Daniel said.

"You hungry?" I was hungry, very hungry and the "Hunger moon" was starting to rise making me a little more irritable. "Hey Mauro, I'm going to go ahead and pedal" he stopped taking pictures and we continued to ride. I didn't talk much, I just wanted to get to this town and eat.

It seemed like hours of climbing and then we biked through a bunch of campers and hikers. They waved and we made it into a clearing. It was a beautiful clearing and looked like a giant prairie on top of a mountain. This was known as Fleecer Ridge.

As we climbed up Fleecer the sun was out, it was warm and I still had all my winter gear on which caused me to sweat profusely. I noted that Fleecer Ridge started to pitch up quickly and the climb became extremely difficult. As I started into it I felt something bump my helmet. I thought it might have been a rock from the wind that had suddenly picked up. Then something hit my helmet again, and again and again and then I felt a horrible sensation sting my legs and arms. Hail, and not just a little bit. We got caught in a full on hailstorm. The sky quickly turned grey and now mixed with the hail was the onslaught of snow and rain. "The hell??" I said as we trudged through. Daniel was able to climb to the top of Fleecer while JD and I pushed our bikes up the now muddy hill. My feet got wet from the stream that had now formed and was coming down; Mauro was way in the back pushing his bike up too. I was in good spirits and was even laughing at one point about how crazy it'd gotten. JD and I made it to the top, I looked back and not 15 minutes ago the sun was out and the ground was lush green. Now it was completely covered in snow. As the rain and snow continued to come down Daniel screamed:

"SO! I HEAR WE NEED TO TAKE CAUTION GOING DOWN THIS BECAUSE THERE'S SHALE AND SHARP ROCKS. SO BE CAREFUL!"

He hopped on his bike and flew down the rocky shale that looked like a series of razor blades. JD dove in after him and I tenderly took it down the mountain grabbing a fistful of brakes at all times.

The shale never seemed to relent and only get worse. While I knew how to take a rocky section, I don't like doing it and I especially don't like doing it in rain and snow. A super rocky area quickly came up on me and I grabbed my brakes to pick a better line down the mountain and that's when I heard "KAH-CHUNK!" I closed my eyes and sighed for a moment, I knew what had happened, the brake pads had twisted and snapped. I glanced down and sure as I'd guessed, the pads were ripped in two. *"Christ..."* I muttered and now with only the back brake to really control my bike, I continued to maneuver down through the rocks going even slower and more careful only to hear "PAH-SHHHHHH." I'd ripped my tire.

As my tire rotated I watched the liquid latex inside spew out like a whale coming up for air and blowing water out of its blowhole.

With each rotation I'd hear *PSSSH! PSSSH! PSSH!* and my tire started to go flat. I said the word "Christ" again but also added in a potpourri of offensive profanities to it. I saw JD and Daniel stopped near one area where it'd flattened out. I screamed at them and with a now flatted front tire, headed their way as quickly as I could.

"Do either of you have a pump?" I said in an animated state. Since my pump had broken to pieces a while back, JD Let me borrow his and I tried to get the tire to catch and inflate.

"Dude, what's wrong with you? It's just a soft leak, you'll make it to town" Daniel said nonchalantly.

I heard him, and a rational me would have said, "Yeah you know, you're right" But the Hunger moon had arisen and the werewolf was coming out.

"HOW LONG UNTIL TOWN?" I barked.

"I uh, bah… dah I dunno? 10 miles?" Said JD.

"HOW LONG! I NEED TO KNOW DAMMIT!" I screamed irrationally.

JD looked taken aback and looked at the map, yeah just a little over 10 miles.

"Christ I'm going to have to walk all this!" I said trying to pump some air in the tire, with my hands numb and still getting hit by small chunks of hail.

"You'll be fine," said Daniel.

"No I won't! I don't even have front brakes!" I fired back.

"Well who needs front brakes?"

"Let's just get a move on!" I snapped.

Who was this barking orders at people I had no authority over? Who was this person using my body? I truly felt like I was changing into a wolf being bitey and nasty towards people that were truly trying to help me out.

Mauro showed up behind us, asked what was wrong and looked at my bike. He said he'd stay behind me and make sure I got down off the mountain. JD and Daniel did indeed drop me and I was pretty angry about it. As we finally got off all the shale, the Divide turned back into a dirt road and it went down. I at least felt a little better about that but then a new problem arose, I was wet and it was below freezing...and we were going downhill at a rapid pace.

I tried to steel my nerves as much as possible telling myself I wouldn't die and that I was just being whiny about the cold however now my core had gotten fairly chilled and I found myself chattering uncontrollably and my hands would not stop shaking. I felt the sudden urge to fall asleep, a sign that hypothermia is coming on and I started to panic. Given I'd now had a whopping half of a candy bar and 15 Sour Patch Kids over the course of 7 or 8 hours and I was doing well to not be in "raving lunatic" status.

Mauro and I rounded a corner on the dirt road and in the distance I saw a home with smoke coming out of the chimney.

"I'm going to stop there and ask for shelter," I told Mauro.

"Oh come now, Scott. You can't do that; we only have a bit left to get to Wisdom, Montana. Keep your spirits up man!" He said in a chipper voice.

I grimaced as we rode past the house. I thought of a good-natured husband and wife that probably lived in there. They probably had just baked apple pies, would let me sit around the fire and give me beer. I could hear them say "Here, Scott, sleep in our best bed as long as you'd like." But we rode past it and all I could do to keep warm was to pedal as much as possible. We hit a long stretch of open road; it was bitter cold as the wind cross-crossed in front of me. Finally the dirt road t-boned into a paved road, I looked on my gps and saw to turn right. I did and I could see buildings ahead of me, as I continued to pedal I saw that all the buildings were closed except for one that said the Wise River Club.

I pulled in, got off my bike and as my feet hit the ground, I had a new sensation, actually no sensation, as my feet were completely numb. I walked in and stood there dripping wet and it was like the scene where the inexperienced cowboy walks into the saloon with all the rough 'n tumble guys look at him funny. Everyone turned their heads to look at me and there I was, wild-eyed, shaking, skin blue and me not caring.

"I need food and warmth!" I said sharply to the waitress.

"Well… how about you go to the bar area around back", she suggested, looking at me oddly.

I dashed to the back and it was a large slab of concrete, four walls, some freestanding tables and a row of liquors. I started stripping off my clothes. A couple in cowboy hats sat and watched me with odd looks on their faces. I continued to strip off layer after wet layer until I was down to my base layer and bike shorts. I draped all my clothes on chairs and watched them drip water.

"Say laddie, looks like you've had a rough day, eh?" I heard in a Scottish accent.

I looked up, a large man with grey hair and grey mustache looked at me with a big grin.

"Do you have any hot chocolate? Coffee? Anything warm?" I said kind of desperately.

"Actually what he wants is a shot of liquor, sir" Daniel said waltzing in stripping away all his wet clothes as well.

"In fact, shots for all of us, and put it on my tab."

The Scottish bartender left while I sat and muddled over the menu deciding what to eat.

"You look rough," said Daniel.

"I'm completely soaked to the bone and I can't stop shivering," I said.

"Well where's your protective outer shell?" He asked.

"That one." I pointed to my dripping wet jacket that has now made a huge puddle on the floor

"That's no outer shell dude, you would be dry if that was the case." He said laughing.

Daniel talked about how he had done several high adventures and had learned what to do with rain, and that was to have a very nice, and handsomely expensive, waterproof jacket. I asked him what I should do and he said the only thing he could think of was to get garbage bags and use those as water repellent. I shrugged and said, "sure, I'll get on that tonight" and that's when our waiter came over with shots of liquor. Daniel raised a toast to now me, JD and Mauro.

"To the Tour Divide! Where we will come back from this mess tomorrow and catch the front racers!" We all chuckled and knocked back a shot of liquor. It felt like fire rushing down the back of my throat and it was quickly absorbed in my body that had absolutely no fuel in it. I ordered some soup, a salad and a burger.

"Here you go laddie," The bartender said coming back to our table with liquor.

"You say the word 'laddie', where are you from?" I said knowing he was Scottish but I didn't want to say that in case he was just putting on a phony accent.

"Scotland! I'm Scottish," He said proudly.

I wanted to make the joke saying "I'm Scott...ish" but was in no frame of mine to be funny. I grabbed the food and started wolfing it down, I was still freezing. I tried to figure out what to do to warm up and all I could think of was to go into the restroom because it was small and free of roaming cold air. I walked in and it had one of those blow heaters mounted into the wall. I stripped down to nothing and pressed the button, the whirring sound of the blow heater came on and I got under it warming up. Just as I was feeling relaxed someone tried to open the door, then when whoever was on the other side couldn't open it, he started knocking.

"Ju… just a minute!" I yelled and I started putting on my wet bike   clothes.
The knocking got louder.

"JUST A MINUTE!" I said louder and got the rest of my cold, wet bike kit on. The knocking became frantic. "HOLD ON!" I barked and opened up the door angrily. It was a wiry little man with a giant mustache and a cowboy hat that was bigger than him.

"I gotta go!" He said angrily and wooshed by me.

I let him go in, and I waited for him to come out, which was much longer than I'd been in there. When he finally came out I went back in to warm up. When I walked back in I realized that bathroom etiquette was not this man's strong suit. I didn't care and walked back in to warm up. I wasn't in for 30 seconds and there was another knock at the door. I threw my hands up in exasperation and went out to eat.

I wolfed down my food, it was now cold.

"Hey Scott, they've turned on the heater in here!" Said Daniel gesturing to another room in the restaurant.

I grabbed all my clothes and headed there.

"NO! NOT WITH THAT SHIT!" The waiter said. He was pointing to my wet clothes. "You put that shit back in the bar!"

I just wanted to be warm. I went back to the bar where my food was, dropped my clothes and dashed into the restaurant where they'd turned on the heater. It was one of those space heaters and I got as close as I could to it without burning myself. I'd snuck my socks in and put them on the heater to dry out while letting the warmth massage my waterlogged body. I sat huddled in a little ball against the heater; our waitress came by and said:

"We're closing in 15 minutes and you'll need to leave"

I pulled out a 20 dollar bill.

"Listen, I'll even make this 50 if I can just sleep right here for the night in front of this heater. I promise I won't budge, move and will be out by daylight."

"I can't do that, plus the owner is really mean and doesn't like you riders anyway. But you can sleep out on the porch!"

I looked out at the porch. It was a covered porch and a wood floor but it was freezing outside.

Daniel, JD and Mauro were already making their way out there and setting up camp. When my waitress came by I tried to think of a way to delay time so I could sit against the heater.

"Ma'am, can I buy a sandwich and have a glass of milk before I go out there?" I said still looking like a miserable wet dog.

"Yes I can get you a sandwich tomorrow for lunch and I'll go get you a glass of milk." She said laughing.

I let the heat blow all over my face and didn't want to move. The cook came out and kind of snarled at me, I'm sure I looked like some wounded dog curled up in a submissive position against that heater looking to just be put out of my misery.

A few minute passed and the waitress walked out with the sandwich and milk. I guzzled down the milk and grabbed the sandwich. She gave me a sympathetic smile and said:

"I have to ask you to leave now."

"I know," I said and I walked outside reluctantly.

As soon as I did, the cold wind wrapped around me and started to chill me to the bone. I gritted my teeth and walked to my bike.

"Dammit…" I said. "I've now got to fix this guy."

I set up camp on the porch and started to address the situation with my bike. My brake pads on the front were shot to pieces, all my clothes were still wet and cold, there was some weird noise coming from crank arms and my hands were already starting to go numb.

"We're gonna do it," said Daniel. "We're going to make the biggest comeback in Tour Divide history. People will see us tomorrow and be like 'Oh Snap! They are just killing it!' That's right, it's going to be known as 'Tales from the Middle' as we make it from the middle pack to the front pack. Hell yes, we're going to be the front leaders tomorrow!"

Daniel being funny and punchy trying to lighten the mood upon seeing I was a raging wolf by now.

"There's a dryer across the street" Mauro said. "You could dry your clothes there, but if you go over there, can you dry my gloves too? They are soaking wet."

"Sure man," I said and I went across the street (well, dirt road) and opened up a rusty door.

As I walked into what was considered a laundry mat, I felt like I'd stepped into a horror slasher movie. The lights didn't work so I went back and put on my helmet with a headlamp and went back into

"The laundry room." There was a rusty pipe coming out for a shower and a rusty washer and dryer that accepted quarters. I popped in 4 quarters and as I did, one quarter accidentally popped out and rolled under the dryer. "Christ…" I said and I reached under the machine fingering for the quarter I needed to dry my clothes. I felt it and as I started to finger it out, I cut the top of my hand on the rust while two roaches scurried out from underneath.

I screamed a couple of profanities then finally fished it out. I got the quarter, stuck it in and threw all my (still) wet clothes in. The dryer clicked on with a whir of a sound and started to bounce back and forth as it (hopefully) was drying my clothes. I walked back across the street and started to address the issues on my bike.

As I knelt down with my light to see what exactly was going on with my brake pads I heard a yell from across the dirt road.

"Hey, hey who is using the dryer? You gonna be long?" I looked over and saw Peter Kraft Sr. looking at me. He and his son, Peter Kraft Jr. had gotten a room (if you could call it that) there at the Wise River club. I don't know the condition of the room but given the slum area of Wise River in Wisdom, Montana, it certainly wasn't the Ritz Carlton.

"I… I just started it. I just need my clothes dry. A few minutes?" I yelled to Peter across the dirt road.

"Well let me know, I need to get my clothes dry too before I go to bed." He yelled back.

"Okay" I responded and went to work on my bike.

I removed the old brake pads. They were completely hosed and torn up. I grimaced and looked at how bad they were. I fiddled around in my bag and found the new brake pads and tried to slide them in. They wouldn't slide in because the pistons on the brake mechanism were too muddy and it was too cold to make them move. I jammed my knife in there twisting and turning, the knife folded back and dug into my finger. I screamed several long words of profanity and tried to conceal my yell since everyone was asleep.

"What's going on?" Daniel said and I explained the brake issue. He came to help, fiddled around with it, which made me nervous.

"Stop! Stop! STOP!" I said scared he was going to mess my bike up.

He backed off and I thought of what to do. I tried messing with it again pushing things in and out, one time I thought I had something working easing the new pads in, I thought I'd gotten it when I heard Peter yelling across the street

"Hey you done yet?" I heard Peter yell across the street not even ten minutes after we had last conversed.

"I got an idea about your bike's brake pads, I'll just twist this knife in it here." Said Daniel fiddling with my bike again.

"Are my gloves done?" Said Mauro sleepily

I tried to answer everyone at one time, which was impossible.

"Hey I'm just going to take your clothes out of the dryer!" Said Peter.

"Hey Scott, I got something moving on your bike. I...oops, I dropped the new pads, let me look for them" said Daniel.

"Scott if my gloves are dry can you go get them for me?" Said Mauro.

"Scott..."

"SCOTT"

"S C O T T !"

If there ever is a zombie apocalypse, I'm your guy. I can handle hordes of zombies and will survive for months if not years. But put me in a situation where the UPS man is knocking on the door, the phone rings, the water is boiling over on the stove and the kids are badgering me about what's for dinner and I melt down. I melt down hard.

I was frustrated while everyone is grabbing for my attention was just more than I could handle and that's when a new voice came through my eardrums.

"Hey, hey Scott." It was Drew from Knoxville and the only racer riding a fixed gear (a fixie) bike.

"Hey Scott, any place on that porch that I could sleep?" asked Drew.

"Are my gloves dry, Scott?" Mauro again.

"So, I... I think this piece fits here on your bike" Daniel added.

"So I'm just gonna put your clothes on top of the dryer…oops a few things fell off!"

At this point and time all I could hear and see were white hot flashes of anger and frustration in front of me. Drew started to open his mouth again to politely ask if he could sleep on the porch with us and what came out of my mouth was something you'd find in a movie about exorcising demons. I completely unloaded on him and melted down badly.

As the words were uncontrollably coming out of my mouth in front of Daniel, JD, Mauro and Peter, I instantly felt better letting the steam go that was swirling in my head but I also felt horrid that I'd let Drew have some undue anger and frustration. I threw my hands up in exasperation, crawled in my tent and instantly fell asleep not giving a damn about my bike, my clothes or anything else. I just didn't care anymore and honestly just wanted to quit this stupid race.

As I angrily crawled into bed Daniel said "so I'm setting an alarm at 4am. You're gonna love the alarm buzzer."

I looked down at my watch and it was already 1 a.m. I angrily laid down without going to the laundromat to get my clothes. I knew I should have gotten them but I didn't care. I knew I should have fixed my bike, but I didn't care and I should have apologized to Drew but I honestly DID NOT CARE. I fell asleep, and fell asleep hard.

Day 9: The North Star

It seemed like only minutes had passed when I heard "On the Road Again" by Willie Nelson emitting out of Daniel's iPhone speaker. I heard people stirring out of their tents and sleeping bags. I peeked out and it was pitch black dark. My somewhat warm body was instantly surrounded by cold as I watched everyone switch into their warm bike clothes while mine were still across the dirt road. I forced myself out of my sleeping bag and ran to get my clothes. They were piled on top of the dryer, freezing cold and stiff as a board. I threw them on quickly then went back to reassess my bike. Daniel came over and said again "who needs front brakes anyway?" Trying to make light of the situation. I cut him a cold glance and shoved the old brake pads back in the bike. At least they would fit even though they didn't work well.

I put on every bit of clothes I had, then made a waterproof jacket out of two extra strength garbage bags. I stuffed my camping gear in my bike and was ready to roll. Daniel and JD quickly worked their camping equipment in their bags too and were ready to go as well. Mauro? Not so much. He was having a few issues with his camping gear and was just a bit more methodical packing up I guess. We waited around; I rode my bike around to see if everything was working as best as possible. As the sun started to come up, Mauro was still not ready. Daniel and JD said, "Hey, we're going to go ahead and pedal." I knew I couldn't keep up with them so I decided to just wait for Mauro instead. Another 10-15 minutes went by and finally Mauro made his way off the porch. He was ready to go and we started out on a long flat road.

Mauro talked a lot. Me? When someone else is willingly opting to chat, I'm happy to let them do the talking and save myself the energy. So we rode for some time letting him tell me about how he'd decided to do the Tour Divide Race, his training, the differences between here and Britain. He'd stop to take pictures here and there. I was happy to accommodate him taking a break and nibbling on some candy to get my calorie intake back in order. We rode on like this for a while when I looked down on my GPS only to find we were off course, and we were off course by about 6 miles. That meant 12 miles total of backtracking. I was livid because we'd wasted so much time.

I looked down the road and saw a dark speck way ahead of me. As I continued to ride the dark speck got a little larger, then a little larger. As I rolled forward, I realized it was a skunk that had decided to play chicken with me on the road. I started to move to the left and it got disoriented and confused and also went to the left, so I decided to quickly dodge right and then I saw it hunker down with it's tail in a defensive position. I stopped and started easing away from the skunk saying "Oh come on now, don't spray me. Save it for Mauro, ha-ha!" The skunk was freaked out but finally it ran off the road and into the grass never to be seen again. I sighed a sigh of relief and looked back for Mauro. I saw nothing; apparently I'd dropped him by a long shot and never knew. So after waiting for a few minutes I hopped my bike and continued to work my way on the paved road. It started to pitch up, however my legs were doing well so I didn't get off the bike.

The road turned worse going even more up and then it started to rain, which had started to turn to sleet. I pulled up my bandana around my mouth and ears to keep them warm and continued to climb. An oncoming vehicle slowed and stopped. The person rolled down his window and snapped a picture of me. I thought it was odd, like really odd but I sort of smiled and waved and kept pedaling. The rain turned into sleet, which then turned into snow, like a lot of snow. The heavy dusting pelted me in the face as I continued to climb, a climb that had me heated internally and causing me to sweat all the while with the snow hitting me externally causing me to be dripping wet. I rounded a corner and found myself at the top. In the distance I saw JD and Daniel, I'd caught both of them and started to pedal towards them a bit faster as the snow and wind hit me sideways and completely chilled me to the bone. I dug my numb feet into the pedals to try to catch them, but it hurt and I started shivering. The storm would not let up and the wind started to howl.

I saw a sign that said "Tour Divide Racers, Welcome! Just Ahead!" There must be a town close by, oh my, it must be the town of Polaris! I can do this! I braved the wind and saw a lodge. IT WAS A LODGE! I was saved! Heat, food, rest, sleep, it was all in my grasp! As I got closer to the lodge I could see its wooden paneling just bursting with heat and cookies, just for me. I got closer and I saw no lights, then I got even closer and realized it was a museum that was closed. I started to tear up and cry. "No. NO! NO !" I screamed and the wind pelted me harder chilling me even worse. I continued to pedal through the snow now with spirits in the toilet and any hopes of positivity completely gone.

The wind continued to chill me inside and out. I'd made up my mind, this was the last stop. I'm quitting here. Screw this stupid race; nothing is worth this much suffering. The wind and rain continued to hammer me and I was shaking uncontrollably. I was crying involuntarily and was ready to throw in the towel. The road started to even out a bit and I saw a sign for "Ma Barnes' Country Store." Here is where I'd quit and throw in the towel. This was the end for me. I pulled down a dirt road and bumped a mile down to Ma Barnes' store.

It was a tiny wee-bitty store a mile off the Tour Divide route. There was a bike leaning up against the outside and so I knew at least one racer was there. I walked in and a dignified elderly lady looked up at me, snickered and said,

"Well that's the fanciest outfit I've seen today!" She was referring to my double-layered garbage bags used as jackets. I looked at her, dripping wet, a few tears still in my eyes and my teeth chattering and said,

"Does this jacket make me look… fat?" She erupted laughing and said,

"Come in son and warm up, we have coffee." I grabbed some donut holes that were at least a week old and some coffee that was on par with black tar. "Hey Scott" a familiar voice said and I looked behind me. It was Matt Slater.

"Hey man," I said trying to smile as my teeth chattered. "Nice to see you again."

"Man this store has everything, first and foremost you need a jacket, lookit, and she has one", said Matt, as he was getting ready to leave.

I looked back and she had some disposable rain jackets. I bought one and some candy, salty treats, cokes and more coffee.

Ma Barnes was from same the town in Mississippi as my dad. She pointed over to a corner where a leathery man sat watching Fox News. "That's my husband." I smiled and waved; he tilted his head, sipped his coffee and continued to watch the media channel.

"I hear there is a place for racers, but apparently I missed it?" I said.

"Yep, it's a mile up from here." Said Ma' Barnes.

I looked out and the sun was starting to peek out but all I could think about was taking my tired body back up the hill again.

"Is there anywhere else?" I asked.

"Well, yes, there's a ranch down the road that is taking in racers. You could go there, it's a mile and a half from there and look, and the sun is fully out." She said.

I started to walk out and soon as I did the bottom fell out again. Montana is a rather unpredictable state. It's 70 degrees or it's 7, it's sunny or it's raining and it changes on a moment's notice. I walked back in and took out the disposable jacket. As I put my arm through the sleeve I ripped it.

"Whoops" said Ma Barnes. "Do you want to buy another one?"

"Do you just have any duct tape?" I asked, upset that I'd have to buy a second rain jacket.

She said she did not have any tape so with one ripped sleeve on a rain jacket I dumped back out into the deluge of a storm and looked for this ranch. I pedaled on the road trying to mitigate the agony of the rain and the dropping temperature. I saw another sign that said "Tour Divide Racers, turn here" and I looked down a dirt road and there lay a huge ranch and lodge. I wearily pedaled down the road still with the rain pelting me and then pulled in underneath the covered carport. I leaned my bike up against a wooden support beam and looked at it. The brand new shiny red bike was covered in mass amounts of mud and looked like it'd been through four or five wars. Then the bike slipped and fell on its side sending everything out of the pockets. I didn't even care and just walked inside.

When I went in the main hall was huge with deer and elk heads mounted on the walls. It was warm, you could smell someone cooking food and for a big lodge, it was, by every bit of the definition, cozy.

"Okay, strip." I heard a lady's voice say.

I turned to the right and a red headed lady holding a spatula was looking at me.

"Go on, take off all that wet garb you have and I'll wash it. I'm making breakfast, you eat eggs and sausage?" The lady said.

I looked at her still trying to come back to life.

"I..uh...yes?"

"Get those wet clothes off of you before you catch a cold! There's a bathing suit downstairs you can put on, and some fresh towels for you to take a shower with. Now, do you eat eggs and sausage?" She said sharply.

"I...yes" I replied and went into the bathroom.

I stripped down to my chamois leaving a pile of sopping wet clothes on the floor, took a shower, dried off and put on the swim trunks. I looked at myself in the mirror. My eyes were sunk in, my laugh lines were so pronounced that I looked 20 years older and I was just grey looking all over.

"This all your clothes?" The lady asked.

"Yes" I said flatly

"Well go on in the breakfast room and eat, you look grey and with no life in you." She demanded.

I walked out to my bike and grabbed my Columbia Falls RV t-shirt and slipped it on and with borrowed Hawaiian flower swim trunks I walked into the huge dining hall and attempted to eat breakfast.

I'm not sure how a zombie feels inside, if it feels at all. But I think I have an idea now. I just sort of bumped my way into the breakfast hall, pulled out a chair and slumped down. I poked at my sausage for a moment and took a few bites. Generally I would have said, "mmm mmm this is delicious!" But I honestly didn't care. I ate a few bites of eggs, some pancake and another bite of a sausage; mainly I just poked at the food on my plate with my fork.

I then checked my phone and noticed I had zero service.

"You like the breakfast?" The lady asked.

"Do you have a telephone?" I said as I was gearing up to say "I quit" on this race.

She pointed to a private room over across the master room and I walked over to it leaving all my food.

This was it, I was calling Kate and telling her I quit. I was sick of this race, sick of dealing with the changing weather patterns and sick of being cold.

I picked up the phone and called.

"This is Kate." She said in her professional tone.

"Hey…" I said as my voice cracked.

"Scott? Baby is that you?"

"I…" And then the floodgates opened and I started weeping on the phone horribly and uncontrollably.

"I'm sorry," I told her. "It's just so hard."

"Just get it out." She said empathetically.

I sat and cried on the phone not saying anything for a good 5 minutes. Then I collected myself and said "I'm just having a really bad time, baby."

"It's okay, we all have bad days." She listened to me sort of work myself out. I was getting ready to tell her I quit, however Kate was prepared to not let me back out. My coach, Tracy, had well prepared her that this phone call might come, and stressed to her that at some point, she was going to have to be strong for us both. Turns out this wasn't a problem for her, since we had gone through two years of intense training with me waking up at unheard of hours to get my miles in and having me be gone for days at a time on a bike. The intensity and frustration we went through during that time was not going to be all for naught if she had anything to say about it.

Surprisingly the next words that came out of my mouth were not what I was expecting.

"I'm not quitting," I said. "But I want to."

"I know, it must be tough. But we're all rooting for you here, you should check your messages online and see what I'm talking about."

I told her about Fleecer Ridge, the storms into Polaris, Ma Barnes, being wet and cold. She listened to me but never once gave me an out.

"I'm sure I've lost my place and I'm probably now in the very back" I said dejectedly.

"Baby, no… noooo, I mean you've slipped a few places but you're good."

I'd slipped a few places all right. I'd been in the top 30 position for a fair amount of the race and now I was 80th, however Kate didn't say that: she was pretty ambiguous about it and I didn't really have a good internet connection to look it up. I told her how I had just poked at breakfast and she said for me to go back in and eat, then call her back.

When I hung up with her I used the Lodge's computer and checked online for messages that were coming in. Like Kate said I had people giving me well wishes and cheers.

There was a video posted from a friend of ours. It was of our friend Langston's son, Will. Will was doing some work to earn his Eagle Scout badge and he had to bike five 20-mile routes on his bike. Will is an extremely talented and strong kid, however if I had to bike five 20 mile routes at a young "tween" age I'd be sunk. The video had him saying "Hey Scott, you have inspired me to ride these 20 mile legs on my bike to earn my Eagle, thank you!" Then another message came in from a friend named Bo saying "I did 50 miles yesterday on my bike, the most I've ever done before and it was Scott that was a huge inspiration!" There was another message from my friend Billy that said he'd committed to doing 12 centuries this year and was thanking me for being a big inspiration. Another one from an extremely fast cyclist, Eddie, who could easily go pro in Birmingham, saying that I was his hero for tackling this race. My friend Mitch messaged me saying that Stewart, another extremely agile and unbelievably fast cyclist at home was just amazed at my tenacity and was super inspired. Followed right after that, another beast of a cyclist whose name is Scott said he just couldn't believe I was doing it and was cheering me on. Message after message kept coming through. I watched the video of Will again and teared up pretty good. Then a message popped up from my hero from the previous Tour Divide race, Eszter Horayni.

"You're at the same place I had a major meltdown last year. The next miles are beautiful out there (especially if the weather gets better)!"

Eszter had a reputation of never feeling pain and was the queen of multi-day endurance races. She'd shattered any previous female records as well as most guys' records too. When I had started keeping an online journal of training for the Divide I'd asked her if I could interview her. She granted me the interview and was very pleasant to chat with. When I did my research on her to prep for the interview I became an instant fan and then watching her traverse the Divide the year before I did was just awe inspiring. So to get this message from her and knowing she too had a meltdown let me know I was not the only one who had issues out here on this race.

I walked back into the kitchen and the red headed lady was in there working on lunches.

"Can I order another round for breakfast?" I asked

"Sure. You gonna eat it this time?" She asked sternly.

"I'll probably lick the plate clean." I said.

She brought out another huge stack of pancakes, sausage and eggs; I wolfed it down in almost five minutes. I said between bites

"So this is a nice place you have here." I said with my mouth full. She responded

"Oh I'm just the help. I'm a retired airline stewardess and just lend a hand here. More food?" She said.

"Yes" was the only word I uttered as I continued shoving pancakes down my throat.

"The owners will be back shortly, they are Karen and Russ. Russ has been out hunting you racers all day with a camera. Perhaps you saw him?" She said.

I remembered the guy taking pictures from his truck.

"Yes, I saw him."

I got up to use the restroom and when I looked in the mirror I noted I had some color back in my skin.

When I came out Mauro had showed up also wringing wet. I told him hello and that the breakfast was amazing here. He went into eat and I looked out the huge windows of the ranch and observed the sun gleaming over the beautiful prairies of Montana. Why couldn't this sun be out when I needed it?

"Folks ask us 'well whaddya bring to wear?' And I tell'em, swim shorts and snow shoes!" I heard a lady's voice say behind me.

I looked around and a small woman with wiry brunette hair and big glasses was staring at me.

"Hi I'm Karen, and welcome to my home. You staying the night?" She asked

"I don't know yet, maybe? I'm still trying to get the willpower to go on from here." I said.

"Oh psh, you'll be fine. It's a beautiful ride to Lima from here, well, that is if it doesn't storm." She said.

"Yes I'm kind of sick of the surprise pop up storms." I said giving her a cold look.

"Well Mister Thigpen, I guess I won't be seeing you again." The British accent of Mauro said behind me. He was suiting up and getting ready to push on.

"Yeah, this might be the last stop for me," I responded as I sunk my head.

He smiled, maybe a little bit too cocky for my taste and then he headed out.

It wasn't until cycling that I knew I had a competitive streak in me. In fact it really wasn't until I started racing the sport known as "Cyclocross" that I knew I had an extremely competitive streak in me. Cyclocross is a short distance race around a skills course that you do full on for 45 minutes to an hour. Your heart is beating out of your chest and you honestly think your lungs are going to cave in as you chase down fellow racers. The camaraderie is awesome as well as the never ending flow of beer served at the races. I've gotten my butt handed to me at almost every cyclocross race I've entered, however I always come back for more. During race season I think about strategies and ways I can best the other guy (or gal) and if I get beat by someone it just ignites a fire in me to come back for more punishment.

I sat in the chair for a moment more and felt the embers burning in my belly, and then it gave way to a fire. Then I remembered Kennedy's speech "We Go To The Moon" with the part that said, "We do these things not because they are easy but because they are hard."

And I said under my breath "You're going to wish you never said that, Mauro."

I marched back into the kitchen.

"Hey, make me some sandwiches to go please? 2?"

Karen got started and I went out to assess my bike. It was a sad mess with bits and pieces strung everywhere. I took everything out, flipped it upside down and started to address the brakes. I went back inside and asked Karen for a screwdriver. She gave me one and I went back out and jammed it between the frozen pistons of the front brake.

After a few grunts and grinds I screamed "COME ON BIKE! WORK WITH ME!" and jammed the screwdriver harder into the calipers, there was click, the sound of pressure relieving and the calipers both eased back into their proper position. "YES!" I victoriously yelled and I threw in the new brake pads, which slid in like a glove. I flipped the bike back over and methodically organized everything and put it back together in their proper places. I went back inside and my clothes were all dry and warm, and smelled wonderful. I went into the restroom and slipped them back on, noting I had a lot of color in my face and less sunk in eyes. I went back out and had Karen take a picture of me. I gave her a big hug and like a cowboy in a western, I screamed "Yee Haw!" and hit the dusty road on my bike towards the next leg of the Divide.

Karen waved at me and I barreled down their dirt road drive onto the road and made sure I was in the right direction when all of the sudden I heard the roar of thunder. I looked to my right and coming my way were huge storm clouds complete with a series of lightning bolts streaking towards me. "No… no no no no no!" I screamed and pedaled harder. At most, I could top out at 19 miles per hour if I was hammering it and I can only hold that type of speed for maybe five or ten minutes before I'm cooked. The storm loomed closer. I let out a series of profanities as lightning struck closer to me, closer than I'd like. I prepared to get pounded by the rain and storm and that's when something happened that had not had happened to me on the Divide, a tailwind hit me.

Like a giant hand smacking my bike I was instantly thrust forward; the howls of the wind whipping past my ears and pushing me forward. I didn't even have to pedal and my bike was moving on its own. I looked down at my bike computer; the miles per hour went from 12 to 15 to 25 to 30! "Holy smokes" I said as I started down a hill. The storm loomed closer; I decided to risk getting back in the aerobars again. I'd not tried since day one in Canada where I wiped out horribly losing my balance. I leaned down into my bike and slid my hands off the handlebars and onto the aerobars. The bike wobbled but I was able to regain my balance. I crouched my legs in, got flat with the bike, gritted and braced for the oncoming storm. I glanced at the bike computer, 32, 33, and 35...38mph! I was now going downhill, still with the tailwind pushing me. A felt a raindrop hit me, then something different hit me... rays of the sun and warmth. I'd beaten the storm. I didn't even look back I just continued to stay in the aerobars flying down the long hill on a smooth paved road.

I saw the turn coming up to the dirt road; I eased out of the aerobars and back onto the handlebars still with the tailwind hitting me. I cornered quickly onto the dirt road and continued hammering into the pedals. I came up on the Krafts, Peter and his son. They were addressing something on their bike and I smiled going by them saying, "I rallied!" And kept going not letting up on the speed at all. The tailwind had gone but my spirits were "full steam ahead." I rode happily for a long time and then the dirt road took a left and once again I was met with the tailwind shoving me faster and faster towards Lima, Montana. A few hours had now gone by since the Montana High Country Ranch and I had gained a lot of ground during that time. I came up over a hill and as I topped it I saw Mauro.

Like a wolf after a rabbit I started to chase him down. Mauro was lean and tall whereas I'm stockier and heavier. Generally having a stockier frame is not the best for cycling but having large legs does have its advantage and that's that you carry a fair amount of muscle on them. I continued to hone in on Mauro and we hit a hill that dipped down and quickly pitched up. As soon as it pitched up I used every bit of my leg muscle to pass by him. Without looking at him, I passed and uttered the words "beep beep" and continued pedaling as hard as I could for a good while. A climb finally slowed me down; but looking back along the prairie there was no sign of Mauro. After only about a one minute break, I was back on the bike going as fast as possible, and then hit a patch of mud that was extremely thick.

Pushing all the weight on the back of my bike and jamming the back wheel deep into the mud, I grabbed the handlebars and gently pulled up on them and started chopping my feet. My friend Maaike, who is a cyclocross badass, had told me this tip and sure enough it worked. "YEAH!" I screamed still tanked up on adrenaline through the slop. Like a mixing bowl kneading through a thick batter, I went to town through the mud without letting up. Adrenaline can only take you so far until your body says, "yeah I'm done" which mine was aiming at. I started to slow down only to notice something in the mud that caused a new emotion, fear.

Slogging through the mud were the enormous paw prints of a mountain lion. The tracks criss-crossed the muddy road and then they went on up a rocky ledge. Bears scare the living hell out of me however mountain lions are just paralyzing. Someone once warned me that if you see a mountain lion, it's already too late. At least with a grizzly you've got a chance that he's just not really into you. A mountain lion has already stalked you for hours and at 220 pounds of all muscle, you're a goner. I tried to lighten my mood a bit by wondering if I'd packed a laser pointer and I could just make a giant cat chase after it instead of me. Fortunately fear was enough to keep pushing me through the mud and back onto the dry parts of the road. I took the next downhill at record-breaking speeds (at least for me) only to come face-to-face with the real danger on the Divide; one that would be the ongoing danger for the rest of the race: cows.

Simple minded, aloof, enormous, easily startled and able to steamroll you at a moment's notice, cows are not fun. As I continued to pedal around a bend I nearly took out a herd of cattle just standing in the road. They wouldn't move, they just stood there and swayed back and forth. I took my whistle out and blew it a few times, nothing.

"Hey!" I yelled.

No cows moved.

"YAH!" I yipped.

That at least got their attention.

"I said MOVE!"

Nothing.

I took a few pedals forward and started to roll towards them. This got the attention of many of them and they raised their heads towards me.

"Alright guys, I'm just going to ease right past you."

I could reach out and touch one.

"Easy big fella, don't you... doooonnn't you..." It jerked its head up and stampeded away.

"NO!" I screamed.

This started a tornado of cattle barreling off left and right away from me flicking dirt (and god knows what else) at me. As the Cownado settled and the bovine all ran off, there stood one lone cow there in the middle of the road looking back at me. Apparently this one wasn't so simple minded and I don't know if it was a he or she but IT looked a teensy bit pissed off and would not budge. So I breathed deeply and pushed my bike up to it, and it continued to huff and puff. Generally people don't think of cows as that scary. They don't have razor sharp claws or fierce teeth but they are one majorly intimidating animal up close, especially when they are perturbed. It continued to huff and nod its head at me as I walked by it. It wasn't moving and I tenderly pushed my bike by it. It made a warning moo... I guess it was a warning moo? Whatever it was, it caused me to tense up and move quicker and it jumped and moved too.

Out of anxiety, I finally said "I'M DONE WITH THIS, SCREW YOU COW" and hopped on my bike pedaling as hard as I could. I pedaled one way and the cow ran the other. I didn't hang around to see if it was going to do an about face and come after me. "Beef is scary" I said with my heart beating out of my chest. Then I rounded a curve in the dirt road that took me to a big open plain.

It was beautiful, the sky was lit up with purples and blues as the sun was setting. There was a gentle descent to go down so I really only had to pedal a bit to keep my speed, life was pretty good. Pretty good until I met up with another herd of cows. I got off my bike and did the same thing again with pretty much the same results. All the cattle would disappear as I got closer, one would hang around and make intimidating moos at me until I hopped on my bike and then it'd take off.

As I rode on into the sunset I was faced with this situation once again, a herd of cattle aimlessly standing in the road. I started to slow down and put my foot down to walk my bike, but then I'm not sure what came over me except I was really tired of braking for beef. I sped up and aimed straight for the herd.

"YAH! YAH! YAH!" I screamed and then I yelled

"YAH!" again loudly. All the cattle bolted and I rode right through them sometimes biking right next to some very scared cattle.

"GIT! YAH!" The cattle continued to run so I shot one hand in the air making the western gun gesture and said "Pew Pew!" As I continued barreling through the mass stampede and never even gave a thought that one of these powerful slabs of beef could bend my bike up like a piece of aluminum foil.

After my little initiation as a cowboy, I rounded another bend in the prairie and saw a huge line of rocks that apparently I was heading towards. Like a scene out of the very first Star Wars movie (the one from the 70's) or Indiana Jones I noticed a large crevice that I'd be biking through. I pedaled faster and hit the windy and rocky road now with the sun fully gone. The wind howled as I zipped through the base of the rocky cliffs. My mouth was open in amazement as I took in all the scenery that was like nothing I had never experienced in my life. It was then I whipped around yet another corner and was almost taken out by an RV with a busted headlight. The one headlight he had was on bright; it hit me in the eyes and blinded me. I lost my footing and almost crashed, but then regained composure on my bike and kept going.

A few miles down the road in the darkness I saw a fire. As I got closer I saw it was J.D. and Daniel setting up camp and making dinner. "I rallied!" I yelled and didn't even slow down... partially because I didn't want to stop and partially because I was so damned embarrassed of how bad I melted down back at the Wise River Club. I started to turn on my lights, but then I didn't. I slammed on my brakes in the middle of the road, frozen at what I saw next.

There past the jutted out rocky cliffs, in the sky above another prairie with miles of winding road, was the super moon. The super moon or "lunar perigee" is a full moon that is closest to the earth. It was huge and I gasped for a moment and a tear came to my eye. No camera I had on me would do it justice, no artistic piece would even come close and no amount of me describing it would begin to illustrate what I saw. It was the most beautiful thing I'd seen in my life and I had front row seats for miles and miles watching it rise into the sky followed by a chorus of brilliant stars. I kept my speed, but I certainly didn't try to break any records because I wanted to soak this up for as long as I could. Hours went by as the supermoon and I got acquainted with one another. And predictably as the Divide goes, solitude turned into farms and farms started to turn into sparsely populated housing.

My phone beeped. "Whoa…" I said realizing I had service. I took out my phone and had three messages. The first was from my mom saying

"Slow down mister! You're gonna get a speeding ticket!" The second was my wife cheering me on in all caps screaming

"WAY TO GO BABY! YOU ARE TOTALLY KICKING ASS" and the last was from Eddie Turkely saying "Hey, I'm in Lima, I'm in room 104 at the only hotel here. Come stay if you want." I looked down and had 11 miles left according to my gps. I texted my wife and told her how much I had rallied. We exchanged "I love yous" back and forth over texts and excited to have a rest, I ramped up my pedaling.

I was tired but happy. The day had started off absolutely rotten but had turned into something else amazing. I continued pedaling and the rocky dirt road turned into somewhat of a well traveled dirt road. As I continued on the road I noted it was connecting to a paved road and major artery to town. In fact I could see the lights of Lima! I was so excited, I was going to get a room, I'd find food, and I could have a Coca-Cola. Life was going to be good and that's when I saw Satan.

My lights hit two green glowing eyes in the middle of the road that were staring back at me. I could make out horns and a long face and that was it. The face moved and bobbed as I headed to it.

"What...the hell?"

I said and I turned my lights on bright only to be faced again with yet another cow.

"Go on boy, you scared me to death!" It slowly got out of the road and moved into the prairie.

I methodically worked my way to Lima. I couldn't believe I was going to be hooked up with the Bromansion again! I was so excited to be with "my peeps!" The lights got brighter, there was movement of traffic here or there and I couldn't wait to tell everyone of how much I missed them and was glad to be with them again. I pulled up to the hotel, when I did I saw Drew, the racer on the fixie bike and the guy I'd unfairly cussed out also getting a room. I ran over and said,

"DREW!"

He looked at me horrified.

"Man, I owe you a big apology. I am so sorry about the other night. I was just not in a good place." I said full of remorse and apologies.

"No worries" he said and moved on to finding a room.

I rode around the motel until I saw "Room 104." I banged on the door. Nothing. I banged again. Nothing. "Hmm, must just be Eddie in there right now while everyone else is eating." I took my light and flashed it in the room. Since Eddie was deaf in one ear and a particularly loud snorer, I'm sure he couldn't hear me, but my light was enough to wake him up. He opened the door and was completely naked.

"Hey, I'm naked." He said sleepily.

"I see that," I said and walked in.

"Where is everyone?" I said.

"Oh the rest? Oh they just wanted to keep on going, I just didn't have the legs to keep up with them. I need some rest. What time is it?" Eddie said.

"1:30 in the morning"

"I'm leaving here at 4, you're welcome to tag along."

"Well, okay, I'm pretty tired but okay. I'll ride on. Is there anywhere to eat?" I said wishing Eddie said he was going to leave around say noon, 1pm or in three weeks.

Eddie said there was a gas station that might be open. I walked out to it only to find it closed and the coke machine busted. I looked around and everything seemed like a ghost town, in fact it looked like a dump from my perspective (I'm sure Lima is a lovely town). I walked back to the hotel really bummed out to not find food.

I shoved Eddie one good time and woke him up again.

"No food," I said. "Do you have any?"

"Dude I have a ton of food, eat what you want, I can't eat anymore junk right now."

I looked down and he had 2 giant bean burritos, a Snickers and some Sour Patch Kids. I made quick work of it all and then realized I had a jar of peanut butter - it soon disappeared too. Completely exhausted now, but full, I went into the shower I leaned over the showerhead and turned on the water. As the water poured out of the faucet below two roaches scurried out of it and fell into the tub near my feet. Generally I'd be on the ceiling squealing like a little girl but I just stood there watching them drown. I was so exhausted I didn't even care. Eventually they keeled over and circled down the drain.

Day 10: It's True, Idaho sucks.

I do not really remember finishing up the shower and making it to the bed. I think I honestly sleep walked from point A to point B… which wasn't very far as the room wasn't even big enough for 2 single beds and 2 Tour Divide bikes. It was very musty smelling and the sheets were like paper but at that moment I thought it was the most comfortable bed ever. For around 2 hours I slept as hard as I could and as Eddie had warned, his alarm went off at 4am. I really thought about sleeping in but I wanted to gain some ground so I reluctantly pulled my carcass out of bed.

"You look like hell, man," I said to Eddie.

He was tired, his eyes were also sunk in and he seemed pretty beat up.

"I just need to do...what do you call it? Soft pedal?" He said.

"Ha-ha! Yes, Soft Pedaling!" I said laughing.

We wheeled our bikes out and there were rays of sun poking out from the clouds.

"Looks like we're going to have nice weather while we go through the Basin," Eddie said.

"Wha?? The Basin! I thought that was in Wyoming!" I said surprised.

I'd been dreading the Basin for some time now. 170 miles through a desert with no access to much of anything scared me more than Mountain lions or Grizzly bears. The thought of running out of food and water was just terrifying and now here we are, at the Basin and I didn't know.

"No not THAT basin," Eddie said. "The Montana Basin, it's like a mini basin! Come on, let's go."

We pedaled out of Lima, hit a soft dirt road and the land and sky opened up to a giant mix of prairie and desert. While we were on the desert part I looked over and saw a lush prairie with elk and deer grazing in the field, and then we saw a moose. I'd not seen a moose since leaving Canada, and I had no idea how large moose were. We startled the giant beast and I watched it run. Generally I'd thought of moose as this dorky and wobbling beast... not so much. The moose galloped at lightening speeds and then as if it was trying out for Santa's sled team, it leapt into the air clearing at least a good 5-6 feet and leapt over a fence. It landed and continued to tear off across the prairie.

"Day-um" I said and looked over to see another sight. As Eddie and I climbed into the desert, a cloud had settled over the upcoming descent. It looked as if it were a mysterious evil queen ready to draw us in and cast a spell on us.

"We have to go into that?" I said to Eddie but he didn't hear me. As we got closer we rode straight into the cloud or fog. Instantly the bright sunny sky went completely grey, the air was heavy and hard to breathe. We could barely see in front of us and we were collecting moisture from the heavy cloud.

"What is this craziness?" I'd been in fogs before while biking but nothing like this. I could feel my body getting colder and wetter when all of the sudden it lifted and we were back in the desert again. It was the wildest thing.

Hours passed and we hit a very, very hard hill to climb. I got out of my seat, dug my feet into the pedals and started grinding up the hill. It got steeper but I was not going to give in and walk my bike. The climb seemed to go on for forever, the heat generated both from the sun and the constant movement of my body was really making me sweat. I love climbing, this is my sweet spot. It hurts but it hurts so good. I love giving it all I have and hoofing it up a hill because when you hit the peak, the rewards are always wonderful with the utter relaxation of your body, the ability to breathe normally again and you see a big, giant sign that says "Welcome to Idaho."

IDAHO

Getting into another state was a huge mental hurdle. Getting out of an enormously huge state like Montana was an absolute burden off my back. I'd heard that Montana was infamous for stopping Tour Divide racers from finishing and I was told if you could get out of Montana, the race was yours.

We rode for hours through single-track, paved roads and dirt roads. As we neared a small town, I saw a convenience store, a fast food chain and then some rustic looking restaurant with some bikes parked in front of it. I headed towards the bikes and recognized them to be Joseph, Taylor, Kristen and Ty's bikes! The Bromansion! I was back!

"HEY!" ! I said dashing through the doors.

"Knew you'd catch up. Soft pedaled did ya?" Joseph said laughing

"Soft pedaled." I said laughing.

Taylor and Kristen looked up, nodded and then burrowed back down into their phone. They weren't ignoring me; they were listening to a message. "Put it on speaker" Kristen said. Taylor flipped on the speaker and I heard the second place leader, Craig Stappler throwing in the towel. He sounded bitter: apparently Mike Hall, the leader, had gotten far enough ahead of him and he'd had enough.

Eddie and I ate an enormous burger with the gang and then dashed over to the convenience store for groceries. Inside they had a deli, rows of canned food and snacks. I loaded up my bag with as much as I could physically handle, ordered a Philly cheesesteak and checked out.

We walked out and I saw two riders we had met in the basin named Jamie and Josh. Jamie was hugging Josh, who looked rather downtrodden.

"I'm out. My knee is shot." Said Josh

"Sorry to hear that, man," I said patting him on the shoulder.

Eddie also gave his regrets and that's when I barked at my bike.

"Dammit! Soft tire again and my pump is broken!"

My tire was going out again and we were still around 1,000 miles to the next bike shop and that was a lot of miles to be pushing a bike.

"You can have mine," said Josh. "If you promise to mail it back to me."

He wrote his address on the pump in a sharpie marker and handed it off to me. I gave him a giant hug and said, "thank you man, I appreciate it."

"No worries now finish this race!"

The sun was setting but we still easily had three hours of daylight, I figured we could completely clear Idaho and hit Wyoming by nightfall. As we rode, it was a pleasant blacktop through a middle class neighborhood. Many people came out to look at us and we waved like we were in a parade. Eddie said "The turn is coming up here in a second."

The Turn. I'll never forget that, the turn was like going into the mouth of hell. Now I know why so many Tour Divide racers say "Idaho Sucks..." As we turned onto what I thought would be a dirt road my front tire started to sink. It didn't sink because it was low on air; it was sinking because it was slid into a foot or foot and a half worth of sand and pebbles. Black sandy pebbles as far as the eye could see. It was an ATV trail and we had to go straight through it. I tried to gain some momentum and I crawled out of my bike standing up only to fall over and bite it one good time. I stood up and my shoe sunk into the black sand. I got back up on my bike and chopped my pedals gaining some momentum. As I gained my balance and started moving, several ATVs buzzed passed me causing me to lose my balance and fall again. Eddie and Jamie were a bit ahead of me but were also struggling. I finally caught up with them and was out of breath by now.

"You... guys... struggling... too?" I barely was able to speak.

"Well, not so much," Eddie said and I saw him shifting gears back and forth to accommodate the soft terrain.

I revved up as much as I could on my one gear only to just barely make it over the top of the sand, where I bit it again.

"Hey man, how long do we have of this crap?" I asked Jaime.

"12 more miles." At the rate we were going that was going to easily be two to two and a half hours. It was hot, dusty and dry and to make matters worse sometimes a cow would aimlessly be standing in the middle of the trail.

Hours passed and as I continued to pedal sleep would overtake me and I'd have to fight against it, which was difficult, then I had a sudden thought. Packed away in one of my pockets were caffeine pills. I'd never tried them but I thought I'd give it a shot. I popped two in my mouth and swallowed some water. Nothing. So I popped two more. Nothing. "Well these things are crap," I said to myself and continued pedaling and then I saw it, the Grand Tetons in the distance.

I'd been told that it was a sight to behold. It was beautiful as these purple snowcapped mountains and all I could say was "wow" and sort of took it all in. Then my stomach rumbled and I realized I'd not eaten in a while, I looked at my GPS and noted it was a solid eight miles to the Squirrel Creek Lodge. "No Problem" I said to myself out loud and I buried my head in my handlebars and pushed on.

"Hey Eddie" I said chugging past him. "How ya doing?"

"Where are you off to in a hurry?" He said.

"Oh me?" I said rushed. "Um, I'm hungry?" And kept pedaling.

Things were moving much faster now, yes much faster. My legs were chugging along at full steam, I was singing a tune and singing it loudly. I thought about Kate, no wait, I thought about Kate and I together, no actually I thought about what I was going to do when I got back, that's not right, I thought about food, wait, something else. Boy, I'm having a lot of thoughts!

I rounded a corner through some farmlands and continued pedaling through the rolling hills. I was singing loudly at this time, in fact I noted I was just singing certain lyrics over and over out of my saddle dancing back and forth. I took another left by an old dilapidated farmhouse.

"Howdy Mister Farm House!" I said "What's mooovin'" I looked up and saw a sign on the road "Lodging in one mile." I picked up my pace.

"Lodging!" I sang "Lodging in a mile" I continued to sing badly.

I wasn't paying attention and almost plowed into an oncoming car. The car honked and I said "Same to you, and your mom!" I was acting like a child at this point in time. I whipped around another corner where it said "To the Squirrel Creek Lodge" and as I bumped down the windy road I noted bicycles, bicycles everywhere surrounding the Squirrel Creek Lodge main hall. When I walked in it felt like a homecoming party. At least 20 cyclists were there all resting for the eve, drinking beer and eating burgers.

I yelled loudly "HEY EVERYBODY" and threw my hands up. There was a cheer that erupted and people came slapping me on the back, giving me hugs and cheering me on that I'd caught up with them. Many racers were there and huddled in a corner were Taylor, Ty, Joseph and Kristen. They kept cutting their eyes at me and laughing, I had no idea why. The staff came out and asked what I wanted; I said I'd take a couple of bud lights and a couple of burgers. I scarfed one burger down without even thinking and talking at the same time about the day's events. In fact I was talking, and talking about everything but nothing but I was doing it loudly and finally in a roar of laughter from Taylor's table, Joseph said

"Dude, how many caffeine pills have you had!?"

They knew that I had them tucked away for moments when I needed them. I got the idea last year from the 2012 Tour Divide winner, Ollie Whaley who had put caffeine pills in his equipment bag.

"Sorry, I just wanted to make it through the long haul." I said embarrassed.

"Dude just settle down, how many pills did you take at once?" Laughed Joseph.

"Oh, not many" I said trying to downplay it.

I'm pretty sure four caffeine pills is like 1,000 cups of coffee...maybe a million.

As I ate the second burger and attempted to eat it slowly Ty came over and said "Hey, we got a room, there's going to be a ton of people in it, but we saved you a bed if you'd like. It's cheap." How was I going to turn this down? Of course I wanted a bed. It was around 12:30am and we all meandered over to our cabin. It was a giant a-frame with every nook and cranny taken up by cyclists however up the ladder there was an empty bed. I grabbed my Columbia Falls RV t-shirt, shorts and went into the shower to clean up.

The cabin shower had zero pressure and you had two choices, one was extremely cold or scalding hot. I tried adjusting the pipes behind the shower that gave no solution so I said a few choice words and walked out. As I started to climb up the ladder to my bed up top in the a-frame I noted Kristen and Taylor snuggled up in a corner asleep. Instantly I thought about Kate and I missed her. In fact I missed her so bad that it made me ache inside. Couple an aching heart with very bad indigestion of two greasy, greasy hamburgers and "sleep" was going to be difficult. By now it was 1am and I started to finally lie down and probably around 1:30 or 2 I fell into a deep sleep, only to hear alarms going off at 4 a.m.

Day 11 And Wyoming Is Not Much Better

"Oh god... seriously?" I said awoken but half asleep. Everyone downstairs was stirring. "But..." I said under my breath, grimaced and got up too. I went outside wearily and started addressing my bike. I just wanted to rest so badly but didn't want to get dropped with all the ground I'd gained. The push from Polaris had afforded me with very little sleep and now I was dealing with some mental fatigue that meant thinking clearly was going to be a tougher challenge.

I stopped, fiddled around in my bags to see if I had any food. I had about 5 Sour Patch Kids left, a half of a beef jerky stick and some melted M&M's. "Mmmm..." I said to myself sarcastically and shoved what food I had in my mouth chased by some tepid water in my water bottle. My phone beeped and strangely enough I had service.

"Hey man way to go helluva job! You're in my backyard now; I may come out and see ya! Roll Tide!" (Saying "Roll Tide" is pretty much a salutation if you're from the south). It was from John Foster who lived in Alta, Wyoming that was near Flagstaff. He'd done the Tour Divide a few years before and was rooting on the other guy with Alabama roots. I tried to respond back however service was so bad that I couldn't get a message off. So I hit "send" and kept riding.

Wyoming was not what I was expecting; in fact I had no real expectations. All I had been told was that it was weird and it had a big desert. Currently it was dusty and hilly. There were many pitches up steep climbs into Flagstaff. When I finally got up on a ridge I went through an area where there was an entire forest burned to the ground. Trees were still smoldering, dark and black, with a dusty road winding through it. Then I heard a vehicle behind me. I eased over to let it by, but it was one giant of a pick up truck and it almost ran me off the road. Frustrated, I decided I was going to give this guy a piece of my mind (because we all know how well that goes over when you aggress an aggressive person). I started to dig into my pedals to catch up, however when I got closer the truck gunned it.

Arid temperatures, no rain, large trucks kicking up dust and me in anaerobic state found me off my bike coughing up a lung from swallowing so much airborne dirt.

"I guess"

::cough::

"I showed"

::cough cough::

"him!"

I finally caught my breath again and hopped on my bike. I started to ride by a riverbank and I could smell the cooler (and much fresher) air coming off the water. There was one better downhill coming up, after my triumphant victory with the truck I was feeling very frisky and decided to take the descent quickly. It pitched down and it was steep. I crouched into my bike, getting my butt off the saddle, legs hunched up and barreled down the rocky mountain like a mad man. Once I hit a rock and felt weightless as my bike used it as a ramp to leave the ground at least four or five feet in the air (or, in actuality, a half of a centimeter, but it felt like four or five feet). My tires hit the ground and I could feel them soaking up the landing.

Mulberry Gap, 2010 - My Very First Visit

"Your bike is designed to handle downhill and rough terrain, Scott." My friend Monty was teaching me how to go downhill on my first very hard descent at Mulberry Gap Mountain Bike destination in North Georgia.

I'd never been outside of Birmingham on my mountain bike and I'd certainly not been on any huge downhill descents either. At the top of Bear Creek Trail I sat terrified watching our mountain bike group "BUMP" barrel down the hills like bats out of hell.

"Come on Scott, you can do this. Just get your butt back and let the bike do the work." I left off the brakes and descended into Bear Creek, terrified."

WYOMING

Going down some backwoods road in Wyoming and hopping off rocks had me screaming many "hell yeahs" and tons of "yee haws." I hit one rock, launched off it and heard something rattling on my bike. Descending at around 18-20 miles per hour does not leave you a lot of room to avert your eyes from the trail to something on your bike, that is unless you'd like to eat a mouth full of dirt or fly off a cliff. I glanced down and saw nothing. The rattling noise grew worse and I glanced down again this time seeing my GPS, my one thing I couldn't lose, rattling loose as one screw had wiggled free and was unhinging. "No... no no no no" I said trying to will it to stay on. Even as I started to apply the brakes and safely come to the stop, the steep descent was still thrusting me forward and it was not very ideal to try to skid to a stop.

Sometimes the Divide will tear you down, eat your soul and leave your mood rotting on the side of the road. But then sometimes you can even try to mess up and come out on top.

As I started to slow down to 15, 14, 13 mph (still fast on a mountain bike) my GPS wiggled free. Everything went into slow motion and the stars must have been aligned just right because what happened next was definitely not practiced skill or talent.

As the GPS broke free from my bike, I attempted to pop the handlebars at the same time to try to knock it back up towards me. As it went up, it flew into my face, and I opened my mouth to reach out and grab it. It gently touched my lips, but I couldn't get a grip on it and it started to fall. I reacted and took one hand off my handlebar - not the smartest thing to do while going down and fast on a rocky descent - and managed to catch it. I quickly grabbed the handlebar and regained my balance. My heart gave a sigh of relief and with a palmed GPS, I flew down the mountain. When I got to a flat area I stopped and cheered immensely jumping around in victory relieving some much penned up anxiety. Then I looked over at my bike and sadly my cheers were dampened.

My bike had been stuffed to the gills with food, items, camping equipment, and I.D., money and bike maintenance tools. When I looked down at it, both zippers on either side on the frame bag had given way, split open and items were just spilling out. I looked back up the giant mountain I'd just come down and thought about having to climb that again and play Sherlock Holmes looking for all my gear. I surveyed the damage. I'd lost my spare spokes, my precious multitool (you know, the thing all guys carry and rarely use, but they carry it anyway for that one moment they know they are going to be confronted with a horde of zombies or have to open a box... the box that could contain the horde of zombies, thus you're prepared with your multitool already out). Also, my knife was gone as well as all my beef jerky and peanuts. Fortunately everything else seemed to be intact, and I'd retained my GPS, so while it was upsetting, it definitely wasn't ending the race for me.

I continued to pedal on the rocky road and as like all towns, I saw a farm, which led to a house, and then eventually there was a road that led to civilization and the promise of the "Lodge. Breakfast. Lodge. Breakfast. Lodge. Breakfast." That's all I could think of.

Seeing the sign for the lodge reminded me of Mulberry Gap, and instantly imagined Diane and Ginny serving me pancakes with tons of friendly mountain bikers still shaking off hangovers from the night before, laughing and talking about today's big ride. When I pulled up to the lodge I saw a huge amount of buses, then tourists coming off the buses in droves, they were all Asian and speaking an Asian language. "Exc... Excuse m... Excuse Me," I said trying to weave around the lines of people who I don't think understood me. They were clean, well dressed, were taking pictures; taking pictures of me who was completely covered in dirt, sporting a seriously badly kept beard, and probably looking something like a haggard a hobo on a bike.

I found everyone sitting at a place in the fancy lodge now with a new person at the end of the table, he looked up and said,

"Hey Scott, I follow your blog. Nice to finally meet you." Rich was around my age and we hit it off pretty well for conversation. Rich was a fellow singlespeeder and a well-seasoned one at that. A nurse from Utah, he rode what was called a Black Albino bike. It was possibly the most awesomely awesome constructed bike I've ever seen. Its unique build is a showstopper and the way Rich had it packed made him look like a pro.

I finished up my meal and the gang except Rich still lingered around chatting.

"I'm going to ride on guys, I'm sure you'll catch me" I said.

"Yes, with your slow soft pedaling? Right! Ha!" Joseph said laughing.

We all laughed and I went into the convenience store annexed to the lodge. They had everything you could guess a store would have but all with a "down home corporate country feel, you all." Of course with that "down home feel" you paid uptown prices so a 99-cent strip of beef jerky was now 2.99. I didn't know the next time I'd see a town so I figured it wise to stock up here no matter what the price. When I laid down my cokes, candy, beef jerky and a few other items I could find I didn't even look at the price, I just signed away on the receipt, wadded up mine and threw it away. I just couldn't bear the thought of what I paid but I'm sure it wasn't cheap.

I went out to my bike and started to load it up with all my goodies. I also took out some zip ties and addressed the split zippers, cinching it up where I could. "Please hold together bike," I said. Rich was loading up his bike. It was neat, tidy and well kept. I looked back at my bike and it was stuffed to the gills, things were slipping off every which way but loose and now was beginning to be held together by zip ties. "Man you seem to have this down pat, Rich" I said with a smile. He nodded and said he'd practiced a bit but had bought many items and tried them on until he got what he liked.

"Hey do you want to ride together? But if one of us drops the other, no hard feelings?"

He agreed and said he felt the same way that he didn't want to be bound to anyone. We hopped on our bike and immediately we were thrust up a giant hill but at least it was on a paved road. The Grand Tetons were now on my right. I'd look up and glance to see the mountains but needed to concentrate on getting up the hill, it was a rather daunting task. What's more, there were RV's and trucks aggressively driving up and down the hills. Generally they were respectful of us cyclists but every so often I'd get run off the road by one. One zipped by me pretty close with me feeling its draft blowing me left and right a bit. "Must be from my neck of the woods," I grumbled. In Alabama it feels as if motorists hate cyclists. I actually have sold my road bike because I can't take the aggressiveness of the drivers. I abide by all laws, obey all rules but the final kicker for me was when a state park employee ran me off the road, stopped, cussed me out. When the cops were called, they were more sympathetic to her because I was "slowing her down" and they were unconcerned that she put my life in jeopardy by speeding up and going by me, narrowly missing my kneecaps.

In Wyoming there were giant LED signs that said "Warning: Cyclists are everywhere. Please drive slow!" This was somewhat comforting and most people abided by the rules, just not all.

Rich was a climber, so as we went up the hills he'd drop me in a heartbeat, however as soon as we hit a flat surface he'd slow way down and I'd pass him. Also, he liked to take pictures of historic marker signs and he'd stop to do that. If I stop my knees lock up badly and I start to hurt so as he stopped in front of a marker, I waved at him and kept going. The climbs finally ebbed and now there was a long winding descent down the road. It was great until "WOOSH!" Another RV about took me out. "THE HELL IS WRONG WITH YOU GUYS" I screamed and I pulled over to collect my wits. While I'm no small guy, a very large RV is quite the force to endure with it whipping by you so close. As I stood there I heard "LOOK ALIVE" and Joseph wooshed by me at a lightening pace. Not 5 minutes later Ty, Kristen and Taylor all zoomed past me. I sighed and watched them disappear around a corner.

Another portion of the route, another long stretch of mountainous and unrewarding climbs. Eventually I caught up with the group and we grabbed some food. The race started to wear on us all, however it seemed Eddie was really starting to buckle under the stress the most.

"I'm…. I'm going to have to break. I'm going. I'm going to see how much that lodge is over there." Eddie looked pretty upset and angry and I do think his engine was out of fuel and needed some well-deserved maintenance and rest. He looked like I did back at the Wise River Club in Wisdom, Montana.

"It looks like smooth sailing from here to Union Pass" said Joseph. Then it's Pinedale and the Great Basin!"

I had no concept of how many miles that meant, but it was nice to hear "smooth sailing" which of course is all-relative. I looked at my GPS and it pointed towards a nice paved road again. "Yes" I said in victory and started into the long winding road that immediately started to go up. "Why does this always happen?" I groaned. "Why can't it just be miles and miles of flat road for once?" I started in on the climb and I heard the clicking of gears coming behind me. Eddie and another fellow were coming up.

"Lodge not good?" I yelled to Eddie.

"I just... I... no. Not good. There's another lodge up ahead. Going to be better. Need rest."

Eddie looked like he'd had enough but was going as hard as possible to make it to the next stop. He put some serious distance between him and me and then eventually disappeared over the rolling hills of the road. I continued at a steady pace, alone, listening to some music. My wife had turned me onto Brandi Carlisle's "Bear Creek" album and there was one song in particular I loved on it, "Raise Hell." Imagine Johnny Cash in female form, and this is what Brandi sounds like.

As I continued to sing along to Brandi I looked down and my GPS was beeping "low battery." I stopped and went to fumble around for new batteries, there were none. "Oh no..." I said. I knew a turn was coming up and I didn't want to miss it. "No...no no no no" I said as I stripped my bike apart looking for batteries. I found one, I popped the back off and pulled one battery out hoping that I could have at least half a charge." At most, all I had was a little bit showing my GPS was going to die any minute but I was at least able to see that I was to take a turn soon, a mile? Wait no, now. Wait, is it a mile; no it's not a mile. I have a hard time reading maps to begin with, I confuse things easily and transpose stuff in my brain thanks to my keen talent of dyslexia and get things flip-flopped easily, especially when I'm stressed.

I heard a voice behind me, I looked back and it was Rich pushing his bike up the road talking on the phone. He had service. I checked my phone and I had service but it was also drained so it died in my hands too. Gadgets. They are great until the batteries are dead in them.

"WHICH WAY RICH?!" He pointed straight which was way down a mountain. "You sure?" He was still on the phone but nodded confidently. I looked to my left and there was a little dirt road there, maybe that was the way and Rich was wrong? Rich pointed again showing me downhill. He said, "I'll be there in a minute, I want to finish talking with my wife." I started to roll down the mountain, it was steep and I rode the brakes down it. Something wasn't right, this wasn't the way. I rode a mile down it and stopped; there was no left turn at all. I stopped and looked at my dying GPS. I'd missed the turn; it WAS indeed that dirt road. I said a host of 12 letter profanities and started back up the mountain.

I don't mind climbing, but I do mind wasting energy climbing when I don't have to. I grunted back up the mountain to already see Rich looping the dirt road. "SORRY!" He yelled. "uh huh…" I said under my breath and dumped into the dirt road. I was met with the washboard ridges carved into the dirt road. It was extremely unpleasant and not very ridable. Basically your teeth chatter to death and no matter which way you hit them, it's still painful and annoying. We went up and down a winding dirt road for an hour and then dumped back out on the road, not very far from where I turned around. This is where DeAnna, a previous tour divide rider got disqualified because she missed the turn and didn't go back to re-trace the correct route.

We rode along and finally came up to a little hotel/diner on our right.

"Hey, I know we're supposed to be roughing it but I just don't think I can pull another pass tonight and get to Pinedale. Wanna get a room?" I said.

"Sure," Rich said.

I went into get a room for both of us and looked in the restaurant. There sat Joseph, Kristen, Taylor, and Eddie, Mason, Paul and Ty. They were getting ready to order in the crowded restaurant.

"I knew you'd make it here." Laughed Joseph .

"Well I do have a way with that super soft pedaling." I smiled.

Taylor talked about ripping his tire on the washboard road and that's one reason they were staying the night here so he can fix it.

"What washboard road?" Asked Eddie

"The one on the turn off just before the giant downhill." Taylor said

I watched Eddie's face turn red and he got very upset as he realized he'd missed a turn. He stormed outside and walked around I'm assuming trying to keep his temper. We all sat in silence watching him. If it were me and this would have happened to me, I would be have been on the next flight from "Wherever, Wyoming" back to Birmingham. Eddie came back in and started asking people if they'd drive him to the top so he could take the right route (that is legal in the race). No one would help him. I thought he was going to blow a gasket, then something happened that I had not expected.

Joseph got up from the table and went out to talk to Eddie. I saw them chat for a few minutes, Eddie being red faced and upset and Joseph calmly chatting, trying to slide in a few well put jokes and ebbing Eddie's temper. Joseph walked back in and said "Hey, I'm going to go ride up the road and do that section with Eddie. Get some food for me?" Joseph didn't have to do this, in fact the thought had not even crossed my mind but he spent some precious energy to go ride along with Eddie, get him up to the top and go back down the rough terrain so he wouldn't be disqualified. While no medals, trophies or physical swag is given out for completing the race, I think Joseph should have gotten a medal for "kindest act on the Tour Divide."

Day 12: That's No Moon

I was still pretty impressed at all the mountains in Wyoming, I was under the assumption that it was a flat area; it had been anything but flat or smooth. Rich and I left the hotel early. Eddie was standing out of his door rubbing his eyes.

"Gonna rest for a while, I'll see you guys later. I didn't get done until late last night." Said Eddie.

"Take care of yourself man, I hope to talk to you soon." I said empathetically.

Rich and I took off towards Union Pass which was particularly difficult (there could be a book written on how hard Union Pass was). Hour later, I got ahead of Rich and decided to stop and wait on him, I'd enjoyed his company thus far and didn't want to get too far away. Even for mega introverts like me, a little company is nice sometimes, especially when it was company you could enjoy, like Rich.

I saw him in the distance just standing there near a stream that ran by the dusty dirt road. I waited a bit longer and finally he started to move, he caught up to me and said"

"My granddad and I camped there one weekend." I looked at him and blinked.

"Really? In this dry area of nothingness?"

"The desert is my home, man, I love it here!"

"Well, at least it's not cold!"

"Oh just you wait."

We continued to pedal through the hot sand and windy environment.

"I think there's some services up ahead" Rich said. "I remember reading about a couple of places."

I was so excited, finally, some food and a place to rest! We dumped off the dirt road and onto the paved road. We picked up some speed and I was delighted to see cars, some houses here and there and… there it was, *a restaurant*! I was going to feast, no, gorge on food. I would order three hamburgers and one to go. I was going to drink soda until I popped I…

There were no cars parked out in front, all I heard was a lonely crow in the background mocking us.

"No…" I said "Nooooo…. no no, it HAS TO BE OPEN!"

I ran up to the door and banged on it, nothing. The lights were all off but I could see the soda fountain machine was on.

"Maybe they'll be here soon, Rich?"

"Not likely, looks like they are closed for some auction tonight."

I sighed, I didn't have much food but I decided to dig out what I had. As soon as I got still to eat my feast of five sour patch kids and one Slim Jim Beef Jerky, I was met with a host of mosquitos, that was awesome. At least there was a hose that I could fill up my bottles and drink water liberally. Rich sat in a rocking chair on the porch of the restaurant and rested his legs.

We talked about life, family, politics, interests and hobbies for a while. Rich was truly a jack of all trades, was quite the family man and pretty damned perceptive about stuff. I was about to continue our conversation when a tiny little car pulled up, parked and a tall skinny man with a weathered face got out. He walked up to the door of the restaurant and started to unlock it.

"Y'all about to open???" I said excited.

"Nope. Auction tonight."

"Oh…Well hey, can I at least buy a coke from the fountain machine inside?"

"Nope."

And he walked in, shut the door.

"Well damn," I said outloud "Wasn't expecting that."

And walked back to my delicious meal of Sour Patch Jerky bars.

Moments later I heard the door open back up and the man popped his head out.

"Hey, I just can't do it. I'm the chef here and I can't let you boys just sit here. You folks want a burger and a coke?"

"Uh, HELLS YES!" I said excited and ran in.

The inside was cool with air conditioning. The cook beaconed us back to the kitchen and he made us burgers.

"You boys are part of that bike race huh? We've seen a bunch of ya."

We told him some stories while he cooked us our burgers. I filled a water bottle up with coke and got a paper cup and downed a few gallons worth of soda. We went outside on the porch and waited for the meal to come out. The cook walked out with burgers and fries and I launched into one big bite.

I generally don't eat burgers, they are horrifically bad for you and all that charred meat is generally cancer causing so I stray away from it. But today was a different day, it was the best food I'd ever eaten. Long live the burger! Whatever cow gave it's life for me that day, I hope has a nice comfy pasture in cow heaven.

YUM-EE!

I started to take another bite and Eddie pulled up. Still wild eyed he walked up and started to go in to eat assuming the place was open.

"They are closed" I said, " but we scored sweet burgers!"

I could see Eddie eyeballing my burger like a shark circling a helpless victim, a helpless victim dripping with cheese and ketchup.

My first primal reaction was to hoard the burger and eat it for myself but then humanity took place and said:

"Here Eddie, eat some of this, man."

"I can't…it's your burger I, well maybe a little bite."

Like a vampire to blood he couldn't stop eating it. He took several big bites and gulped it down only handing me back a shred of burger left.

"Sorry man, I was really hungry. I can pay you!"

"No need, it's cool."

I think Eddie needed food worse than I did and I was happy to see his demeanor change when he got in food. The goodwill gravy train continued when the chef brought us out ice cream as well and we all lapped that down too. Now with sugar, carcinogens, bread and cheese in our bellies - we were good to make it to Pinedale, Wyoming which was the last city before the mouth of the great basin.

Climb after climb, small town after small finally led Rich and I to Pinedale, Wyoming, the start of the Basin. We made a stop and as with most places someone inevitably asked you:

1. We saw some bikers here the other day, are you guys in a race or something?

2. Where ya heading to? (Followed with "MEXICO!?")

Then you'd spend 20 minutes explaining yourself. When question #2 was asked I'd usually go into great detail about the race, the ride, the people and the length of the trip. However that started to really get old so I just started making up stuff. I told one person I'd traveled from Africa by bike and was looking for my son in Brazil just south of Texas. I told another person that I was part of a Harley Davidson gang but was poor and could only afford a bike but if he saw any of them tell them that "Danger Roberts" had stopped by. Lastly I told someone that Michael Bay was filming the 8th installment of the "Transformers" series and that they were filming just down on the next mountain pass and I wanted to use a bike to sneak and see them. If you think this is horrible, then hey, you ride nearly 3,000 miles on a bike and try not to make up things that are recycled over and over to keep you from cracking.

I'd agonized for weeks about the Wyoming Basin. Alone, sand, no water, and extreme heat for a little under 200 miles? Yeah, it frightened me. My goal was to hit it at night and ride the entire thing busting out one of the longest rides I'd ever done, but I could get through it, be done with it and recover in the next town Rawlins.

As we made it out of Pinedale and entered into the Basin, we rode up on an entire herd of cows standing in the road. They looked at us motionless and wouldn't move. Now with my newfound cowboy skills I started yipping and making noise as we rode into them. The cows parted and we continued on. We dipped into a dirt road as the moon was rising and the sun was setting. The basin: we'd arrived in it.

It was a lot cooler than I'd guessed temperature-wise...and hillier, a lot hillier than I'd guessed. We rode on into the night through the Basin; I could not see a thing except the moon, which was oddly colored.

"Blood moon" Rich said. "It's reflecting the fires they are having in   Colorado."
I looked at the large moon for a while; it was indeed orange at the bottom and lighter at the top. I'd heard murmurs of the fires in Colorado as well as Matt Lee, the race director, saying that there was a mandatory reroute for us Tour Divide Racers due to the fires. After riding and gazing at the moon for some time during through the night

of the desert, we made camp near some fence post and promptly fell asleep in our bivy sacks.

Day 13: The Meaning of Life is about 58

Most of the day was a series of climbs and descents in the desert. We'd find a trickle of water here and there and fill up our water bottles then sterilize them. One time we came up on some water that was low lying and littered with cattle tracks. Rich stopped to fill his bottles up.

"Uh uh, no way" I said looking at the filthy water.

"A bird in hand..." Rich said.

I surveyed my water, I figured I had enough left for a few hours. I didn't feel like drinking water, even sterilized, after what a cow did in it so I decided to skip it.

After a fairly hard push to the top of a mountain, we spotted a tiny little town on a muddy dirt road. We got up to the welcome sign that said:

"ATLANTIC CITY: POPULATION, about 58."

I snorted and asked Rich to take my picture then we rolled into Atlantic City. It was as if time had stopped in this town. The buildings looked to be something from yesteryear being made out of all wood, no bricks, chickens running across the dirt road, hardly any cars and it really felt like you were on location for the filming of a western movie. We rode by the community center which was where they held town meetings. Apparently the city official would let you sleep there for the night should you need to rest; they were used to Tour Divide riders coming through their town and spending money. There was a library, a few shops that looked to be blacksmith shops and then the greasy spoon restaurant. We pulled up to it, parked our bikes and went in.

After a quick bite, Rich and I headed off to the more difficult section of the basin. I was rather intimidated but was glad to have Rich's company. He was always pretty sure of himself, confident, and the desert seemed to not bother him. This was good because I was still a little gun-shy about the basin. We rode out of Atlantic City's booming metropolis of 58 people and were met immediately with a huge climb.

"What the hell is up with these hills? I thought the desert was supposed to be flat!" I yelled.

We finally crested the top and there it was, or more so, there it wasn't. It was just a vast sea of nothingness. A dry dirt road and yellow sand as far as the eye could see. The wind was howling and pretty strong as nothing was there to block it. I got to see my first tumbleweed zip by and I could look down the road and see small dust devils spring up out of nowhere. It started to become afternoon and just ahead I saw the city of Rawlins.

"Well just like that, we're out of the basin" I murmured to myself and took a giant victory sip of water.

"So Rich, check it, there's Rawlins, we did it, and we're not far from cold sodas and a nice room for the night!"

"Obviously you've never seen a mirage before," he said.

I looked again and rubbed my eyes. The reflection of the sand had made it look like there was a city in the distance. I winced and said "oh..." We pedaled on for a while and I realized what a big mistake that "victory sip" (more like a good two gulps) was. I was getting low on water and I had no idea how much longer we had in the basin.

"Rich, my mouth is dry and I'm starting to feel woozy, I think I'm dehydrating." I said as the sun continued to beat down on me.

"Pinch your hand." He said.

"What?"

"Pinch the top your hand." Rich said sternly.

I pinched the top of my hand. I grabbed the folds of my skin, brought it up off my bones, pinched and let it go. The skin spread back into its place without even struggling.

"If you were dehydrated your skin would have stood up straight and then you'd have known you were in trouble."

"Really? How do you know that?"

"I'm a nurse, we have to do these things at work, testing people for dehydration."

Still, whether I was dehydrated or not, I was thirsty as hell.

"How many more miles do you think we have, Rich?" I said.

"About 60 or so."

I started doing the math saying to myself if we could keep at a 10-mile per hour pace that puts us in Rawlins in 6 hours which is around midnight where we could sleep in a hotel and be refreshed. I told Rich this and he said he doubted we'd make it to Rawlins. I told him it was worth a shot and we continued on. The sun was still out beating us down pretty hard. I took one of my last sips of water and wondered how I was going to get out of this alive.

I looked up and saw another mirage, or another town. I wanted it so bad to be a town and it wasn't. But it was. It was indeed a town as I moved my head left to right making sure I wasn't seeing things. I could see it was a small town with buildings and people, and cokes, beer, pie, burgers. We were saved!

"Look Rich! IT'S A TOWN!"

"Obviously you've never seen a ghost town"

My heart sunk, how could it be a ghost town? Ghost towns are only in movies!

But it was a ghost town, as we rode up to it you could see all the abandoned dilapidated windows and buildings.

"Hey Rich, you know what, screw it, I'm going down into that ghost town and looking for water."

"You're not going to find anything, he said"

"I DON'T CARE I NEED WATER!" I barked and I turned my bike to the left and rode down into the town.

It's like any start of any horror movie with the windows flapping in the wind, the buildings creaking back and forth and the hint of shadows moving behind the buildings. I honestly thought I was going to die here for a moment. That was until I rode by one alleyway, looked down past the creaking buildings and saw one house with an ATV vehicle parked near it and a modern truck. Someone lived there.

I tore down the alleyway and straight up to the door. Desperate for water I knocked on the door and heard movement inside. It was then I thought this was a really dumb idea and anyone that lived in a ghost town was surely not going to be offering cold beer and a nice slice of homemade apple pie. I heard someone come walking toward the door. I tensed up thinking over and over "this was dumb, this was dumb." A shadowy figure came to the door and opened it. "Yes?" The man said. He was shorter than me, brilliant blue eyes (possibly cataracts), dark brown skin and a foreign accent.

"Hi," I said. "So I'm out here in this desert and I've run out of water. Is there anyway I could have some of yours?"

"Follow me around back." He murmured.

I thought to myself and said "hmm… 'Around back' is where the axe and the torture chamber is, I know where this is going." I followed him around back and there was a single pump and about 300 sheep. Apparently this strange little man was a sheepherder in the middle of nowhere. I filled all four of my water bottles up and thanked him profusely.

As the sun beat down on us, We made our way through the dusty washboard-eroded roads. We saw a figure way up in the distance, another rider. As we closed in on the rider I noticed it was a female, but which female rider? On the roster there were only two that I had known of, Kristen and Sarah. She was pushing her bike and it was loaded out with saddlebags and tons of gear.

"Hi" I said.

"Hi" she said quickly and dismissively.

"Doing the Tour Divide Route?"

"Yeah, kind of. On my own. You guys?"

"Yeah. We're racing it."

"Well if you guys need water, there's a reservoir down the way. I stopped there and refueled and swam in it. You can camp there too!"

I thought about camping there, maybe there was a coke machine or a shower! But I knew better, I'm sure it was just a patted down area where people camped.

"How much longer until Rawlins?" I said.

"I dunno...50-60 miles?" She said.

"Dude, I told you already it was 50-60 miles!" Rich snapped.

"I know, I know you told me but I just wanted to hear it from someone else."

I think I offended Rich not trusting his math, he was dead on accurate but I was starting to go stir crazy not seeing a town. We continued riding and the sun started to fall.

"We're not going to make it to Rawlins tonight" Rich said.

"But it's less than 50 miles away" I said firing back.

"You're just afraid to be alone out in the wilderness."

"Not true" I lied.

Rich was partially right. I didn't like being out in the elements where I was basically a bear burrito wrapped up in a tiny little sleeping bag/tent smelling like a beef jerky pizza Oreo smorgasbord for animals to dine on. Or for some hillbilly to ride up and decide this would be the night he and his boys would use me for batting practice while I was asleep. Honestly? No sir, no thank you, I'd rather be in a ratty hotel with a shower than camped out on the side of the road alone. But I'll do it if I have to.

Rich said, "Here is where we go off course to get to the reservoir."

The road winded down and and when we got to a certain spot Rich veered off into the sagebrush. When we ventured into it a few chickens flew out of nowhere. "See those?" Rich said, "those are sage hens, they are like wild chickens and are prized by hunters. I watched the wild chickens fly off. Much like the old Looney Toon cartoons, they looked like little cooked chickens ready for me to sink my teeth into. We kept walking through the sage up a long hill and when we crested it, there it was a, a large lake. It was a large lake and had about 8,000 cattle standing in it. Cattle in water meant poop; poop I was going to have to have in my water and sterilize.

"Jeez…" I said and walked down to the edge of the lake. By now the sun was waning and it was starting to cool off. I stuck my feet in it and the water was freezing. I washed some of my clothes off and when I got back up and to the campsite the wind was blowing to the point that it was nearly knocking me down. I carefully pulled out my tent and it flapped in the wind. I grabbed it and stepped on it to prevent it from flying off. I managed to get the tent poles in the top and I slid inside. I grabbed my last remaining sandwich and ate it along with some Oreos. I washed it all down with some water with which   I   hoped   was   free   of   all "whateverwasinthewaterthatijustfilledmybottlesupwith."

The rest of the night was a hard sleep for me; and I actually started dreaming for the first time I could recall on the Divide. It was this odd dream in which aliens were landing near the campsite. The sharp-pitched yips and lasers emitting from the spaceship were deafening and loud… and really realistic. So realistic that I realized this was no dream and the loud sounds were not far from my tent! Yes, aliens were invading our campsite.

As the sounds grew louder I started to panic as it did sound like some form of alien machinery, but then the sound changed for a moment and I heard a lone "awwwoooooooooo" and I realized, Coyotes. Their high-pitched yips and yells almost sound mechanical when they are all together in a pack. The rest of the night I didn't sleep because I was unsure if coyotes, as a pack, would come around humans. Humans with food, mind you.

I could hear them run from place to place yipping and howling. Eventually the sounds died out and just when I was going to fall back asleep, the sun poked its rays right into my tent. "Oh god, seriously?" I said and that's when I heard Rich stirring in his tent.

Day 14: Knee Deep

"You hear those guys last night?" I said.

"Yep," said Rich.

"They didn't bother or worry you?"

"Nope." Rich said matter of fact.

He was a little cold in his responses but I didn't pay it much attention. We packed up and continued out of the Basin.

We were passed by many people in trucks going at unheard of fast speeds, which I assumed they were getting to work. I assumed we were at last not far from Rawlins since the mass running of trucks. The washboard roads, the trucks and the howling winds made for a miserable morning but eventually the dirt road gave way to a paved road which was slightly more pleasant but still horrible as it was cracked, hard to ride on and now we were dealing with cars flying at high speeds either way. The scenery was flat and barren with nothing in sight for miles. I let Rich in front of me and he slowly chugged along. I was a lot faster than him on a flat straightaway but I didn't want to get separated, however he was really slowing me down. "You can go on ahead if you want, I know you like to go fast." He said. I did and I got ahead of him and pedaled at a fast pace. I looked back and he'd disappeared out of my vision. I kept riding for hours on the hot paved road and then I saw a large, round and dark black object to my right. As I got closer I realized it was a dead cow that had bloated. When I passed it, its skin was crawling and moving - that's because it had tons of maggots crawling around it. The stench was just absolutely revolting and I thought any minute now this cow was going to explode into piles of nasty. As I went by it I gagged and almost threw up, it was one of the grossest things I've ever seen.

I rode on for a while, hours actually. I'd pass an RV or two parked out into the middle of nowhere. It reminded me of the hit series "Breaking Bad" and I wondered if they were running a meth operation or something. Eventually the nasty paved road gave way to a busy highway that said "Rawlins 10 miles." I was elated until I saw a climb up.

I was looking at the GPS and it showed me to go straight; I did and then I realized I was off route. "Hey!" I heard a distant voice say.

It was Rich and he was on the correct route. I retraced my steps and caught up with him and we stopped at a grocery store.

"Boy, for someone who wanted to see civilization, you sure missed a big turn!"

"People make wrong turns, I made a mistake. I was a little sunbaked, low on water and I simply missed a turn." I said angrily. "Are...are you joking or is there a problem"

"Oh I'm only picking on you. Let's go in and get some groceries." He said brushing off my concern.

I am a person who likes harmony, peace and no animosity between two people and will go to great lengths to "keep the peace."

"Hey, sorry about not believing you about the mileage. I was just anxious, that's all." I said trying to mend things over.

"You're done aren't you? You're ready to quit, right?" Rich said mockingly.

"Huh? I... huh? Wha?" I said baffled.

"You're mentally done, right? You're going to give up, right?"

"Well, no. Of course not. Sunbaked? Yes. Quitting? No." I said defensively.

We ate our food in silence of the restaurant and I started listening to this girl and guy talk to the girl's mom."

Guy: "Yeah, I've been in jail three times now. Can't seem to stay out of there."

Girl: "Awww psh... whatever. I been in jail three times myself and you don't see me never talkin no big stuff about it."

Guy: "Yeah but what'd you do? Drink and drive?"

Girl: "So? So what if I did?"

I couldn't believe my ears; they were honestly trying to one up each other about being in jail. I scooted closer to Rich and murmured "What is it with this weird place called Rawlins!" Paul had told me that he thought Rawlins was an odd and quirky place too. Rich said that it was a place that courted a lot of young, blue collar people to come "make it big" working for Big Oil. Apparently there's oil in the basin hence all the trucks, and very nice trucks to boot.

We finished up lunch and headed out of Rawlins and making our way to Colorado. I was so elated to wrap up another state. I went into the next climb, seated and didn't have to push. There was yet another climb up which was painful but I made it up that without pushing. "I gave a little fist bump" and started into yet another horrible climb that I pushed up which I was doing fine and then I felt something slip in my knee.

Searing pain forced it's way through my kneecap surrounding my leg with some of the most intense pain I'd ever felt. I drew a sharp breath in and about fell over not because I was hurting so badly, but because I couldn't breathe. Colorado was known for it's harsh elevations and people at that high of an altitude have trouble breathing. I drew another breath which made me have to heave. Between me feeling like I had to gasp for air and the new found pain my knee, I was dying.

I tried to ride and at most if I didn't put much pressure on my knee I was okay, but it hurt and would cause me involuntary to emit yelps and sharp barks each time I had to push with it. I took a break waiting on Rich to catch up.

When he did show up I hopped back on me bike and shrieked as the pain seared through my leg.

"You okay?" Rich said and I told him about my knee giving out.

"Dude, you need to learn how to ride a singlespeed! You don't sit and climb, you stand and climb!" He said sternly.

If I stand and climb, I burn out all my energy quickly; however seated climbs I can save some energy and be okay. I've always done that on a singlespeed, I've never done anything else but that. I was trained on seated climbs because they require less energy and let's face it, climbing on a singlespeed is bad enough as is. I dismissively said, "Let's go" and we dove into the downhill dodging construction vehicles and crew. On the next climb, my knee really let me know it was there. Rich got a fair distance ahead of me and I stopped to rest. I saw some snow a few yards away; I grabbed some and rubbed it on my knee. It helped enough to allow me to keep going, and I then found myself completely alone.

I started entertaining the idea of quitting. I mean after all I'd conquered half the Divide as a rookie, no one else currently living in Alabama had ever done that. But then I started thinking about all the people that had leant a hand helping me out and giving me so much love and support. I'd saved some messages on my phone for when I would get down on myself to pep myself up.

"We're praying for you, Scott, you rock!" A message from Sunny and Owen came through on my phone just then.

Sunny embodies her name, having one of the brightest and most positive dispositions ever. She's broken both her ankles before on rides and runs but still can outrun most people in a race. Owen is one of the nicest and fiercest competitors I've ever met. In whatever he competes, he gives it his all leaving no reserve. Kate and I had fallen in love with their friendship and they were always quick to bestow blessing and prayers to us. I figured if Sunny can continue to run races on two broken ankles, I could ride out this pain in my knee.

Sunny and Owen's message was enough to at least temporarily get me back on my bike. I kept riding through the shadows of the daylight until I almost plowed into a truck not seeing it because I'd had my head in my handlebars.

"Son you okay?" The elderly driver said.

"No, no I'm not. I'm hurt and I'm hungry. Have you seen any bikers lately?"

"I seen a pack of you folks about 2 hours ago. You guys are a crazy bunch."

"Any towns close by?" I asked.

"Noooo, none that I can think of. You're pretty far out in the sticks."

I gritted my teeth and thought for a second. The man responded,

"You need a ride to town or something?"

It was so easy, all I had to tell him was yes and I could load my bike up and be done with the Divide. I wanted to, I wanted to so bad. I felt my knee, it hurt. My stomach was rumbling. I looked at the man and said

"Yes, I'd love to…"

"… But I can't" and I hopped back on my bike and kept riding.

I entered into "Aspen Alley" which was a series of beautiful aspen trees. I tried to take a picture of it but was beaten alive by mosquitos. "Dammit!" I screamed, swatting mosquitos and dealing with knee pain.

"Scott!" I heard a voice and Rich popped out. "I was going to camp here and then I heard you coming. You know, there's a lodge just inside the border of Colorado. It's Kirsten's Brush Creek Lodge and we could make it, I think."

"Yes, I need a place to formally rest. Let's go."

We hammered on through the waning hours of daylight. As the sun started to dip behind the mountains we saw a sign, "You are now leaving Wyoming." We crossed it and did a small victory dance.

Two states left.

COLORADO

Look up the definition of "awesome" and you'll see that it says this:

awe·some

'kall or ah doe/

adjective, noun, verb, adverb, hell...it's the entire enchilada of grammar

Extremely impressive or daunting; inspiring great admiration, apprehension, or fear. This is what Colorado is, the most awesome place in the world.

"The awesome power of Colorado"

As we transitioned from Wyoming to Colorado I could instantly note a change. Sure, the scenery had not really shifted that much but you could just feel John Denver singing "Country Roads" in the distance things started to just feel better.

"We have 12 miles until Brush Lodge, I just don't know if I can make it, Scott. We may need to camp," Rich said.

"12 miles? Screw that, if we pedal quickly we can be there in an hour and a half!" I said sternly.

Rich looked tired, haggard and really wanted to stop. Not me, I wanted a shower and this mythical lodge that Rich had mentioned.

My knees were hurting horribly and I constantly had to shift places but I was bound and determined to get to Brush Lodge. As nighttime came upon us I could see a light way off in the distance. It was the lodge, and I was so excited. Sadly, as I got closer, I realized it was a camper fiddling with his light. We rode on for a while and a truck passed us going way too fast. As we pedaled a little further we saw the deer he'd taken out. It was freshly killed and there was blood trickling out of his mouth. These are images you don't want to see in the middle of the night and it caused me to think about every horror movie I'd ever seen. We rode in darkness for a while and we were coming up on mile 12 with no lodge in site.

"Are we getting close? Are we there?" Rich asked.

I looked down at my GPS; it now said that we were at mile 12.74.

"Uh…" I said

"If we don't get there soon I'm camping!" Snapped Rich.

And that's when we rounded a corner and saw a series of lights illuminating a quaint little lodge.

We couldn't see much but I noticed Ty, Joseph, Taylor and Kristen's bikes were leaning against the wood railing. A man stepped out, he was large, had a lot of frizzy salt and pepper colored hair along with an untamed beard.

"I hope you boys aren't vegetarians," he said.

"I could eat a live horse right now" I said.

"Well that's good because we've been tracking y'all and put in some pepperoni pizzas in for you; they'll be done in a few minutes. Welcome to Brush Creek."

Relieved, I walked into the lodge. It was dimly lit, there was a giant dining table and over in the corner were some board games. We started to sit down and Kirsten, the lady who ran the lodge, walked out. She had on a blue beret, flannel shirt, looked tired, but smiled and said

"Hi, I'm Kirsten."

I held out my hand to shake hers.

"Oh no, no, I don't shake people's hands. I give hugs." Kirsten said with her arms stretched out. She gave Rich and I these huge, wonderful hugs and then we sat down.

"If you boys don't stop coming in here, I'm going to have to shut this place down, you guys are wearing me out."

"Been a rough day of racers? I can't thank you enough for the late night pizza." I said empathetically.

"This is like the 4th or 5th run to the city I've made to keep you guys taken care of. So many of you this year."

I stood up to thank her and my knees screamed in agony.

"Um, Kristen… would you happen to have any ice? My knees are killing me."

She brought me some and I put the ice on my knees, then took a picture of them and posted it on the Internet for my friends to see.

Birmingham, February 2012

A message popped up one day while I was on the Internet. It was from Eddie O'Dea, one of the Southeast's pro racers.

"I want you to come to Atlanta to get a bike fit by me, if you're going to do the TNGA and the Tour Divide, you need to be fit right on your bike." He said.

"Yes but they are so expensive, Eddie."

"You won't make either of these races without a proper fit, my bike fits are perfect. Come to Atlanta so I can fit you."

I had known about Eddie for some time now and was rather star struck that a big fish like him would even message a small fish like me however he did and I went to Atlanta to get fit by Eddie's coaching and bike fitting service at Endurance House in Atlanta.

When I showed up Eddie was a person of very few words. That made me nervous because I hate long pauses and awkward moments of silence.

"Boy, this sure is a cool setup you have here for mountain bikers to get trained for long distance instead of those stupid roadie guys and their silly shaved legs!" I said awkwardly trying to break the silence.

Eddie remained silent as he took measurements and that's when I glanced down and saw he had shaved legs. I couldn't even back pedal on what I said and just did a small face palm hoping he'd just forget I ever said that.

I spent many quiet hours with Eddie in his office. He barely spoke to me while he did all my measurements uttering occasional directives for me to hop on my bike, hop off of it, get my feet stamped so he could see where to place this, that and the other. Finally he asked me to hop on the bike and explained all these variables, numbers and reasons why he did this to my bike and that to my bike. But it was magical and a huge shift in performance as climbing as well as comfortably pedaling at a high speed.

167

Brush Lodge, Colorado

A message popped up on my phone "What's up with your knees? They shouldn't hurt. Something is wrong with your bike, my bike fits are perfect." Eddie's message was direct and blunt. "Go out and measure your bike, something is off, your knees should not hurt at all." We talked it over and I grabbed a measuring tape and went out to my bike. Sure enough my seat post had slid an inch thus the problem with my knees cramping up. I messaged Eddie back and said "Thank you" then said "You'd totally love it out here man, I mean you could really just kill it racing." There was a long pause and then a one-sentence response "Of course I would."

Kirsten sat down with us at her table. She looked tired.

"I just don't think I can keep this up. The Tour Divide keeps growing every year and I'm just wiped out from tending to you guys." She said wearily.

"You know next year I'd love to bring my wife out here and help. I doubt we could do it that soon, but this is so awesome!" I said.

Rich also gave her a heartfelt compliment and then a smile came across her face.

"Awww then nice people like you show up and just make everything better!" Kirsten said

"Okay, I have a room for you all the way down on the end."

This was great, but my cash reserves had taken a fair beating since Canada and I was starting to run low. Given I had two more states to go I got concerned about shelling out for this stay at the lodge. I wolfed down another piece of pizza and then Rich and I wheeled our bikes past Ty, Joseph and Kristen's bikes. I peeked in their room and saw them all sound asleep. Rich and I made it to our room. It was huge, a kitchen, a nice bathroom, four huge beds although we only needed two. It was like the Taj Mahal.

"This is going to cost a fortune, I just know it. I was too afraid to even ask." I said.

"Scott, she doesn't charge you anything. She just asks for donations."

"Really??" I said baffled.

"Yes... really." Rich expecting that I knew this.

Day 15: Big Hearts of Humans

Kirsten made an unbelievably huge breakfast, and then showed us all the snacks and sandwiches she'd made.

"Take what you want, I made the pbjs this morning!"

Kirsten took pictures of us, and I gave her a big hug. She waved and wished us well as we rode off. I let Rich get a bit ahead of me and I dropped back to riding alone. I grabbed my earphones and popped them in. I had a specific playlist ready for Colorado that was a mixture of John Denver and Mumford and Sons. It was bliss and I hummed along serenely down the dirt roads.

A few hours later and I could sense the presence of others and sure as the sun coming up, Joseph, Ty, Kristen and Taylor rode up next to me on the dirt road.

"Again! Again with the soft pedaling!" Joseph said with a laugh. "How are you doing this?"

"Because I'm a stubborn one and you guys aren't gonna drop me!"

As we rounded a corner I saw rolling hills of sage. The fragrant smells hit my nose and it was the most amazing scent and sight I'd ever seen. As with each time riding with the four kids, my speed was quickly being outpaced by the strong legs of my competition. Joseph looked back, laughed and said:

"So you'll pass us tomorrow?"

I smiled and watched them disappear. The rest of the day was a series of up and down hill, going through the forests of Northern Colorado. It was absolutely blissful and wonderful, except the altitude was killing me though I'd somewhat adapted to it.

The afternoon started to creep up and I went down a giant dirt hill. As I came screaming down it I saw lots of extremely nice homes built along the dirt road. A mother and her two kids were at the foot of the hill that turned into a paved road. They had signs up that said "GO TOUR DIVIDE RACERS" And they cheered me on as I whipped by.

Alabama is quite a bit different than Colorado. First there is the humidity vs. the arid climate. That was a fair amount of adjusting especially getting my lungs around the fact that they were just not going to get the air they were used to. In Alabama we have the humidity and it can be rather daunting at times feeling like you are wrapped up in a wet hot blanket. Also us Alabamians struggle horribly with our waistlines with all the delicious bbq and comfort foods we have here. In Colorado there were plenty of fast food areas but most areas had a healthier fare readily available. However the one big difference between Alabama and Colorado? The motorists in Colorado don't try to use you as target practice if you're on a bike.

In Alabama I've been run off the road, had cars come so close to me that I could almost feel the door whoosh by me and I've almost been in two physical altercations that being with a person driving a van that represented a popular cellular service company and a State Park employee. As much as I love Alabama, especially Birmingham, the motorists here just can't be bothered to give a cyclist struggling up a hill at least three feet and slowly drive around us. We have a lot to learn.

Contrast to Colorado and it was the exact and utter opposite. As I pulled onto the busy road on a muddy bike, with my muddy self looking more like a hobo I heard the familiar sound of a car come up behind me. I gritted my teeth, prepared to feel the "whoosh" of the car come by me closely. But it didn't happen, in fact the car swerved into the other lane giving me an entire eight feet of clearance. In fact the car in the oncoming lane slowed down, letting the passing car get around me. I blinked and thought, "What world is this?" I initially just thought I got lucky and this was an isolated incident… but nope, in fact it happened multiple times with Colorado motorists giving me all the room I needed as they got around me. I have never felt safer in my life while on the road riding a bike.

As I made my way into Steamboat it quickly turned into a busy area littered with very fancy cars and suvs and extremely perfect buildings that had a somewhat rustic feel mixed with "Hey we're extremely wealthy but also very rustic...in an expensive way." The route led behind a series of kitsch buildings that paralleled a stream that was apparently a popular tubing destination.

I rode around the perfect town of Steamboat and had trouble figuring out where Orange Peels Cycles was to get some much-needed attention for my haggard bike. The paved scenic trail whipped around the river where multitudes of people were tubing. Finally I saw it, the cycle shop. I had been 1,000 miles since the last cycle shop and had worried myself sick with rickety brake pads, weird clicking noises and things on my bike that didn't look right. As I pulled in I saw several cyclists such as Rich, Joseph, Ty, Kristen and Taylor. I was going to ride up and make the soft pedal joke when I saw another person, Prentiss. We had not seen each other since he pulled away from me in Whitefish. I threw down my bike and ran up to him.

"PRENTISS!!! Holy cow man! I wasn't expecting to catch you, wh...where's Ron? How are you? Dude so good to see you!" I bombarded him with questions.

"I quit." He said with his eyes heavy.

Each time, someone I knew and liked (or didn't like) quit, it stabbed me right in the gut.

"No, noooo man, no come ride with me! Come on, we'll have a blast dude! I need a riding buddy!" I tried to coax him out of giving up but I could see that he was done.

We sat down in two chairs staring at each other. I looked down at his feet, still sporting his signature Converses. His ankles were completely swollen and honestly looked like they were spilling right over his shoes.

"Jesus man, what's up with your ankles!?"

"Man I don't know, they just blew up."

"Is this why you're quitting?"

"Naw man, I'm just not having fun anymore, I'm not going to beat my time last year and honestly I just need to get home." He said.

"Hey well stick around for a few, I gotta go check in my bike."

I went into the cycle shop and started to open my mouth to say I need my bike looked at. Ahead of me was a sea of Tour Divide bikes being worked on. Mechanics were chatting with the other racers about their bikes and what needed to be addressed. One mechanic quickly came up to me.

"Tour Divide? Okay strip your bike down throw all your garb in that basket there and tell me what's wrong? Want a beer?" He was a pro, he'd done this so many times before that it was a no brainer for him.

"My bike needs some attention." I said as I started to strip away everything except the bare bones of the bike.

"Uh huh, okay, need some more info than that." He responded not missing a beat. "Well there's some clicking noise coming from this thingy here, and then there was some clicking going on back here around the wheely part, I think. Oh and I think the chain is slipping a bit, too."

At this point, he already had my bike in the clamps of his repair station.

"It's going to be 30 minutes before I can look at your bike and probably an hour to fix it. okay?"

"Sure" I said shrugging.

I sat down outside where Taylor, Kristen, Ty and Joseph were grazing on some food.

"There's a great organic shop where you can get healthy stuff just down the street, Scott. I'm sure you could just 'soft walk' over there since your bike is in the shop." Laughed Joseph.

I looked over at Taylor, who didn't look the least bit tired or worn out.

"How are you doing it?" I asked. "How are you going so blazingly fast on a singlespeed? I try so hard to keep up with you guys and I just can't seem to do it

"Oh, you just spin up, rest and keep the spin up." He said.

I let the thought marinate in my head.

"Okay so I just rev up the speed until I cannot sustain anymore, coast and then when the speed starts to slip just rev up some more?"

"That's right. Singlespeed. It's simple." Said Taylor.

I'll admit, I'd been somewhat intimidated by Taylor and Kristen. They were fast, lean, very level-headed and pretty confident in their skills. Transition to me and I was always groggy, exhausted, emotionally wrought and my muscles felt like they'd been put through a wringer several times. I didn't even feel remotely in their league and having 20 years on them made me feel old and rundown. But the fact that they would both chat with me, smile laugh and enjoy my company made me feel like I was accepted by their extremely fast group. I was just the slowest part of the fast part.

Prentiss was going to stay in a hotel overnight in Steamboat then fly out the next morning.

"Ask to stay with Prentiss, Scott. Actually, end your trip here and just go home. Relax. Go tubing. Enjoy the cool water."

My brain was doing its best to convince me that Steamboat would be a great place to stop.

"No."

My mind warred against my brain.

"No, were going to get to the next town. Shush, you."

My coach had wisely said that the brain does everything it can to keep you comfortable and happy. I think that's one reason we as a nation are so fat, why would you ever want to choke down three stalks of celery when you can have a double bacon cheeseburger for $1.99 at any fast food joint? The Divide isn't won by a strong body, an expensive bike with top-notch parts and fancy gear. Mental fortitude gets to you to Antelope Wells, New Mexico. Everything else is secondary.

I told Prentiss "Hey I'm gonna go catch Ron" and laughed. I knew Ron was at least two days ahead of me. Prentiss looked at me and put his hand on my shoulder. I couldn't tell if he was tearing up or just being dead serious, however what he said was such a turning point for me in the Divide. He looked at me and said;

"Enjoy yourself out there Scott. Stop, look up from the handlebars, and dammit drink a beer from time to time."

"Well you don't have to worry about the beer part!" We both laughed and gave each other the "bro man hug."

I called Kate and said, "I miss you, hope you are well, etc." When I got off the phone with her, I smiled, let the sun hit me and rode through the rest of Steamboat, the perfect city. I went through an area with all perfect shops and found the perfect organic market that Joseph was talking about. When I walked in a lady with perfect long braided hair, a paisley dress and a sweater (despite it being 80 degrees outside) said "We're about to close, we're not making sandwiches anymore." I said, "I'll just be a minute getting some snacks" and quickly went through the little shop. Everything was "locally made" and apparently you paid for the locality of the product. Locally made beef jerky, locally made honey, locally made butter cups, locally made Chap Stick. EVERYTHING was just perfect and locally made.

This is why I think I had such a hang up with Steamboat. It was the most awesome and perfect place I'd ever been in, maybe like say what Heaven was supposed to be like. But it made me miss my imperfect state, Alabama. We have problems here, our politics are shot to hell and we fight against obesity something awful here. There's a high amount of ignorance and illiteracy and much like many places over the "new south" the McMansion Suburban sprawl has decimated beautiful wooded areas all in the name of profit. We have strip malls that give birth to strip malls that contain a Pawn Shop, a church, a nail salon, a Faux-Tex-Mex Mexican restaurant, a ton of chain fast food restaurants and we're ranked last in bike friendliness.

I missed it, I missed it all.

As I rode out of Steamboat and into the 'burbs I noticed tons of people going to a "concert in the park." I was riding on the same walking trail that people were using to get to the show. Many people would look at me strange in my extremely worn out bike kit, ragged beard, haggard face and hobo-like quality, enhanced by the bags hanging off of my bike. Some people knew what I was doing and they'd scream "YAY TOUR DIVIDE!" Which was a booster. I saw a family walking with their kids. The family looked distantly like our family and watching them happily go down the trail to the park I had to question to myself: "What the hell am I doing here?" That's when it sunk in.

I had my sunglasses on which was good, because I started tearing up pretty bad. I had to bite the site of my mouth as people would wave and cheer me on. Generally I'd eat that attention up and would have added to it by doing fist bumps or making corny jokes like:

"Sorry, out of pens or I'd give you my autograph!"

But I was just doing my best to not show that I was a complete basket case. The Divide route turned onto a road out of Steamboat and I couldn't be happier so I could be sadder. As soon as I saw the last person and was on a rural road, I stopped and pulled out my phone to watch the video of the kids' skit again they did for Father's day that was seemingly a million years ago in my mind. As I watched it I let out a flood of tears and sobbed. I was homesick. I wanted to go home.

I heard the familiar click, click, click of a hub as I sat in a ditch drying my eyes. It was the sound of a road bike and when I looked up there was a lady looking down at me.

"Are you okay?" She asked

"Yeah… yeah I'm… I'm fine." I lied.

"You're doing the Tour Divide, aren't you?"

"Yep. Although I'd like to make Steamboat my last stop, it's lovely here. I'm 'Scott' by the way." And I extended out my hand to shake hers.

"I'm Lacey, it's nice to meet you."

Lacey worked for Moots, the bike company that crafted Scott McConnell's bike, the bike on which he was currently leading the singlespeeders on the race.

"Do you need someone to ride with you for a while and just have a buddy to talk to?"

"Thanks but no thanks" I said smiling. "Your conversation and kindness here was enough."

She pedaled on and I was completely renewed with just how nice people could be and how helpful an empathetic ear is.

I rode on the road for a while and then the Divide route took a turn onto a trail that circled around a beautiful lake and these log cabin homes (well, mansions) tucked neatly in the base of a mountain. I was still reeling in the homesick and was working my way through that mental mess so I was more intently looking at my handlebars than anything else when all of the sudden I whipped around a curve in the trail and heard:

"HEY WATCH OUT!"

I about obliterated a wife, husband and two kids. I stopped and said emotionally:

"I am … SO.. sorry!"

"Are you okay?" The lady said collecting herself.

"Well, I've had better days." I said.

She asked what I was doing and I explained the Tour Divide, how I'd biked from Canada and down to here and still needed to make it to Mexico... and that I was missing my wife something awful. The lady, who I had almost taken out said "hold on just a moment dear" and bolted up to her log cabin house (mansion) and 5 minutes later came down with 10-15 energy bars, a huge bar of Hershey's chocolate, 3 Gatorades and some gummy bears.

"Here, have this."

I shook my head and said "Oh no I ca..." And then my brain quickly said:

"Hey dumb-dumb, take the food, TAKE IT NOW!"

So I grabbed it and thanked her immensely. The husband and wife had been to Birmingham numerous times, mainly the suburb of Vestavia Hills. They said they loved it down there and now we had somewhat of a bond. I told them that my suburb was just a few miles south of Vestavia Hills and were welcome anytime they wanted to come. They realized I was dawdling and stalling for time not wanting to leave. The lady said,

"Now what was your wife's name again? Kate, right? Well I'm going to pretend to be Kate and if I was her, I'd say 'get your ass on that bike and come home to see me quick. Now go!'" I smiled, shed a tear and took off.

I rode late into the night through freezing cold weather and then ended up attempting to camp near a stream where I dealt with warbling birds and howling coyotes all night. There was no sleep to be had. The next morning I gingerly stepped through the cold creek barefooted carrying my 55lb bike across it. When I got done, I dried off my legs and looked back.

Day 16: The Beer Of Thor

"HOW?" HOW ARE YOU DOING THIS? HOW DO YOU KEEP GETTING AHEAD OF US?" I looked back and it was Joseph, Ty, Taylor and Kristen. I smiled and wiggled my foot at them as I was putting on my socks.

They crossed the stream one by one. Ty and Joseph were noticeably thinner than they were just over two weeks before. Their bike kits were loose on them and Ty looked especially "mountain man"-ish as his beard had grown out since I'd first seen him in Banff and Joseph had the beginnings of a beard, eyes were bloodshot red and he looked tired, but happy.

Colorado was easily the prettiest state to ride through. The sky was blue with beautiful clouds, the countryside was something like I could imagine might have inspired John Denver to write the songs that he did and everything was just a visual potpourri of awesomeness.

As the day marched on I found myself climbing up a very steep paved road for what seemed to be hours, in fact it was hours climbing it.

"Hey, hey racer!" A person said coming up behind me.

"Yeah?" I panted

"If you want some water, 7 miles up to the top, turn left at the canoe hanging from the sign post and get some water at the house."

"O..."

::Pant:::

"kay…"

The sun beat down on me and the climbs, while on paved roads, were pretty intense. I refused to walk any of them and grinded to a slow crawl on the ascents. I continued climbing the long tortuous mountain when it finally flattened out and then up to my left was a giant lodge and a canoe hanging from a signpost. I got to the driveway, which continued to go up and I was so exhausted I had to walk up to the house. A man was there cleaning up.

"Hey, mister, so there was this guy that said I could get some water here?"

"That was me," The man said smiling. "Welcome, I'm David."

"Hi David, nice to meet you, I'm Scott and I'm thirsty."

He went inside and came out with a tall iced water, which I downed immediately. He went and brought another along with some potato chips and candy bars, which I ate, almost taking off his arm in the process.

It was then he started asking about how the trip was and any stories I could tell. I realized I was to sing for my supper, and being the storytelling kind of guy, I sang. Apparently my "singing for supper" is rather crafty because the frozen burritos started coming out and now my very famished self was now full and happy. I walked out from under the shade to bask in the sun, it was warm and I was sweaty and wet. I sat on a stump and decided to call my wife as I had a smidge of service. When I called it went to her voicemail and I started to leave a message.

"Hey babe, just wanted to say hi and..." And then I lost it. I started sobbing uncontrollably on the phone even to the point I was heaving. It was just another moment where fatigue, mental anguish and overall exhaustion had gotten the best of me. If a reality TV team was filming me, I'd have been America's top star since those shows love it when people turn on the waterworks. I hung up after making some garbled message and the phone rang back quickly. It was Kate.

I sat sobbing on the phone for a while and she let me cry it out. I told her that this would happen at least three more times on the Divide where I'd need to just get all the anxiety out. We chatted for a while and when I hung up I immediately started getting pictures from people back home holding signs that said "Go Scott!" and "You can do it!" Apparently while chatting Kate let some friends know I was having a bad time and to send me a little cheer.

I smiled and went back to talk to David. David's family had all showed up and they too wanted to hear stories. I looked back and saw a big black cloud lingering over where I needed to go next.

"Listen guys, I would love to chat, I really would but I've got to outpace that cloud over there." They all agreed, gave me a soda for the road and I tore off down the

179

mountain scooting past the and of course before I could get too far, the bottom fell out.

I got pelted with rain pretty hard; then it turned to sleet. I stopped to put on my raingear. It took at least 10 minutes to get it all put on and when I got the final zipper pulled up and was like a waterproof sweatbox, the sun peaked back out. This was getting old.

"Seriously?" I said looking at the sun as I put all my raingear back up.

Rich, Joseph and the rest of the gang rode by. Joseph giggled at the familiar sight as he saw me stuffing my rain gear back in my bag. All Divide racers have dealt with the same thing at some point. I hopped up on my bike and briefly caught up with them. Joseph and Ty weren't riding with their helmets anymore and had them mounted on the front of their handlebars like trophy deer. "Too hot to have that damned helmet on, you know? Besides it's all flat here anyway."

Predictably everyone dropped me. Because it was a flat, I dropped Rich and like a line of ants we weaved up and down the backside of Silverthorne.

It took a fair amount of work to get into Silverthorne... Rich was somewhere behind me and while I should have split a room with people, I needed some "me" time, to unwind and relax. I finally saw a hotel.

"I'd like one room please? Smallest you got. Cheapest you got."

"We ain't got no effin rooms here. Biker gangs, you know the ones with motors, already took up every last room." He said curtly.

"Dammit..." I muttered.

"You know, there's a hostel just down the road; it's cheap. Go there." He said gruffly.

I hopped on my bike and tried to find this hostel. It was off the main drag of Silverthorne and it looked like a giant Swiss or Bavarian house. I pulled up into the hostel and parked my bike out front. I walked in; it was dark, clean and smelled like a fraternity house with the scents of booze and... other things legal in the state of Colorado. A man walked out in a sleeveless flannel shirt and a mullet.

"Sup dude, you're one of those racers? Need a room?" he said.

"Yes, one room please. Private, just for me."

"Man this is a hostel, it's dorm room style. 25 bucks and you got a clean bed."

"Listen I'll pay extra if I can just have a room to myself, I need some down time… and a shower." He sat and thought for a moment and said,

"Tell you what, there's a dorm room with no one in it currently, but it sleeps 16. If the other dorm room fills up with hikers and bikers, I gotta let them come in. Ya dig?"

"I dig."

He let me into a room all by myself. It was huge room with bunk beds and single beds sprawled everywhere. I picked a bed by the window, switched into my Columbia Falls RV Park t-shirt and my running shorts. I walked downstairs to the commune area, the manager was watching MTV with his buddy, who had long golden blonde hair and drank a golden blonde ale to boot. Imagine Thor if Thor liked beer, like a lot of beer.

The manager and his friend who now I'd dubbed "Beer Thor" went down to watch TV for a while and they invited me. I figured "why not" they intrigued me. They were glued to some 80's videos on MTv and I sat down relaxed on a sofa that obviously was from the 70's. Beer Thor looked over at me and said:

"Biker man?"

"Kinda. I'm doing a race from Canada to Mexico on a mountain bike."

Generally when I tell people that they get animated and want to hear more. He just drew a long sip of his golden ale and without even looking at me said:

"Right on, brother." I sorta snickered to myself and we watched a run of videos by the 80's hair band "Poison." Somewhere between the top hits of Bon Jovi and Cinderella I decided I should go get some sleep. I bid the manager and Beer Thor a good evening. Beer Thor looked back and said

"Man you ain't gonna stay for RATT? They're up next, brother!"

"No, not today, maybe the next time I race through Silverthorne."

I chuckled up the steps and entered into the hostel's dorm room, which I still had to myself thankfully.

Through "Facetime" on my iPhone I was able to connect with Kate and see her face. She looked so pretty and I'm sure I looked like something run over a few times by an 18 wheeler truck.

Kate had gotten a new haircut, and I begged her to fly out here to Colorado and hang out for a while in my fancy hostel with the mullet manager. She laughed and said "no." After we hung up, I munched on my sandwich I'd picked up close by and looked out the window. Silverthorne was awesome. It was a little less perfect than Steamboat and I liked the people and the vibe here. I decided that tomorrow (Sunday) would be a complete rest day for me and I'd just take it easy getting out of here.

Day 17: Loss Of A Friend

The next morning was an extremely pleasant bike ride on a paved trail that made my love for Colorado continue to grow. Tons of people were on it riding, hiking and running. I rode up on one lady who seemed to be struggling up a hill while on a bicycle. I always believe in being the more passive when being around new people. I'll go out of my way to display courteous cycling while trying to give proper biking etiquette.

"On your left. Ma'am, I'm coming up on your left." The lady in front of me was so terrified she didn't know whether to move right, left, speed up or slow down.

"Hey," I said. "I'm going to get around you in a minute when we get around these curves. She stopped, got off the bike and was panting in frustration.

"Just go!" She yelled.

I stopped and asked if everything was okay. She looked super stressed out and upset.

"My husband decided today was the day he'd play Lance Armstrong and roped me into this crazy bike thing, I hate it. I can't stand it!"

"Hey I get it, it's really stressful. Just rest and breathe for a moment."

"I bet your husband is no more than a half mile in front of us, I'll zip on up and see if I can find him for you."

She breathed, relaxed a bit and then looked my bike and me over.

"Well you look different than most people I've seen today." I decided to just downplay what I was doing given her horrid experience with cyclists for the day.

"I'm... um, camping out in a few places." I bid her farewell and kept going. I passed her husband just a bit up and said:

"Hey I think I saw your wife back there and I think she's having a hard time."

The man was struggling to get up a small hill and winded. He said:

"Thanks, I'll go get her." I kept riding through the beautiful town of Silverthorne and then on into Breckinridge. Breckinridge (Brek) was every outdoorsy person's dream... as long as your dream was being or being married to a CEO who made seven figures a year, then yes, every outdoorsy person's dream. I noticed every outdoors brand was represented there as I wheeled by all the Benzs, Porches, Hummers, Land Rovers and Lexus luxury vehicles. I decided to stop and get a Coca-Cola at one vendor there on the strip but all they had was Organic fresh local grown goji berry juju juice for 14.99 a thimble. Realizing I could not afford to even breathe the air here, I pedaled on.

Plowing my way through the back roads of Colorado, I dealt with a fair amount of rain. Traversing the trails got rather muddy especially when I got onto a long dirt road.

I was wringing wet, in fact most of my clothes were wet so I tried to tie off my rain jacket and rain pants on the side of my bike to dry off. I also tried to rearrange things in my bag and that's when my Columbia Falls RV Park t-shirt fell out of my bag and into a mud puddle.

"Well, damn," I muttered.

I now tied it off on the side of the bike in hopes to dry it out a well. The Columbia Falls RV Park shirt had become my favorite thing on the divide. It was nice, comfy, had a giant wolf on the front of it and ironically funny because I'd never in a million years wear something like this back home. But here? Here on the Divide? It was my favorite thing ever and now it was coated in nasty mud smell, which meant I was going to have to find a laundromat, because I needed my shirt. My Columbia Falls RV shirt had become my best friend.

For the first time in Colorado I experienced something new: flat land. I honestly didn't think Colorado had any flat land but here it was, and it went on and on for forever.

I dumped off onto a new dirt road that lead into a series of rolling prairies. They were absolutely beautiful and seemingly never ending. As I rode over one rolling hill, I could see for miles with nothing but green, a house here or there and... AND A GIANT FREAKING STORM HEADING MY WAY! I dug my feet into the pedals and powered it as hard as I could. Its massive lightning was striking randomly all over the ground.

Lightning. It has no prejudices, is random and kind of likes things that are metal or steel in a giant prairie like, oh, my steel bike.

I don't know if I entered into some beast like mode, turned temporarily to Superman or what, but I outran the storm coming in to my left. I could feel the wind changing and the storm was behind me. The wind, the wind that was changing was now blowing against my back and like something that was alive and wanting to eat me, the storm was now chasing me. Lightning struck closer than I'd like, I screamed and pedaled faster now panting and running out of energy, but had a full tank of adrenaline which kept me going.

I was breathing heavy and my lungs were making the sound of a mix of a chorus of bad violins and pistons pumping with no oil to lube them. The storm's lightning struck close again and fear overtook me. I was screaming and going as fast as my two legs would let me go. I figured I was going to get struck, there was no place to hide and no shelter. It was a giant prairie and I was a damn fine lightning rod.

I looked down at my GPS, it was showing I was going to hit a dead end then turn to the right. I thought maybe, just maybe, the storm will just keep going straight and I can get out of dodge.

I pedaled and pedaled fast, bumping over washboard ridges in the dirt road, covered in sweat, mud and now in tears fearing for my life. The dead end and sign to turn to the right came up. I took the right and dumped onto a paved road and continued going as fast as possible when I suddenly felt the air die down and stop suddenly. I was out of the wake of the storm and I stopped to catch my breath. I looked back to see the monster of clouds and lightening go across the prairie now ignoring me.

"Ha!" I said out breath and heaving. "Ha!"

I was not laughing in victory, but more in anxiety. That said, I was rather proud of myself that I outran a storm. In fact I felt a little smug knowing I'd outsmarted Mother Nature. Or at least I thought I had.

There is no resting on your laurels on the Tour Divide, at all. Nope, you have one small victory and it's like you get punished three times harder. As I leaned up against my bike to regain my breath and smile victoriously at my outrunning of the storm, I saw a flicker or something being carried away with the wind of the storm.

It was grey, cloth and I saw it whoosh by and disappear with the dark clouds. I knew what it was and it was confirmed when I looked down and realized that my Columbia Falls RV Park t-shirt had become dislodged and was now heading towards Kansas or Oz.

Material things don't really have a tight hold on me. However things I have emotional attachments to are an entirely different ball game. Being highly sensitive and in tune with your surroundings also lends you to putting emotions into something creating great value. Maybe it's a stick, maybe it's a bike, and maybe it's a t-shirt you just saw blowing away that you'd never get back.

I felt like I'd been socked in the gut. My shirt that I'd looked forward to putting on every night to sleep in was gone. It was like a friend that kept me company at night. I yelled at the storm irrationally and had a ton of resentment towards the force of nature as it blew away, along with my shirt. I knew logically that it was a shirt made in china, screen-printed by someone local and sold with a 200% markup. But it was the emotional value I'd assigned to it and it was now gone.

I rolled slowly along the paved road that at least was pleasant and easy on my legs which had given all they had trying to outrun the storm. I looked down at my GPS and noticed a town called Hartsell coming up. I looked up and saw that there were a few buildings and thought, "Well maybe they have food."

As I got closer I saw a gas station, well it used to be a gas station. Now it had a spray-painted sign that said "Sheriff's Office" on it.

"Surely this is a joke," I said.

I looked across the street and there was a bar that said "Burritos to go." I laid my bike against the side of the bar and walked in.

Coming into the bar was like any scene you've seen where the stranger walks into the western bar and the locals look at you like "You're not from 'round these parts are you partner?" There were kids with families eating comfort foods, some girls with way too much makeup talking to the local football hero in his letterman's jacket and some odd characters seated at the bar. They all had their eyes on me and had paused in their conversation to give me the once over. I took a deep breath and walked past everyone and headed for the bar.

"I'd like a bunch of burritos. Some for here and several to go."

"They are big. You sure about that?" Said the bartender.

"And a beer, like a really big beer" I said.

As I waited, I checked my messages and responded to a few texts when all of the sudden I felt the eyes of someone staring at me.

You know this feeling, the feeling when you're being stared at. It's like a sixth sense us humans possess or maybe it's like our primal instincts when we know we're being hunted by a predator. I looked up and around then down the end of the bar where an old man sat staring at me. He had breathing tubes attached to his throat and nose. He had an air tank attached to that and he was sipping vodka on the rocks with a cigarette in the ashtray. He was rail thin, about as old as Moses and had a bolo, giant horn rimmed glasses and giant turquoise belt buckle. I looked at him, nodded and then buried myself in my phone hoping he'd stop looking at me. He didn't.

I really needed a moment to regroup, drink my beer and collect my thoughts and really didn't want to have to engage in conversation with anyone, especially this guy at this moment.

"Whatchya doin?" He said in a raspy old voice.

"Oh, um, I'm in a race called the Tour..."

"SPEAK UP! I CAN'T HEAR YOU" He yelled.

"I'M IN THIS MOUNTAIN BIKE RACE CALLED THE TOUR DIVIDE." I yelled back.

Since the bar was not soundproof my voice bounced all over the walls and now the entire bar was looking at me listening. I looked around, the families at the tables, the heavy mascara girls with the jock were all now staring at me.

"WHAT'S A YOUR DEE VIDE?" He asked.

For the millionth time on the trip, I explained it, which also meant I was explaining it to the entire bar. I told a few stories which got a few "oooh's and ah's." I heard the jock say to the girls "I ride a bike too, you know" trying to one up me and impress his girlfriends. After I felt like I'd sufficiently told the entire town of Hartsell about my story I went back to nursing my beer. The man kept staring at me.

"WHERE YA FROM?"

"Alabama"

"WHERE?"

"ALABAMA." I yelled with now the whole town of Hartsell knowing where I was from.

"No son, WHERE in Alabama"

"Oh, um, sorry... Birmingham!"

The man sat and nodded for a few minutes in silence then said

"Used to live Huntsville."

Huntsville, Alabama is 80-90 miles north of Birmingham. It's where the Space and Rocket center is as well as the Redstone Arsenal. I grew up about 30 minutes from there and here I was 1,100 miles away from Birmingham and I've met a 1,100-year-old man who used to live there 1,100 years ago.

"Used to work for Mister Von Braun as an electrical engineer and gettin' people on the moon." He said.

I blinked, Wehrner Von Braun , the German rocket scientist that moved to Alabama and is credited with being the father of Rocket Science.

"So I'm assuming you got to meet Neil, Buzz and other astronauts?" I asked.

"Of course." He said nodding.

I was enthralled and now started asking him questions and telling him that I grew up in Guntersville. He'd spent many vacations there on our lake (we're famous for our lake) and even knew where my dad's pharmacy was in the heart of Guntersville. I got so wrapped up in conversation I said,

"Why the hell did you move to this place?" When I realized that maybe this wasn't the smartest question to ask and followed up quickly with:

"Because it's.... lovely!" And he laughed and nodded saying,

"Yes, it is lovely and I moved here to retire. I like the simple life here." It was great to meet someone from your home state, even cooler to meet someone out on the Divide that was 30-40 miles from where you grew up.

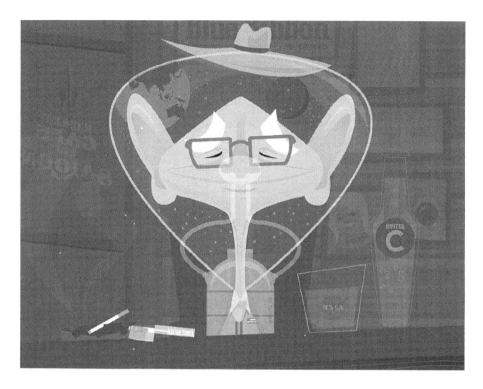

I got back on my bike and continued pushing on through the night, I knew Salida was not far away and I had a fresh new bike kit mailed there waiting for me at the post office. I was so excited because the bike kit I had on was, to put it nicely, not doing so well for the lower regions of my body.

I continued riding and noted it was 3 or 4 o'clock in the morning. I'd been at this now since 10am the day before and not taken many breaks. Sleep deprivation was starting to have its way with me. I saw the lights of Salida off in the distance and knew I had enough left in me to make it. As I crested the top of a mountain I started to go down the windy road. It was a little windier than I thought as I nearly slipped off the mountain since I was so tired. I had whipped around a corner and taken it too fast. I had not realized how sharp of a turn it was and my front tire started to hit loose gravel and go down. Figuring down meant 300-400 foot fall I screamed, dug my feet into my pedals and by some miraculous (or utterly stupid) move, I escaped a nice tumble down the mountain.

That woke me up enough to get me to Salida. Well, I thought it woke me up enough but I missed the sign for Salida completely and biked on until I got to Poncha Springs instead. I pulled into an open gas station and walked in, famished, grabbing stuff up from the aisles and stuffing it into my arms. "You're one of those bike people, aren't you?" I heard the clerk asking the infamous question I'd heard a million times by now.

"Yep! Going to Salida, if I can find it. I think I missed a turn."

"You're almost to Poncha Springs, man... Salida is 5-6 miles where you came from. You've missed it"

"Oh... well this Poncho Springs..."

"PonchA Springs." She interrupted.

"Yes, Ponch-AH Springs, so do they have a hotel or motel?"

"Yeah there's a placed called the Poncha Lodge, they may be open although it's really late." I found the Poncha Lodge, it was cool with the neon pink lights, and neon pink lit flamingos and neon pink office area. I went to the door and it was locked

"Oh no..." I said to myself and knocked a few times. Nothing. I pressed the buzzer and I heard some faint rummaging around.

"Ves?" A lady said in a strange accent coming through the intercom.

"Uh... um, is there any vacancy?"

"Ves."

There was a long pause.

"Uh, okay I'll take a room?"

"Ves." The voice said "Von moment."

I waited, and I shivered and... why the hell is this lady taking so long?" Finally an older lady came to the door and unlocked it to the office. She had on a pink robe, an impressive amount of white blonde hair stacked on her head, pink makeup and a heavy dose of eyeliner.

"You vant a room?" She said.

"Yes, please. One. Single. Cheapest you have, I'll take the worst possible room you have."

"All of our rooms are vonderful, ve do not have worst rooms." She said sternly. I couldn't place her accent, but I loved listening to her talk.

I paid for my room and wheeled on over to it. It was indeed, awesome. When I walked in there were pink lights everywhere, the pictures hanging were of all pink flamingos, the TV looked like something from the 50's and the entire room should have been placed in some magazine called "Retro Today." It was awesome and I felt like I'd landed in the lounge of Tiki.

I took off my shoes, stretched and reviewed what I'd do for the next day. I had a nice bike kit waiting for me now 8-9 miles behind me in Salida; it was worth it as I was starting to get into some bad situations in my nether-area of my body. I had also shipped myself a motivational letter to push me through to Antelope Wells, New Mexico (the finish line). I pulled open my clothes now only having a pair of shorts as my Columbia Falls RV Park shirt was now probably somewhere in Japan. I grimaced about not having a shirt on and climbed over the covers. The sheets were hard and felt like sleeping on sand paper. If I'd had my Columbia Falls RV Park shirt, this would not be a problem.

Day 18: I Got Your Nose

That morning I awoke to the sounds of roaring Harley Davidson motorcycles. Generally I'd have been pretty pissed off about this but I wanted to wake up because I needed to trek back to Salida. I got up, packed my bike and then looked down noting it was almost 8am and that meant it was almost time to pick up my new bike kit in Salida! At 8:00am sharp I called the Salida Post Offic,

"Hello? Salida Postal, can I help you." A friendly man said.

"Yes. I'm Scott Thigpen and you guys should have a package from me?"

I heard some rummaging around.

"Nope, don't see one."

"Um, I sent it a month ago. It said, "Racing the Divide, don't discard!" On it." I said with a heightened alarm in my voice.

"Nope, don't see it."

My heart sunk, I needed a new kit, and mine was in some serious bad conditions.

"Can you check one more time?" I begged.

"I'm sorry, it's just not here. We have you guys ship packages all the time, not sure what's going on." I needed this news about like I needed a random email saying that the Tour Divide was going to be rerouted.

I checked my email.

Subject: Detours ahead

Message:

Very sorry to report two fire closure detours ahead.

1st: Abiquiu to Cuba must be travelled via hwy 84 / 96 / 550

Map 5-A existing cue: 145.5mi or 234.2 km "Abiquiu. Just past Bode's Store, turn left onto paved Co. Rd. 189. Enter Abiquiu Grant private land; no camping next 10 miles."

New Cue: Keep straight on hwy 84 to Left on 96, to Left on 550 into Cuba. (about 60miles).

2nd Detour, The Gila is closed. Detour is as follows:

Map 6-A. This is the warning cue (next cue is the actual route departure) Mile 68, or km 109.4, the cue reads: "Bear left on FR 28 into Collins Park; FR 94 goes right". Here you will execute cue

normally. 1.6mi later you will depart from TD route by going right when route sweeps left (SE).

Point of departure, TD Route cue reads, "* Mile 69.6 or km 112, At "Y", bear left onto FR 30 toward Beaverhead instead of right toward Willow Creek and Snow Lake"

You will take a RIGHT onto 28 (also known as Bursom Rd). You will be following 28 / 159 all the way to Hwy 180 (approx 50mi), where you will go LEFT / south (approx 65 miles) to Silver City. Along 28 are a couple 'potential' turns to make. They may be signed 28 / 159 and also may be signed Bursom Rd. Not entirely clear. Proceed with adventurous spirit!

End of Message

"PROCEED WITH ADVENTUROUS SPIRIT?" I yelled. I can follow a line on my GPS but I failed orienteering three times in a row as a Boy Scout and can't find my way out of a paper bag.

Proceed with an adventurous spirit, *MY ASS.*

I angrily got on the phone and called Matt Lee.

The phone rang and Matt picked up.

"Hello, this is Matt."

"Hey Matt, this is Scott Thigpen."

"Heeeeeeey Scott, the TNGA guy right? Yeah I'm at the beach on a family vacation. What's up?"

I felt guilty for calling him on his vacation but I was in directional trouble trying to follow some garbled email message.

"Hey Matt," I said. "Listen, I get confused very easily with written directions and can get lost in a paper bag. I was doing awesome with following a GPS but I'll surely get lost with just these directions… plus your email really don't make sense."

"Oh, oh that's bad, Scott. Well, just pay close attention; I'm sure you'll be fine."

::Click::

Fine!? FINE???

No! I was not fine, in fact I was upset, mad and really panicked but I thought,

"You know, maybe I can just tail someone through the reroute."

My coach, Tracy had mentioned drafting off the intelligence of others. While physically drafting behind a fellow racer was against the rules, mental drafting was fair game.

I got my stuff ready and pulled out back to the intersection of the busy highway. My GPS pointed left and as I started to turn left I saw a biker with an orange bag on the back of his bike. "HEY!" I screamed. He didn't hear me. I got my whistle out but it was too late, he was already gone. I'd not seen someone move that fast on the Tour Divide route and he was hauling some major cargo to boot, and he made it look effortless.

After spending what felt like an eternity peddling up a mountain against the wind I found a tree that I could nestle up against and bear the brunt force of the wind. I sat and watched the sun go down and thought about taking a picture but it just wouldn't do it justice. It was a beautiful sunset and like magic, as soon as the sun went down, the wind died.

The rest of the climb up the mountain was easy in comparison. I climbed quickly and when I got to the top I was rewarded with a lovely downhill albeit it was pitch black dark. As I made my descent I couldn't make out much in front of me other than shadows, tree lines and the sky. I kept a fairly good speed due to the wide-open road but I could not see much in front of me. As I rounded a corner on my bike I saw a shadowy figure, a large shadowy figure and I was heading straight for it. I slammed on my brakes and my lights hit its eyes lighting, which glowed a brilliant green. I heard the scream of a "MOOOO!" And the black cow darted off confused and that set off a whole host of fun problems for me.

That was a younger cow, now mama cow was very concerned and I heard the hoofs of her running to her calf... with me in between each of them. This also startled other cows and I heard the pounding of a lot of hooves.

Bears are scary, I hate when I'm in close proximity of spiders, going in the ocean knowing there are sharks swimming around turns me to ice but shining your light and seeing many green eyes stampeding your way mooing has got to be one of the scariest experiences I've ever been through. I took off like a rocket screaming like a small child (okay, a small girl). When I got to the bottom of the mountain, I was sort of amazed I was still alive. I've never gone that fast in the dark but figuring I had the McMafia after me, my adrenaline left me no choice but to risk flying down a hill at lightning speeds.

I was completely exhausted but at least it was a pleasant ride in the night after that. Sometimes there was a small climb, mostly it was just flat. The air was nice, but chilly and all was still and quiet. I looked down on the GPS and realized I was not far from a town, I had considered stopping there and spending the night but the town looked pretty sparse. Then I saw I was not far from Del Norte, the second to the last town of Colorado. It was 12 miles away.

"I could do this, you know."

It was some ungodly time in the A.M. and I'd been riding for what had seemed like forever. I thought about camping but I loved making it from town to town. The town I was closest to seemed to have a school, a church and that was about it. Del Norte had hotels, gas stations, restaurants and when I looked up, I could see the glimmer of lights way far off; it was Del Norte. I was tired, but super excited and I pedaled on south anxious to get to the second to last town in Colorado.

Nothing is easy on the Divide. You never get the easy route, it's always the hard way. As I continued to pedal, the route led me off the nice paved road straight onto a dirt road, a dirt road with washed out divots which means miles of getting vibrated to death while trying to pedal on them, a road that went up and then a road that veered off onto an ATV trail.

I could see the lights closer to Del Norte; I only had 8 miles left at this point. I was so excited I couldn't stand it but as I hit the ATV trail, my nightmare began.

If it'd been daytime, I'd not been riding for 20 hours and I was not lugging around a 50+ pound bike, this would have been fun. However when I hit the soft sandy trail I found myself flying off my bike left and right. Focused on getting to Del Norte I gave all my strength I could to get through the miles of ATV trails and the more I tried, the more I'd bite it.

One time I rounded a corner and my bike washed out in the pebbly sand. I lost control of my bike and fell with the bike landing on me and then the handlebars flipped and smacked me in the nose. White flashes of stinging pain hit me all over my face. After the whack by the handlebars, a new sensation hit me; a cool liquid was on my face. I put my hand over it and then looked into the light coming from my handlebars. I'd smashed my nose and it was now bleeding profusely. On top of that when I tried to get the bike off of me, I had landed on my ankle wrong and I was now reeling in pain.

Hurt ankle, bloody nose ... I didn't care, I wanted to get to Del Norte. A few thousand more crashes later and I was back on a dirt road and finally a sign that said "Welcome to Del Norte."

I could see blue hues developing in the sky as the sun would make it's appearance sooner than I would have liked. I biked over to a gas station, which was closed. I then biked past a fancy hotel and I knew that it was not even in my now extremely small budget. I kept going until I found it, The Country Family Inn & Restaurant. It was very run down, which meant it was in my price range. I went to the front desk and rang the bell, then knocked on the door. I'm sure people were sick of me waking them up in the middle of the night.

A young man walked to the front door. He had a ponytail, a sleeveless shirt that said "Megadeth" and some stubble around his chin. He unlocked the door and before he could say anything, I said:

"I know, I woke you up, you're probably full and you don't have many rooms. I'll take your worst room you have and I'm not even going to stay the whole time, so can I get it for half price?"

Sleepily the young man looked at me and with a confused look. Then I realized, I must have blood all over my face. I quickly said:

"Oh! Hey, nothing bad happened, I just took a tumble on my bike. I'm okay. Now about that room?"

"Uh, oh...okay. We serve breakfast and lunch if you want."

"When I wake up, I'll take you up on that."

I went to my room; and he indeed did give me a pretty horrible room. The walls were paper thin so I could hear people snoring on either side. The entire room was kind of at an angle; and it was so small that me and my bike could barely fit in it. In the bathroom one the handles to the shower was gone. I had to use a washcloth to grip it with enough torque to turn it on. It smelled horrible with scents of cigarette smoke and... other things. I showered off and before I went to bed I did check under the bed to make sure there were no dead hookers stashed there.

Day 19: Girly Men

I walked over to the restaurant that was part of the lodging "experience." An older man came over to me and poured me some coffee.

"My boy do you good last night?" He said. I looked over and the young man, still with the Mega Death shirt on. I nodded and said yes.

"My help ain't here yet but she'll be along shortly, you can't miss her, she's got red hair."

Can't miss her? I was the only one in the restaurant! How am I going to miss anyone that comes through the door? I looked over the menu and settled on eggs, sausage and pancakes, you know, a light breakfast.

The man went to put the order in and three other older gentlemen entered the facility. They were obviously locals as they nodded to the young man, huddled around the TV and turned it to Fox News. I quietly read my messages on my phone and texted my wife. I could hear them murmuring over the news when a road cyclist zipped by on the street in front of the restaurant. The owner and cook brought out my food and went to sit with his buddies.

One of the old men, a wiry bitter looking guy said loudly:

"THEY SHOULD JUST ALL BE ROUNDED UP AND SHOT IF YOU ASK ME. STAY OFF THE DAMNED ROAD YOU BUNCH OF GIRLS."

By now the father and son were saying "shh shh!" and motioning back to me. The wiry old man looped around and eyeballed me. It was painfully obvious that I was a cyclist as I was still in my bike kit and my jersey said "Cahaba Cycles" on it (It would said "Columbia Falls RV Park" but that shirt has now sadly found some new home… probably rotting in the dirt somewhere in France by now.)

The man looked at me, he had more lines in his face than a sketch drawing on a piece of paper. His skin was leathery and I don't think he'd smiled in the last 400 years of his life. He shriveled up his nose and said,

"I DON'T CARE IF THAT GIRL IS LISTENING. WHAT YOU GONNA DO GIRLY. COME ON, SPEAK UP."

I personally hate confrontation, it's not my strong suit. I like harmonious situations and for people to just be happy all the time. I'm a happy guy, so don't poop on my happiness.

The guy was staring me down with this beady little eyes huffing and puffing. I looked up and swallowed down a large piece of pancake and stared back at him.

"Yeah, I got something to say" I said and ate a piece of sausage after that. The man intently stared me down as I started on my next sentence. I opened my mouth and said,

"Do you know if these pancakes are high in fat or not, I'm watching my figure?" And I patted my stomach, which was now rather pronounced by the enormously large amount of pancakes I had just gobbled down.

There was silence, the man continued to stare at me, and then his eyebrows lifted and the wrinkles started to melt away as the two muscles on either side of his mouth pulled east and west and I saw a smile and then a roar of laughter from the old geezer.

"YOU ARE ONE FUNNY SON OF A BITCH, YOU GOT BALLS, BOY." I laughed (nervously) and I balled up my fist and shook it at him. He continued to laugh as the rest of the table did. I secretly was sweating bullets because I knew I was about to get the hell beat out of me by someone that knew Moses as a child.

I settled up my tab, got ready and pedaled out of the lodge and back to that gas station that was now open. When I pulled up there was that bicycle with the orange bag on the back. I leaned my bike near it and started to walk in, when I did, a kid met me at the door still in his helmet. He had olive skin, wore a pair of shorts (not skin tight bike pants like me) a large backpack and a loose fitting shirt.

"Hey!" I said recognizing him as a cyclist. "Hey," he murmured with his head down. I tried to get his attention.

"Hey you're with the Tour Divide, right"

"Yep, you are too?"

I said yes and that I'd been on his tail for the past few days. I asked him if he'd like to ride together and he said sure. The kid's name was Mike and he was actually one of the front pack of the Tour Divide, but extreme saddle sores had done him in pretty bad and he had to take several days off to let them heal. I could relate to that as my soft tissue areas were now feeling the sting and burn caused by a worn out bike kit.

One of the number one questions I was asked when prepping for the Tour Divide was "Are you gonna pack heat?" or "Are you going to carry a gun?" I'd say the same thing over and over, which was:

"I don't know how to use a gun and I'd blow my leg off trying to ride with one."

I got many people telling me I was crazy to go on a race through the backwoods of many small towns without protection but I honestly was going to believe that 95% of the population is comprised of really cool folks and the other 5% needed to be rounded up and thrown to the bears.

The heat beat down on me as I trailed Mike up an enormously steep mountain and eventually Mike disappeared around a bend and I was once again alone. As I continued climbing, I noticed two figures walking down towards me.

Fear surrounded me and I tried to move to the left only to have them move to the left. Then I moved back to the right and they moved back to the right. Adrenaline, difficulty breathing and extreme panic were all starting to set in. Also irrational thoughts like:

"What was in that big backpack of theirs they had? Oh god, what if they offed Mike!?"

I started to really get scared and thought that when they got close enough, I would just try to out muscle them. I mean after all I'd only been climbing the side of a mountain for over an hour, I'm sure I had plenty of steam in me, right? Right?

They got closer and I started to think about how I would be left for dead in some backwoods part of Colorado. Their hands started to stretch out and I gritted my teeth. The larger one moved in towards me and said,

"WAY TO GO MAN! GO CATCH THE OTHER DUDE HE'S WAY AHEAD OF YOU, MAN!" Reaching out to give me a high five.

I tried to return it while on my bike. When my hand left the handlebar I lost balance on the mountain and between the sheer force of the climb and fatigue from the situation I almost fainted but regained my composure enough to lose my balance and fall anyway, but at least I didn't black out. I think.

The two men helped me up, asked me how I was feeling, gave me a pat on the back and I kept going. It took a lot of mental energy out of me but I felt relieved that I was safe.

The day was starting to turn to eve and I felt something hit my helmet. Then another pelted me. Then another and another and another - hail. All of a sudden a torrent of hail and then ice cold rain started coming down getting me soaking wet. It continued to chip away at me and my warm day had now turned into a festival of freeze again. I looked as far past the mountain as possible, hoping to catch a glimpse of Platoro. I saw a few houses on a muddy road, which meant I was close, or so I thought. Maybe I was closer than I thought when I saw the sign "Welcome to Platoro." It was comprised of some houses in the mud and an extremely large lodge with smoke coming out of the chimney. I quickly leaned my bike against the railing as the rain continued to hammer down and dashed inside.

When I got into the lodge it was rustic feeling, kind of. It also had that:

"Hey we could make money out here as the only place to have a lodge and charge people and arm and a leg" feeling too. I walked in and was greeted by a large man in a camouflage jacket and neon orange hat.

"Welcome, are we just having a room for one tonight?" He said with a giant toothy grin. "I...uh...huh?" I said shivering.

"A room, is it just you tonight?"

"I...I'm really cold can I just..."

"We're running a discount for you racers, save lots of money and you can warm up! So we'll put you down for one?".

I hate pushy people, I do, and they bring out the snippy in me pretty quick.

"I'm not ready to commit to a room, sir. I'd like to eat first." I snapped and I walked into the lodge dining area. There was a guy buried in his Tour Divide map pouring over the information. I sat down at his table; we were the only ones there.

"Hey" I said still shivering.

"Oh hey, didn't hear you walk in. I'm Greg, who are you?"

"I'm Scott, Scott Thigpen"

"Ooooh yeah, the guy with the blog! How are ya?"

"Very cold. I'm going to go sit by that fireplace."

The big fireplace was roaring and it instantly warmed me up. The man in the camouflage jacket came in and said,

"You'd be warm all night if you got one of our cozy rooms."

"I'm not paying 100 bucks to stay less than 24 hours in one of your 'cozy rooms!'" I barked while I made air quotes saying "cozy rooms."

"Just put it on a credit card!" He laughed.

"No room. Not tonight. Not ever. Stop pushing me around.!" I said with my teeth gritted, angrily snapping at him.

"Well..We'll be closing soon, you better order quick. We don't stay open all night for passing travelers." He said with a completely different demeanor knowing he wasn't going to get a sale from me.

I looked on the menu and saw the "Bigfoot challenge." It was a $30 burger that if you ate it, the fixings and the fries, you would get it free.

"Game on, Camouflage Jacket man, you're about to lose 30 bucks! As I'm about to show you how us Alabamians can put away some food!"

"What would you like to eat?" The waiter said coming up to our table.

"The Bigfoot."

"Uh, okay? I mean, it's getting late I'm not sure we have time to cook that," he said nervously.

"I suppose if I were staying the night you'd made three Bigfoot challenge burgers for us, right?" I said sharply eyeing him down.

He nodded and went back to make the Bigfoot challenge.

Several minutes came by and finally I heard the door swing open. They brought the burger down; it was huge, several patties of meat stacked way high dripping with cheese. I had this and would be done in 10 minutes (I only had 30 minutes to finish the meal). Then the "gotcha" moment happened, they sat down the plate of fries. It was enormous and twice the size of the burger.

"I...I can't eat... I can't eat the burger and the fries man... I'll burst wide open." I protested.

"That's the rules." He said nonchalantly.

"It says 'with fries' not 'a small continent of fries!'."

"You got 30 minutes. That starts now."

Something tells me if I'd committed to a room that plate of fries would not have been so large.

I did clean the burger in 10 minutes and started to work on the fries. It was impossible and at the end of the 30 minutes, I had to concede and had to pay the 30 bucks. The service was good too so I tipped my regular 18% since the help doesn't really make that much. I sat there attempting to let the food digest and the man in the camouflage hat, now with his brother standing next to him came in.

"We're closing up, last chance for you guys to get a room, because we like ya, we'll knock the price down to 90 bucks."

"NO!" I said sharply.

"Well then we're closed and you need to leave!"

"Fine by me!" I snapped!

As I was getting ready to walk out, I heard the door jingle and a tall thin figure walked through the door. I heard the Camouflage Jacket guy squeal, "BILLY!"

I looked and there he was, Billy Rice. I'd passed him at the end of Canada while he was going to Banff and he'd not only gone to the start, turned around and come back, he'd caught me. He sauntered in like a rock star and was treated like one too. The Camo Jacket Man was relaying information to him giving him all this courtesy and telling him he'd laid out fresh blankets for him, *yadda, yadda, gag...* *WHAT EVER*. I sort of smirked at Mister Rock Star and the Camo guy ogling over him like a squealing girl at a Boy Band concert.

I looked over at Greg and said:

"You ready to make it to New Mexico tonight?"

"Sure!" He said

I was getting to walk out the door and had to pass by Billy "Rockstar" Rice. We made eye contact and I thought it to be polite and at least say hello. Maybe he'd sign my bike kit or something.

"Hey, I'm Scott, we met back in Canada."

"Oh yeah, hey how are you?" He said while his fan boy club was getting his room ready.

"Oh fine, can't believe you even know who us no name riders even are Mister Wonderbread" I said in my mind... loudly.

"I'm good, I'm cold," I said audibly.

I was surprised he remembered me or even talked to us commoners. I hated to be so bitter but the Bigfoot challenge fail, the overly pushy Camo Jacket guy and the rain had, pun intended, dampened my spirits. I walked outside, it felt like I was in the arctic tundra, it was freezing and not 4 hours ago I was burning up hot. I shook Billy's hand; I was surprised it wasn't covered in diamond rings the way people were fawning over him here in Platoro.

"Nice to meet you, again… I'm heading to New Mexico." I said starting to shiver.

"Alrighty, I'll be watching you!" He said earnestly.

"Right…" I said rolling my eyes.

Greg and I hopped on our bikes and rolled out.

At least it wasn't raining anymore, but it was no fun seeing my breath. Greg was faster than I was as but I could always keep him in my sites watching his little blinky light. A good hour or two had passed on this dark and bumpy dirt road when I saw Greg's bike stop and move sideways. I caught up to him and he was looking over to the side of the road.

"What's wrong?" I said.

"Look…"

I looked over on the side of the road. It was July 1 in south Colorado and blanketed as far as the eye could see was snow, snow everywhere.

"Oh God…"I said.

"OH GOD!" I screamed and yelled again "

IT'S FREAKING FIRST OF JULY! AND IT'S SNOWING!!! DID I ACCIDENTALLY KICK A PUPPY OR SOMETHING TO DESERVE THIS!" I said now reaching drama queen status on par with Diana Ross.

We continued to ride for several more hours into the darkness. I caught up to Greg where the dirt road turned into a paved road.

"We need to get onto that and then we have to climb La Manga pass, the bad climb."

I thought to myself "*Oh because all the previous climbs were so easy?*"

I remember hearing about La Manga pass. A north bounder (someone going from New Mexico to Canada), Cjell (pronounced Shell) Money had put a lottery on the mountain pass and whoever got up it the quickest, won the pot of money. Let's just say it wasn't me.

The climb, while paved, was grueling. Greg and I started up it together and then he had an issue with his tire going soft. "I'll catch up with you in a bit" he said.

I stuck in my earphones and started climbing, always looking back seeing if Greg was coming and never did. When I finally got to the top it was around 4am, I was absolutely exhausted and was looking for a decent place to camp. I found one soft patch and quickly said "nope" when I realized it was soft because it was covered in snow. I kept falling asleep and honestly I'd been awake now for around 48 hours with only lightly snoozing. I decided to just get down the mountain and get into New Mexico. I needed to get into New Mexico, it had to happen so I could mentally only have one more state to go before dozing off.

I started to go down the hill. The cool wind wrapped around my face, my eyes and then all of the sudden I was back home as a kid drawing and showing mom my creative pictures I'd come up with.

Mom has always loved my art like I guess all moms love their kids' art. She was careful to never say "you're special" but she would say what was great and what needed work.

I handed mom a picture and she started shaking, violently and then she said something:

"Rot Take Yup!"

"What, mom?"

"Sock Cake PUP!"

"What!? Mom you're making no sense!"

"SCOTT WAKE UP!"

That's when I realized I'd fallen asleep while on the bike going down the hill and was running off the road at a very fast speed. I almost lost control of my bike and it was enough to startle me awake however not 10 minutes later I was nodding off going down hill again. Sleep deprivation, and sheer exhaustion had finally caught up with me.

My mind was starting to play tricks on me, as a near 24-hour day of cycling was becoming a realization. I started seeing shadows move out of the corner of my eye. Those shadows became zombies, the howls of coyotes became werewolves and the devil himself was creeping over the mountain to take my soul to hell for eternity…or at least Platoro, Colorado.

I looked at my GPS and it said I'd made it into New Mexico, I did a small "whoop whoop" fist bump and collapsed on the ground near a pack of birch trees and soft grass. I was asleep in mere seconds.

NEW MEXICO

Day 20: Mister Wonderbread

I'd always envisioned New Mexico as flat and sparse, and parts of it was, however the part I was trudging through was anything but. Everything was dry; everything was a giant hill to climb and everything was on those stinking washboard roads that had permanently jarred me to pieces by now. I could no longer feel my pinkies in either hand and I had no feeling in the sides of my hands either. Riding 2000 miles had jarred my hands to a new state of damage.

I was trying to navigate through the washboard roads to not be so vibrated to death when I heard the clicking of gears behind me. Passing by me was Mike and the blonde-headed surfer looking guy I'd seen back in Elkford, Eric. They rode by me like lightening and danced across the washboard roads without missing a beat. I watched Eric; as he would get out of his saddle, bend his elbows and "*bump bump bump*" glide over the divots in the road without even missing a beat.

"Huh? So that's how you do it?"

I attempted it myself. I leaned out of my saddle, crouched my elbows and knees and bumped through the next patch of nasty washboard roads. To my surprise I comfortably bounced through them. Now if only I'd known about that back in Montana.

I watched Eric and Mike ride away until they were tiny ants. I watched them fly up a hill that took me 10 minutes to get up pushing my bike. Their talent and speed was absolutely amazing. I tried to mimic it only to be completely depleted of energy and I burned through more food and water than I needed to. The dirt road dumped into a paved road and my GPS said there was a campground ahead with water services. I breathed a sigh of relief because I was out.

I eagerly got to the campsite. There were tents, RVs and SUV's everywhere. I navigated to the facilities only to find the water pump completely inoperable. I fell back on the ground upset and exasperated. I looked around hoping someone would say "Hey do you need water" but no one even paid me any attention. There was a family eating at a picnic table, their food on the table looked limitless and they had sodas and drinks galore. I started to ride up to them to ask if I could have some water and the father leaned into his kid protectively putting his arm around him and glaring at me. I moved away. I went past some other campers and they looked at me then turned away. What the hell was going on?

I rode out of the campsite area dejected and upset only to find another campsite with another facility station including water. Maybe it had water. As I went to the pump a mother and daughter were walking their dogs. When I set my bike down the two dogs came towards me to sniff me.

"Hey fellas, hey doggies!" I said attempting to pat the head of one of the dogs.

The daughter hid behind the mother while the mother looked at me protectively. I backed off with hurt feelings and said "I'm sorry" and they walked off briskly. Did I have a t-shirt on that said "*I hate America*" or "*I am an axe murderer?*" I don't know, I didn't know what made people so scared of me until I walked into the restroom and looked in the mirror to find the culprit, it was me.

I looked at myself; I didn't even look like me. Red faced, bloated, scraggly and some horrific smells emanating that I was pretty sure were going to be permanent. I usually keep my head neat and shaven, but a razor had not touched my head for weeks now and all these scraggly tufts of hair had grown out in a horrid salt and pepper (and more salt than pepper) fashion. My beard was the fullest it had ever been and it had giant patches of grey and white in it. There were extremely pronounced laugh lines with dirt caked in them and the bags under my eyes rivaled that of a purse store. I officially looked like hell on earth and was even frightened by the site of me.

I looked away from the mirror, put my hands on the sink's water handles and turned. A rattling eventually led to spouted water of some sort. At least it wasn't completely brown and I filled up all my bottles and hopped on my bike avoiding all campers while riding through the campgrounds.

The next portion of the ride was all downhill, which was great because I was 100% spent and out of gas. I continued riding down through parts of New Mexico that were finally lovely. It was a beautiful ride, seeing all the pretty trees, warm air and sparse population. I saw a hand painted sign that said "Entering Villa Locos" and I said out loud;

"Woo hoo! BIG CITY TIME!"

And kept making my way down into the tiny, tiny, tiny town of Villa Locos. Tiny as is in a muddy dirt road with some Mexican man waving at me pointing to a building that resembled a small storage shed. I had no idea what he was talking about, but then it hit me. I'd seen this shed before! I had seen this same location; in fact I'd seen it many times, even though I've NEVER visited New Mexico.

In the movie that inspired me to do this race, *Ride the Divide*, directors Hunter Weeks and Mike Dion film Matt Lee, the originator of the Tour Divide, riding to a small building where a Hispanic lady named Sylvia Gurule had candy bars, Coca-Colas and other goodies for him to buy. They interviewed Sylvia and I remember listening to how pleasant and cool she was.

As I slowed down at the warehouse I looked up and saw her barreling down the hill from her house on a four-wheeler. She hopped off her ATV and fumbled with her keys to open up shop.

"I know you," I said standing on the muddy road.

"From the movie?" she grinned with her eyes lit up.

"From the movie indeed, I'm Scott."

"I bet you're hungry, well let me open up for you."

She opened the tiny store and in it was a potpourri of food, canned goods, dry goods, and a fridge with frozen burritos, ice cream and milk. I had $50 dollars in cash and I spent every last bit of it there in her warehouse.

She looked at me, cocked her head sideways and said,

"You're from the south, right? Alabama? I recognize that accent"

"How did you know?"

"Oh I have relatives in a tiny town there."

"WHICH tiny town?" I said quickly as being from a tiny town, I know tiny towns well.

1989 Friday, Guntersville High School Football Stadium

The Wildcat football team was doing their routine end-of-summer practice. It was still sweltering hot in all those football pads and garb, but generally those of us from Alabama could handle it. The coach had us running sprints saying, "Those Knights will be tougher than you, you don't want to lose to Arab!"

The coach was referring to the Arabian Knights, Guntersville's hated rival. Arab, Alabama, pronounced A-rab, was no more than 10 miles from Guntersville and for some reason, we hated each other. I remember one day at practice where an older player, Scott Tillman, was not having a good day and a teammate said, "You play like a Knight, man." Scott turned bright red and tackled the other player and began to try to tear him limb from limb.

--

On a dirt road, New Mexico

"Oh, it's this town that sounds like it's from the Middle East, it's called Arab." Sylvia said.

"I'm from Guntersville!" I exclaimed.

Here a zillion miles away from my hometown a lady in Nowhere, New Mexico had relatives near my hometown. Sylvia and I talked and played connect the dots. She'd actually been in my dad's pharmacy in Guntersville once. I can't believe I had met two people on the Tour Divide that had been to my tiny hometown in Alabama! I heard a voice outside the warehouse.

"NO WAY! UH UH! NO NO NO! HOW!?" I looked out of the warehouse and Joseph along with the rest of the kid gang sat there stunned.

"Okay Scott, how'd you do it? How the hell did you catch up with us THEN PASS US? No wait.. I know what you're going to say," Said Joseph.

"You know, soft pedaling." I said with a big grin.

Everyone erupted in laughter.

"I don't know how you're doing it man, but that's awesome." Said Taylor.

That made me feel good, here was someone that was 15 times faster than me as well as 20 years younger, patting me on the back for keeping ahead of him.

Night started to fall and the kids rode off. I didn't even try to keep up, as I knew I'd get dropped anyway. As they rode away, Joseph said "I guess we'll see you ahead of us tomorrow?" We laughed and they disappeared. Greg said "I'll be happy to ride out with you for a while if you like, I just need to get situated first." Greg took his time and it was more situating than I would have liked so I said "Hey man I'm just going to pedal on ahead of you. I'm sure you'll catch me." Before I left, Sylvia gave me a big hug and said,

"Watch out for the little brown dog in Cuba, he nips at your ankle!" I bid her farewell and rode off through a tiny town in New Mexico heading towards Abiquiu.

The night was exceptionally dark and our lights illuminated the trees, which gave a scary "Legend of Sleepy Hollow" feel, you know the feeling where something is galloping up behind you, galloping up to take you down and... there was a light shining behind us. I glanced back and in the distance I saw the peak of a light and it coming fast. Like Ichabod Crane I tensed up because I didn't know who it was or who was following us on this deserted lonely road to Abiquiu, New Mexico. The light got closer. Was it a backwoods hillbilly here to take us down? A drunk driver not paying attention with one light out on his truck? The headless horseman himself? No... *worse*, it was Billy Rice.

"Sup fellas," he said as he caught up to us. I frowned, stopped and turned around. I wanted to say,

"Okay Rockstar, just... just get ahead of us so you can once and for all say you caught someone else passing them in Canada, going up and then turning around and catching them in New Mexico. Go ahead, brag, brag, brag!" Billy looked down at my bike,

"Wha? Ho... HOLY COW man, you're on a... single speed!?" He said in an elevated voice.

Taken aback, I then in a puffed up in a peacock way and said, "Yeah, yeah it is."

"Hey can I ride with you fellows into Abiquiu?" He asked.

"Aren't we too slow for you?" I said sort of taken aback.

"Ha, no, I'm not that fast, I just ride for long stretches at a time."

At the time what I didn't realize is that Billy had been riding 40 hours straight with no sleep, he was also mentally wearing down and was trying his best to get to Abiquiu so he could get a room.

We rode along for a while and Billy had an issue with his bike so he stopped and Greg stopped with him. Anytime I stop my legs lock up, freeze and it's very painful to get going again, so I said "I'm sure you guys will catch me, see you in a bit" and I rode on by myself. The dirt road finally turned into a paved road and the paved road dropped into a seedy little neighborhood. I stopped to take a break for a moment and Billy and Greg pulled up. Greg said he was full of energy and was going to go past Abiquiu and try to make it to Cuba, New Mexico

Billy said "Hey man, let's get a room in Abiquiu, I know this great place and you'll love it. The next section is 8 miles of steady downhill; you're going to love it! I'll get ahead of you, get the room and see ya there! I'll hang my helmet on the door, so you'll know which one it is, just come on in!"

Greg and I said our farewells and I told him just how much fun I had riding with him and that we should keep in touch. He left and I never saw him again. We started out onto the road, a little bit of flat and up through the dilapidated town and then it eased into a nice rolling downhill. I looked to my left and saw the blood moon again. The fires were still illuminating it from Colorado and it was an orange hue behind the mountains. The fires looked immense and now I could see why we had reroutes.

As I continued towards the hotel I could smell the smoke, and while it was nowhere near us it was thick when I breathed it in. It took a good hour to get into Abiquiu but true to Billy's word there was a very nice motel, and hanging on a room door was Billy's helmet. I grabbed it and wheeled my bike in. I sort of froze when I walked in.

This was no room; it was more like a honeymoon suite with a fireplace, pinkish orange walls, frou frou throw pillows, ornate lamps and a bed that looked like it belonged in a palace, not in a motel in Abiquiu. A single-only small bed tailor made for cuddling and snuggling.

"That's a tiny bed," I said to Billy.

"Yep. It is"

Billy was a large guy, skinny but he was easily 18 feet tall.

I thought about sleeping on the floor then my stomach rumbled and I realized I'd not eaten in quite some time. I looked into my food bags, nothing. I rumbled around in my backpack and my hand scraped some aluminum foil and I instantly remembered I'd had a chicken sandwich I picked up in Del Norte, which was now ripe with 2 days of sitting on my back in the hot sun. I unwrapped it and looked at it.

It had mayonnaise and cheese on it. It looked delicious but I worried about what bacteria had taken up residence in the meat. Then I remembered I still had all those fries from Platoro and that's when I hit my most depraved moment on the Tour Divide Race. I took the chicken from between the buns and tossed it in the garbage and wiped off all the mayo from the buns. I then took the cold, stale fries and shoved them in between the buns and made a French Fry sandwich.

"Still healthier than McDonalds"

Billy stepped out in a towel and got on his side of the bed, which was most of the bed. I took a shower then got on the very edge of the bed without falling off. We laid there in silence and I sat looking at the ceiling wide awake at the awkwardness of being in a tiny bed with an 18 foot tall man who was sprawled out everywhere. I thought I'd diffuse the situation with some humor so I said out loud "So no snuggling okay?" And something much worse happened, Billy started snoring. *Loudly.*

I am such a light sleeper and need to be in total silence to get any good deep sleep. Billy not only was loud, but if his snores were a lumberjack, he'd be responsible for clearing out national forests.

Day 21: Seeing Red, Bull

While at the breakfast table I asked Billy,

"How are you doing this? These huge massive miles in long strides?"

"Well, with two things… Red Bull Energy Drinks and staying positive. As long as you can keep awake you can pedal, and if you can keep your spirits about yourself, you'll keep going."

I wish I'd had breakfast with Billy in Canada and he'd told me this. The Tour Divide would have been an entirely different race for me. It was one of the most meaningful things I learned on the race…hyper caffeinated drinks and a smile do get you a long way.

Billy and I continued to chat and he was probably one of the coolest guys I have ever met. He was super excited because he'd gotten his permit to go through the original route instead of the reroute despite the fires and smoke in the Gila. He wanted his back and forth ride to be pure. We said our farewells and I felt a tinge of pain judging him like I did. He was indeed a rock star, but not the conceited kind. With a new attitude about a new friend, I began the 100-mile stretch towards the Indian reservation through Cuba, New Mexico.

As I rode out of Cuba I heard the high pitch yips of something demonic and moving at lightning speeds. It was brown, low to the ground and heading straight for my ankles. The little brown dog that Sofia warned me about really did exist 70 miles down the road. I outran it, but it really wanted to make quick work of my ankles.

I reached the reservation about 5:00 p.m. I had read and heard rumors that the Indian reservation was not necessarily very welcoming of my demographic. I probably should have just camped out in Cuba and started out fresh for the next day, but I wanted to bank some miles and armed with my new secret weapon of Red Bull, I was ready.

I rode into the reservation, which was both beautiful and somewhat scary. It was beautiful because as the sun was setting it illuminated the red clay mountains and valleys creating an awe-inspiring site that is just too good for a photo. It was scary because every drunk driver in New Mexico was racing up and down the road at speeds I wasn't comfortable with.

The Indian Reservation was odd; there is nothing to see for miles and miles and then all of a sudden you'll happen upon a tiny community. Then another lonely stretch of nothingness, only to repeat the cycle.

Somewhere around the 30-mile mark in the pitch black dark I had a sinking feeling.

"What if I went the wrong way?"

I compared my map against my GPS... my dyslexia in high functioning mode since I was fatigued and sleep deprived. I started to get confused not knowing which was right. The map said I was off course, the GPS said I was... well it looked on course, I thought it was? I don't know, I was so confused.

I panicked, I'd gone 30 miles into the Indian reservation and I was supposed to go through the Gila National Forest instead! I started to get very upset. It had taken me 3 hours to get here, mostly downhill, which means I had to climb back out of this place, back to Cuba and then back on the right route.

Cold sweat started to run down my back and my breathing was hard.

"I should quit. This is not worth it. I don't even know where I am! OH GOD I'M IN HELL!"

I knew I needed to get my wits about myself and it was then I remembered a mile back there was a tiny church with a light on. I thought I could go there and collect my thoughts, come up with a plan and rid myself of this panic. I turned around and pedaled fast due to the fear.

I grew up not thirty minutes from all those backwoods-Alabama-snake-handling churches you hear about. They exist, these crazy folks who willingly stick their hands in a snake aquarium and pull a rattler out and dance around with it. This was considered a true act of faith which some people called a "Come to Jesus" moment. From what I understand, they keep the snakes in a cold area and since they are cold blooded animals, it's safe to pick one up because their muscles are too constricted to bite you. Now get them warmed up and you better have a dear friend up above because you are getting bit!

But I digress ...

In the south the term "Come to Jesus" or a "Come to Jesus moment" has been adopted as a harsh realization of truth that has very little to do with the Christian faith, or snakes. Many of my school teachers growing up would take me into the hall, frustrated as all get out saying "now you and I are about to have a come to Jesus moment, son!" Sometimes I think handling a rattlesnake would have been easier than to be faced with some of my teachers armed with a paddle.

The church radiated an orange light and I said audibly

"I don't know if you're up there, but if you've ever wanted to help me out, now's the time!"

I buried my head in my handlebars and sleepily barreled off the road towards the church, hoping, no PRAYING I wasn't off the beaten path. That's when I heard,

"WHAT THE HELL? MAN WATCH OUT!"
I looked up and I was barreling through a dying bonfire with several

drunken people around it. I was so sleepy I almost went straight through the fire. I stopped, horrified and was breathing hard. I looked at the stoic and angered faces of everyone. They were all holding beers and liquor, one couldn't even stand up he was so drunk. They all peered at me with frowns and frustrations from nearly plowing into them. A large woman walked up to me, no smile and rather bitter expression. I thought:

"This is it. I'm going to get beat to a pulp on an Indian reservation and the first punch is going to be thrown by this stout lady."

My heart was beating through my chest, my eyes were wide and I could barely breathe. The lady opened her mouth and in a calm tone she said,

"Are you okay?"

I about fainted from the tense moment. I rested my weight on my bike.

"No, no I think I'm lost. I think I've gone 30 miles off course. I'm in this bike race and I think I've taken the wrong turn."

"I've been seeing you bikers ride through here for a week now. I don't think you're lost at all."

"Heeeey man, you...you almost rode through the fire! You crazy! YOU CRAZY SON OF A BITCH," A man said, blatantly drunk, laughing and putting his arm around me.

I sort of gave a nervous "heh..heh" and was trying my best not to pass out.

Lots of young children came out of the sole trailer. One kid was rather large, wore a beanie on his head complete with the propeller. The lady told the propeller boy "Go get this nice man some water and fruit." The kid came out with several bottled waters and a few bananas. "Eat," She said encouragingly. The other folks around the bonfire asked me questions about my bike, the race and where I was from.

These guys were great and some of the nicest people I met on the race. I told the woman "You know I'd been warned several times to be extremely careful when going through the reservation but I don't see the need to be worried at all!" Her demeanor changed and a worried look came across her face.

"Our area is peaceful, but the community before us is very bad."

"Oh? What do you mean *'very bad?'*" I said with a cocked eyebrow.

"There are just some bad people there, gangs and stuff."

"Should I be worried going forward?"

She struggled to answer for a moment.

"I'm sure you'll be fine. Another banana?"

After bananas, I bid everyone farewell and got back on the road, retraced my steps and started steadily riding through the rest of the reservation. It was now midnight and I easily had another 6-7 hours to go before I got to the next city, Grants. I decided it was time to take a page from Billy Rice and I popped open a Red Bull and downed it. It was horrific, how anyone leisurely enjoys that stuff is beyond me. It's possibly the worst tasting thing I've ever put down my throat (Okay, Ketchup potato chips are the worst thing I've ever eaten however Red Bull is a close second).

After I finished it off I sat and waited for the hyper caffeine magic to happen. The road was lonely, there was absolutely no illumination anywhere except for two tiny lights coming at me which quickly grew larger and larger. A car passed me at lightning speeds and was swerving all over the road.

"I'm going to die here."

I hopped on my bike and continued to pedal on and I realized I was shivering. I'm not sure why I was shivering, I wasn't really cold per se and I found myself talking out loud a lot and singing to the songs currently playing through my earphones. I saw another car come up and it passed me then slammed on its brakes. It stopped for a few seconds and I could tell they were looking back at me. Panic started to slide in alongside the jittery shivering I was experiencing.

"Please just go, just go, just go. Just go. Just please..."

I heard the screeching of tires and they took off disappearing into the dark. I tried to put my hands on the handlebars and they were shaking so badly I could barely stand it. I realized it was the Red Bull in my system, I was indeed awake but I was shaky and I could barely handle it. I put my body back on the bike and continued pedaling and when I would see the lights of a vehicle I would turn off all my lights and ride off into the ditch waiting for them to pass.

This went on for hours however when it got to be 4:00 am the vehicles ebbed and it was just me, myself and I on a lonely road. Despite two red bulls, sleep was fighting to take over. There were a few times I'd go into this dreamlike euphoric state and I'd snap out of it again. I had to climb a big mountain and struggled to keep the legs going as my brain was saying,

"You must sleep, I'm shutting things down. You're going to bed, now!"

I decided that it was time to sleep, so I found a bit of dirt that looked level and I started to unravel my camping equipment. I got my sleeping bag out and started to set up camp. As I did, my helmet light would shine in the area I needed it to so I could get the tent pole inserted into said loop and so on. I had the tent poles almost assembled when I saw something move out of the corner of my eye. I didn't think much of it because I was sleepy, then I saw another thing move on the other side of the tent. I scuffed my shoe at the movement and that's when I saw a third thing move. I looked down and scurrying left and right, there white and tan scorpions

I hate arachnids, I hate them so much. They freak me out and their eight-legged ick is just too much for me to handle. Panicked, I started stomping left and right trying to kill the scurrying little bastards. I'm sure there were only four or five total but to be safe, let's just say there were 80 billion of them scurrying about wishing to do me harm. I grabbed my sleeping bag and flapped it harshly hoping to God that no scorpion climbed into it. The same with the tent. Now wide-awake I decided there was going to be NO SLEEPING in a scorpion infested Indian reservation and kept biking.

My brain warred with my mind until I got to the top and then it happened. As I crested the mountain the sun peaked out and illuminated the New Mexico vista. It was possibly one of the most beautiful things I've ever seen in my life. Hues of purple, orange and pink illuminated the sky, the plains and hills were sandy yellow and white with the movement of antelope and cattle here and there. I just sat and kind of gasped then descended down. I looked at my GPS and noted that Grants was 12 miles away, that meant usually about an hour or a little bit there over. I started to go down the mountain at an easy speed; I kept going in and out of the dream state so I didn't want to take anything fast. As I was making my descent, my brain won over for a bit and I started to drift off to sleep. As I did, my front tire hit something stopping the bike and sending me sailing through the air.

I did a somersault and lay on the ground for a few moments stunned. I stood up noting just how much pain it was to make a quick connection of my body with the asphalt.

"Aaaah---oowwwww"

I limped back to my bike that surprisingly only fell to its side scuffing up the frame and that was it, nothing broken. I looked down to see what my tire had hit. It was a cow skull. Well, it was a cow skull that the coyotes had not finished dining on, which quickly killed any hopes of me having a hearty appetite. It was horrifically gross and was enough motivation to not dally around and worry about if I'd broken anything because I couldn't take the stench or the sight of it.

As I made my way down through the orange and purple hues of the morning, I saw a stirring in a ditch to the left of the road. A head popped up from the ditch, then another and another and another. It was Ty, Joseph, Kristen and Taylor. They were just waking up from camping and were stretching. Joseph planted his head in his hands as I gave a slightly offensive hand gesture and flew right past them.

The fall from the bike helped keep me awake for the next twelve miles or so and after passing the kids, I ramped up the speed hoping that Grants would have a "home vittles cookin' place" (despite the images of the cow skull) or something authentically Mexican that I could sink my teeth into. The only thing in the town that looked like it had a health rating of 60 was McDonalds.

Pre-Divide, I'd not eaten at Ronald's McRestaurant in over a decade. Now, including breakfast in Banff this was twice. The thought of putting that stuff they call food in my mouth is just downright horrific. However today would be the day I'd break my decade long (And that one time in Banff) stride of eating there and have a McOrgy of food. I ordered the "everything breakfast" and had a feast delivered from the Red Headed Clown. Where McDonald's lacks in health and nutrients, they make up for in taste, bad fats, carbohydrates and sodium. I ate until I about popped and then I went and ordered more to make it to the next town, the most magical and coveted town of all who race the Tour Divide: Pie Town.

Pie town, where restaurants exist solely for one thing, pie. Like the restaurant in Pie Town known as the Pie-O-Neer. I'd heard tales of this place with it's famous tasting pies ranging from any type of berry pie to cream pies. I couldn't wait, my mouth was salivating.

After around 18 million McCalories consumed, I rode towards Pie Town and the ride was wonderful. That was until a storm started to pass over me. I quickly got into my rain gear only to zip the last zipper and the storm shifted and moved another way. Being extremely sleep deprived lead to irritability, and I was there, welcome to Irritableville, population: Me.

I took off my all my rain gear when another storm seemed to be cresting over the mountains towards me so I started to zip up again only to have it change course and go another way. So I screamed some choice words at the storm, took my rain gear and threw it in the garbage and yelled

"DO YOUR WORST STORM! I DON'T EVEN CARE IF I GET WET!"

That was dumb. Really dumb.

Feeling vindicated, I rode along on the hot pavement for a while enjoying the temperatures and humming along to my playlist.

The road turned became a dirt road and that's where *"it"* began. What is *"it?"* Let's say that *"it"* is Karma cashing in on all the sneaky, underhanded and dishonest things I've ever done in my life.

If you're reading this, and I've wronged you in life in one-way or another? This is for you because this is where "Scott meets Hell."

As soon as I hit the dirt road the washboard divots in the dirt road showed back up en masse. "No worries" I said to myself and I got out of my seat and tried to bounce over them like I'd seen Eric do back at the start of New Mexico. It had worked in the past, but not here, the divots were too big and too far apart so it was like riding on hard crusted waves that jarred with each bump, especially with no suspension in your bike. On top of that, the sun was now in full heat mode and was baking me plenty good.

This is fine because I enjoy heat, but one side effect is that when it's unrelenting, it does tend to mess with your mood and your ability to keep focused because you're so hot and sweating profusely. I had to slow to a crawl to not get beat up by the washboard roads and it was painful bumping over each one like waves of stones in a cement ocean.

As I continued to bounce along in the hot sun I realized sleep was taking over and I thought it was indeed time to take a nap. I found one shady wiry bush to climb under and sleep a bit. With the hard packed and hot dirt beneath me I curled up in a little ball in the middle of the day and tried to sleep. I shut my eyes, and as soon as I did I felt something bit me. I looked down and it was a horsefly. I shooed it away and then closed my eyes and dozed off again. Then I had another biting at me. I shooed it away only to have it return bringing its relatives with him. I got up and screamed at the flies, shooing them all away only to have them fly right back on me. So I yelled:

"FINE! I'LL RIDE!"

I stood up and slipped on something squishy and fell into a nice organic landmine a cow had made. I screamed a few choice words consisting of 4, 8 and one 12-letter string of profanities. I angrily went to my bike to find any wipes I had left to hygienically get back to where my hands and body weren't a carrier for cow giardia, but I had none. I did what I could to get clean and angrily went bumping over the large divots in the road again.

There was a pretty nasty climb I had to manage as the sun batted down on my sleep-deprived mind. I finally made it to the top and as I started the descent, my front tire was sliced by a sharp pointy rock.

I heard "pssssshhhhh" and watched the latex squirt out of the tire, as it got softer and squishier.

"Come on, seal, seal up!"

The latex inside the tire was supposed to seal up any hole, it was not doing its thing. *"OH COME ON WORK!"*

Nothing. The tire went flat. I hopped off my bike and started to pump it up to see if I could get it to come to life before I had to take the tire off and put a tube in. As soon as I started pumping, the horsefly and his friends came upon me biting me while the sun continued to bake me.

Twenty minutes and thirty horsefly bites later, the tire finally held together.

"We're ooookay" I said trying to coax myself down a mental ledge.

And that's when I felt a thud hit the top of my helmet.

That storm I dared earlier? The one I said, "Do your worst" too? It was back and back with a vengeance. Quarter sized hail poured from the sky pelting my fly bitten, sunburned skin and since I'd ditched my storm clothes, I was going to have to tough this one out. I rode through it as best as I could and hit a flat prairie area where I heard the crack of lightning to my left.

"OH MY GOD PLEASE NOT LIGHTNING!"

Exhausted, I tried to muster every bit of my strength to go as fast as possible. The lightning struck all around me and I'm sure if I could have seen myself, I would have been as white as the lightning striking from fear.

In the distance, I saw a truck coming down the dirt road towards me. As I approached it, I waved at it to stop. It rode slowly by me as its elderly driver ignored me. I banged on the truck trying to get his attention. He stopped, creaked a window and said *"Wut..."*

I mean, seriously? *"Wut???"* There's the return of God and he's taking out his wrath on me for all the times I cheated on tests in school and your response is going to be *"Wut???"*

I yelled in the window: "HOW FAR TO PIE TOWN?" He responded with a mouthful of tobacco:

"Bout four or five miles. I'm gettin' wet, bye."

And he drove off.

I rode as hard and as fast as I could trying to keep my front tire from seeping out any more air and banging against washboard roads along with a merry host of lightning and hail striking everywhere. I rounded one corner of the dirt road and there in the distance I saw it, I saw the tips of some rooftops on a muddy road.

PIE TOWN!

I wasn't that far now!

PIE TOWN!

I could make it!

PIE TOWN!

I could do it, I could make it on adrenaline alone and not only that, there was a huge downhill to take. The downhill had some risk with it, it was a wide-open prairie and the storm was moving across it. However I had a 50lb bike with that weight and I could hammer it down the hill getting closer to safety and pie. I risked it.

That was *dumb*.

As soon as I hit the downhill I was caught by a headwind. Not just any headwind, but one that completely stopped me in my tracks. I tried with every bit of effort to pedal downhill. I've gone up sides of mountains that were easier. A bolt struck close to me and I screamed in terror, causing me to dig into my pedals and stand out of my seat on a steep downhill while once again getting beat to death with the washboard roads.

I looked over to my left and saw a rainbow. I screamed,

"Oh screw you rainbow! What are you going to do? Save me!?"

Instantly the storm passed and the sun came out. So in exasperation, I yelled at the rainbow,

"Oh and I guess you lead to Pie Town, too, huh?"

It did, right into the tiny, muddy little town. Pie Town, where I'd finally get a slice of hard earned victory pie.

It was closed. Everything in Pie Town was closed for the night.

I slumped down by a railing of a house and the rain started in again. I didn't even care. I was completely depleted. I honestly was just going to spend the night in the dirt at this point I was so frustrated and pretty fatalistic muttering things like:

"I'll just sit in this mud, this is all I'm worth."

Which is total hooey, but when you've gone 300 miles with just a bit of sleep, you don't think straight. It started to rain again, and then it got a little harder. I scurried to a house on the side of the muddy road and squeezed up against the edge in hopes the end of the roof would block some of the rain. I heard the door open from the house and a man looked down at me.

"Are you okay?" He asked.

"Well, no not really." I said covered in mud.

"You want to come in under our deck where it's dry?"

"Yes, thank you."

I wearily walked up to the porch and sat there shivering. The man went back inside and I sat down in one of the porch chairs giving my legs a much-needed rest. About five or six minutes later he came back out and said:

"Hey, my name is Jerry and we're having a family reunion inside but I'd love for you to come eat with us."

I didn't know what to say but one thing was for sure, I wasn't turning this down. I had been told that on the Divide there would be people who would give and give big, this person was one of them. I walked inside; it was homey, warm and full of people. In the kitchen there were tacos, burritos, cake, ice cream and mac n' cheese. They let me serve myself and I tried very hard to not eat everything in sight. They let me go for seconds and then thirds. Like most people who gave of their hospitality, they only wanted to be repaid in stories, so I told them my journey from Canada to Pie Town.

Jerry asked me a few "get to know you" questions.

"Where are you from?"

"Alabama" I said shoving more food down my mouth.

"You want a beer to wash that down with?"

"Oh god yes, thank you."

"Alabama huh? I used to live there, worked at the Red Stone Arsenal in Huntsville, you know where that is?"

"Is everyone that lives on the Divide route from Alabama or something???" I said then explaining about all the people I'd met close to my hometown.

We laughed and cheered to hometowns.

"So what do you do Jerry?"

"Oh I mountain bike for fun and I hunt antelope."

"Antelope huh, so how do you do that when they can outrun a bullet?"

"With a Shania Twain CD."

"I'm sorry?" I said confused.

"You know, a Shania Twain CD. You bring a boom box and Shania Twain tunes when you hunt." He said matter of fact.

I was confused,

"Okay, listen. So it's very hard to hunt antelope, you aim shoot, miss and they run off. But antelope are curious critters and for some reason they love Shania Twain, so all you have to do is press play, turn up the volume and they return. Then you get your antelope." I was completely bewildered of how a Canadian Pop Country singer that was famous during the 90's could attract one of the strangest animals in the United States.

I slumped back in my chair thinking about having to camp in that wet, cold ground tonight.

"I heard there was a hostel close by or something, right?" I said.

"That's just right next door. It's stocked with more food if you need." Said Jerry.

I looked out the door and sure enough I could see a home with tons of bikes surrounding it. I thanked him profusely and rode on over there. When I got to the door, it was like a homecoming with tons of bikers there cheering me on as I rode up. Eric and Mike were there as well as Joseph, Taylor, Kristen and Ty. Other racers I'd just met were there as well as a bunch of hikers, too. Joseph and Ty came up and to me and said,

"Man we are just in awe of your tenacity and never giving up. We just expect you to either be a little ahead of us or just right behind us. Great job."

I looked at both Ty and Joseph, they looked like beanpoles, they were so thin and tiny now. Taylor and Kristen looked about the same and me? Well I'd packed on a pound or two. This Tour Divide *"Eat Anything You Want"* diet? Yeah whatever, I've not lost a pound and in fact I had gained some!

"Did you hear? Matt Lee has re-rerouted us now, we're supposed to go through the Gila again." Said Taylor.

The Gila, I'd heard many of unpleasant stories of its barren, dry terrain and how harsh it was to get through there. I'd been dead set on the reroute, not because it was easier, but all the racers before me up until now had gone that way. I frowned and said,

"He can't do that, he can't split the race up and shove riders one way and then another set of riders another, it's not fair."

Everyone shrugged, not really knowing what to do exactly.

Day 22: Math

This would be my last night in a bed before the race was over. This was the last time I'd rest my bones and relax. From here I would not stop until I saw Antelope Wells, New Mexico which bordered Mexico - 300 miles left. We all changed into our bike kits and went outside. It was cold and I started shivering.

"The sooner we get on these bikes, the better," said Taylor and we rode out of Pie Town and down a muddy, wide dirt road. As usual, Taylor, Ty and Joseph got on ahead and Kristen once again hung back with me while her legs warmed up.

"We started the race together like this and here we are at the end like this again," I said.

"You're right," she said, smiling. As her legs warmed up, the distance between us grew.

I didn't want to be alone today. I needed to be around humans. I needed to laugh with people, talk. I didn't want to be alone with my thoughts—I was tired of me, I wanted someone to crack jokes and carry on. I worked hard to keep up and for once I did keep up, albeit I really had to struggle while it looked effortless for the rest.

During a break with everyone, I was reviewing the next part of the route on my GPS. I pressed my MAP button to see how many miles to the next set of services.

Data Corrupted, my GPS said.

"Oh no..."

I started frantically tapping on buttons, and it kept saying, data corrupted. This was terrible because I would be completely lost without it. Sweat started to form on my head. That's when I realized that I maybe had packed an extra data card that has the maps on it JUST in case this were to happen. I dug around different pockets looking, throwing things left and right.

Oh please, oh please, oh please do not have fallen out.

"Scott, you coming?" Said Ty.

"In... in a minute," I said, heart racing.

If I didn't find that card and they left, I was lost for sure. I grabbed the Ziplock bag that had my ID and passport in it. I flipped through the passport and something flicked out.

The spare map card!

I flipped open the back of the GPS and loaded it up. The GPS lit up and said, "Garmin."

"Yes, yes, Garmin, we know!"

The progress bar slowly inched along loading up what I hoped to be the maps.

"We're going to go ahead and go, Scott," Said Ty

"Just a sec!" I yelped in a panic.

The GPS continued to load when finally—*DING!*—the maps loaded, the Tour Divide route lit up again and I was A-OK! I hopped on my bike to catch everyone, which, at their speed, was no easy feat.

As I spent the hour trying to catch them, there were no clouds and the sun was beating down on me. I felt like I was going to crack, mentally.

Come on Scott, you got this.

Even my self-talk was not working. I thought about what Billy Rice said, how to just keep positive, but I was tired, alone, and sick of this stupid race. Then I heard a faint laugh, and murmuring in the distance.

In the distance there they were—Mike, Taylor, Eric, Kristen, Ty and Joseph. I didn't know if it was a mirage, if I was hallucinating, or if it was for real. As I got closer, it was real! It was them! I had caught the pack! Mike was quietly sitting by himself eating an apple. Eric, Taylor, Ty, Joseph and Kristen were deciding to take the original route, as was I.

"Matt said we are to take the original route now, dude," Eric said. "If you take the reroute, you're like disqualified."

"You don't know that," Said Ty.

"I don't really care, I'm just here to enjoy the Tour Divide, I couldn't care less if I get disqualified, and Matt did not say anything about disqualification," Mike said.

"You know what, I want to do the pure route," Ty said. "Who's with me?"

Eric, Kristen, Ty and Joseph moved over to the part of the road that led to the original route. Mike sat in the part of the road that went towards the reroute.

"Taking the reroute, don't care," Mike muttered.

I'm not one for taking the easy road. If you do something, you do it 110% and the right way. So what happened next was sort of an odd one for me.

"I'm taking the reroute," I said.

"Okay," said Joseph.

Then I went into rationalizing my answer.

"Because I'm tired, I've slept approximately 6 hours in over two days and I just can't take the brunt of going through one of the roughest parts of the Divide and it's not like I'm getting it that much easier here, we have a lot of climbing and you guys are still going to beat me and..."

Kristen interrupted.

"Scott..." she said pragmatically. "You don't have to apologize or defend your position. It's cool whatever choice you make."

There was around a 20-year difference between us, and yet she made one of the most mature comments that has stuck with me ever since. In fact if I took anything away from the Tour Divide, it was to stop apologizing for my decisions. I nodded.

"Well then there's just one thing left to do."

I went up to Ty and gave him a hug.

"Thanks man, it's been a helluva time getting to know you man. Keep in touch?" "Thank you for the laughs, the fun and letting me travel with you," I said to Joseph.

"I don't care if you beat me in Singlespeed, and chances are you will," I told Taylor. "You are one cool guy, man."

"Look if you beat me, it was fair and square." I gave Kristen a hug and tears swelled in my eyes because of the words she'd said just a minute before.

"Thanks, Kristen," I said, trying not to crack my voice. "You rock. Best of luck to you in life." "You too, man!" she said with a smile.

They hopped on their bikes and were gone.

Mike was finishing his apple. I made my plea.

"Listen, I get confused easily," I said. "You are way faster than me. Do you mind sticking with me until we get out of the reroute? I promise I won't ask for a mile over when I know where we are."

"Yeah man, the company would be nice," he said. "If I get ahead of you, I'll wait."

THE REROUTE

The reroute was not easy. Soft pebbly terrain and massive climbs, pass over pass. Mike would get way ahead of me, but wait at each mountain pass. He worked in Vail, Colorado and did all sorts of high adventure. During the Divide Race he had not really called in, made a lot of updates or anything about the Tour Divide. In fact he wanted to be quite anonymous about it and just wanted to finish it. We navigated through one area that was a little tricky making sure we took the correct forks in the road and not going off course. Hours passed, and we got to a point where I knew where we were and Mike and I said farewell and I watched him take off into the sunset like a bullet.

I checked my directions.

Left to Silver City.

I thought about that: Silver City, New Mexico. The last town before the end of the race. I honestly never thought I'd make it this far.

A minivan pulled up next to me and a lady in her 50s rolled down the window. When she opened her mouth she sounded *very tipsy.*

"Well where are you going all dressed up in that tight outfit, honey?" she said, laughing.

"Ain't seen too many boys run around in girl clothes like that!" said her tipsy friend.

"Well it's a bike kit, and I look manly in these girly clothes!" I said, knowing if I had gotten defensive they would have just laughed harder. "Hey how far is the next town?"

"'Bout eight miles, Honey," she said.

"Hey ladies, I need to try to make it to the town before 8 p.m. and everything closes," I said. "I need to get some supplies."

"Well you better hurry, but if you miss it, we all are having a dance at the local high school, and there's plenty of food there if you want to gobble some down. Plus I bet you could cut a rug in that tight outfit of yours!"

They both died laughing and sped off in their minivan.

I also tore off down the rolling hills of paved road, getting as "aero" as I could. My GPS was clocking speeds around 35 mph. As the hill came up, I glided nearly to the top before I had to pedal. I did this for 7 miles and then I started to see bits of civilization, which I knew I was close to the town.

Come on, come on!

I pedaled as hard and as fast as I could.

Come on legs! Don't give out!

The 7.5-mile mark came up. It was nearly 8 p.m. I had to make it to the gas station or whatever it was so I could refill supplies. I pedaled faster and faster until I saw a sign for gas and… a closed sign. I looked at my watch: 7:55pm.

"No!!!!" I yelled. *"No no no! I need food!"*

Then I saw several people walking towards the high school dance. Kids, adults and teenagers all congregated on a catwalk towards the *thump, thump, thump* of music. I actually thought about going. Real food would be worth dealing with the odd stares and looks in my dilapidated and smelly bike kit.

As I rode along through the tiny town I saw a sign: Italian Food and Video Rental.

It also said: Open. I saw Mike's bike and I dashed in.

"Yeah, gas station has been closed since 7," Mike said. "Something about a dance."

A waitress approached our table. "Wut you want to drink?"

"Coke, please," I said.

"We ain't got it for refill, it's by the bottle only," she said. "That okay, sugar?"

"Sure." I said. "Do you guys have Wi-Fi"?

"Yeah you can plug it in over there," she said, gesturing to an electrical outlet.

"No," I said apologetically, gesturing at my phone. "Wi-Fi. Like, the internet?"

"Oh. You mean one of those new-fangled PHONE THINGS that you can look at movies with?" She looked disgusted.

I blinked. The iPhone had been out since 2007. Now it was the middle of 2013. The iPhone was in its fifth iteration.

When I finished gobbling down my food, I packed my bike and saw Mike about to leave.

"Hey," I said. "Nice to see you again. Kick ass to Mexico?"

"Yep!" he said, smiling, and disappeared.

The ride to Silver City was beautiful, but I was extremely sleepy and weary. I popped one of my last Red Bulls. I still thought it was horrible, but at least by now my face didn't contort when I drank it. As I finished the last gulp, my helmet light reflected off a sign in the distance.

Welcome to Silver City!

Nothing was open. I rolled up and down the streets looking for signs of anything. The city was very cool looking at night but I could see nothing, no open restaurants; not even the McDonalds was open.

On one block I saw a lady kicking a drunk out of a bar. I rolled up quickly. She looked like she was trying to rush inside and avoid my seeing her.

"Eh...excuse me!" I said. She acted like she didn't see me and began locking up.

"EXCUSE ME!" I yelled.

"We're CLOSED!" She snapped.

"I see that. I don't want to come in, I just want to know if there was a restaurant or gas station open."

"A gas station about three miles away, that way," she said, gesturing away from the Divide route.

The quaint cool looking town of Silver City sort of got seedy looking as I continued That Way, riding into a not-so-nice area. As promised, there was the gas station, Open 24 hours.

There were a few sketchy characters hanging about outside so when I pulled up on my bike, I took out my cable lock and connected it to an old phone booth. I went inside and plopped down at a table to relax. I was obliterated. I finally got the strength to get up, get a Coke, some food then wearily sat back down nodding off at the table.

I sleepily studied my GPS. From what I could tell, I was around 90 miles from the border or so.

I'll just get some sleep at a hotel and then I'll bust this out! I thought.

Hotel pickings were slim. I wanted a shower so bad, my bike kit was shot to pieces and the bottom portion of it was so so caked with topsoil it was like strapping on sandpaper.

February 2013, The University of Alabama at Birmingham (UAB)

It was 8:30 in the morning and I walked up to the podium.

"Morning class, glad that most of you showed up for your assignment to your last project, I hope you've learned a bunch this year and hey… since you already woke up, downed your coffee and came here to listen to one of my oh-so-invigorating lectures, why don't you take the day off as I've got to prep for this big race and you need the time to study."

My class gave sighs of relief and bolted out of the classroom like mice to cheese.

I taught graphic design at the University of Alabama at Birmingham (UAB) and I always let my class go early during finals. I see no need to keep them there if all they have to do is research and design an awesome project on their own. I started turning off the mic on the podium and shutting down the computer when a lady named Rosie came in who worked across the hall from my classroom.

"Scott," she said. "Would you consider applying with us at UAB Digital Media? I think we can get you in part time."

I'd been freelancing for over 20 years, so working a "job" that required me to come in for a full 8-to-5 workday didn't particularly interest me. I've always been a free spirit, but the recession of 2008 had really done a number on me, and all I'd had left lately was just adjunct teaching for the college.

"I...uh...well, um, yeah sure I'll apply, I said, "Can I wear jeans and a t-shirt?"

"Yes!" She said laughing, "You can wear jeans and a t-shirt!"

Yes! I thought. No *"monkey suit!"*

I was both excited and apprehensive to leave the freedom of freelance, but the thought of a promised paycheck each month was also tempting. Rosie laughed, smiled and said;

"Mail us your resume and we'll get back to you."

I emailed it that night. Never heard back from Rosie.

Some Gas Station, Silver City, 3:00am

My phone beeped, I whipped it out and checked it, and it was an email from Rosie:

Hi Scott,

Congrats on the Tour Divide! I know you must be exhausted - but whenever you're ready to talk work, let me know. I finally got approval to move on the position if you are interested. Let me know a good time to talk.

Thanks!

Well this was fortuitous. I would be finishing the damned race tomorrow, and maybe I could go straight home to gainful employment.

I pressed, "shuffle" on my playlist and listened to the music piping through my earphones, it was the rapper, JAY-Z.

I think one of the most influential musicians in our time is the rapper from New York, JAY-Z. Sure, he may be controversial and many people are critical of him but in my opinion, his lyrics are pretty intense and he's quite the storyteller through his lyrics. He has a song, "Run This Town," with some of my favorite lyrics.

Victory's within the mile

Almost there, don't give up now

Only thing that's on my mind

Is who's gonna run this town tonight

I could drink enough Red Bull and power on, getting another easy 10-15 miles on everyone behind me before they even woke up and started moving. I could place in the 30s amongst the Tour Dividers! I could, in my own little world, run this town tonight.

I went to the aisles and grabbed some painkillers, lotions, and sun block. I knew it was going to be a hot day. The lady at the bar who had given me directions to this gas station had come in to get a soda. I didn't want to leave my bike unattended while I was in the restroom taking care of business. I went to the lady who was about to pay for her items.

"I'll pay for this if you'll watch my bike while I'm in the restroom for the next ten minutes," I begged.

"Uh, yeah sure!" She said stunned.

I went into the restroom and took a "prostitute's bath," which consisted of throwing water on my face and cleaning up with the sink's soap. I took off my kit and observed the damage.

Since I did not have my other kit when I needed it, the padding in mine had turned to sandpaper. With all the abrasion on the soft tissue, very bad things had happened. Things that included, um, dried blood, mixed with sweat and lots of bacteria. I had saddle sores giving birth to saddle sores. My kit was a mess. I grabbed the lotion and did what I could do to alleviate the pain, but in fact I could barely get my kit on without yelping a few times as the harsh abrasive cloth made contact with the soft tissue. I gritted my teeth and replayed the lyrics in my head:

Victory's within the mile,

almost there don't give up now...

I walked out of the restroom, thanked the lady, and walked out to my bike. The cool air and the blue hue of morning greeted me as I prepared to embark on my last journey. I knew as soon as I planted my butt down on the seat I would experience some immense pain. I gritted my teeth, hopped on my bike and tore out of Silver City.

Who runs this town tonight?

I did. I ran this town. I ran right out of it and never saw Silver City in the light of day.

Tarantulas and Asses

The lonely road was illuminated by the sunrise around 5 a.m. My light caught a large lump lying near the road. As I passed it I saw a trail of blood leading to something quite large. It was a donkey; apparently a car had whacked it. I heard the braying of other donkeys and looked up to see a hill full of them standing there.

Asses, I muttered and rode on and hit the desert.

The mixture of the sun peeking over the desert and the sandy white roads was stunning. It was just me, a few tumbleweeds and miles of windy deserted road. I was going at record speeds (for me) and plowing through it all thinking only one thing:

Get to Mexico.

As the sun rose around 8 a.m. the desert was bright and baking. A black critter scurried across the road. It was a giant tarantula. The only things I hate worse than bears, scorpions, and lightning? Spiders. I swerved around it. I figured if I'd tried to flatten it, it would have been my luck to have it jump up on me and bite me.

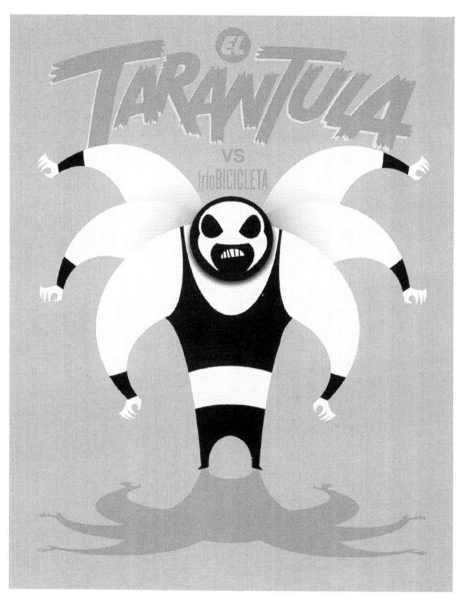

I continued riding through the hot sun, counting down the miles: 50 miles left, 40 miles left, 38 miles left... And then I saw it.

A busy interstate, with cars barreling down it. There was a sign that said, Mexico ahead.

I was so excited. I rode underneath the interstate and saw a "World's Best Gifts and Snacks" store inundated with people. I had 36 miles left until the Mexico border, one empty water bottle, and two full ones with a half-full bladder in my backpack. I had 3 candy bars and some nuts left. I had this. I ignored the store and kept riding.

I can do this, I told myself. *I can beat a slew of people and take a place in the 30's on the toughest mountain bike race in the world!*

I rode on and got on a flat road and saw the sign in the distance: Antelope Wells.

"WOO HOO!" I screamed. And then stopped to call my wife.

One month before the tour divide race:

Hey Scott,

My name is Fred and I'd like to support you after the Tour Divide. As you know, I cannot give you support during the Divide. I'm an old school biker and IronMan triathlete. Let me know how I can help.

Best,
Fred
--

35 Miles from Antelope Wells

"He's a hoot, baby," Kate said, talking about Fred while I made one last phone call to her. "I called him to confirm he's picking you up and he's hilarious! I think you'll be in good hands."

"I can't believe I'm here, 35 miles and I'm done!" I said. "And I'm in 39th place!"

Fred and I had exchanged emails back and forth right before I left for Canada. He said he wanted to help a Tour Divide racer this year and provide support and picked me. Fred told me he was an old guard mountain biker and Ironman triathlete. I was excited to meet him!

Kate and I both gave each other a tired but elated "hooray" to each other on the phone and hung up.

It's serious, it's time to get this race done with. Twenty-something days out on a bike is about to be over for me. I am ready for rest and relaxation!

I pedaled on closer to the sign that said "Antelope Wells," getting ready to see the "35 miles left." And then my heart sank.

Math was never my strong suit. Mom and dad hired tutor after tutor for me to see if they could help me with it. I never did grasp math beyond the basics. Get me into triple-digit numbers and I'm done for. Like, now. I had miscalculated, by like a lot. Antelope Wells was not 35 miles away. It was 65 miles away.

That convenience store was now a good 30-45 minutes behind me. I knew that everyone was heading my way, so I thought it best to hope for a town and get water there. I started pedaling and I could feel the heat sapping all the water out of me. Up ahead I saw a town and said, "Oh thank god."

I didn't care if the water was brown as long as I could refill my water bottles. It was a ghost town. Literally. It's a shame, too; it looked like it might have been a cool place once upon a time. There was a dance hall, a pink church, and what looked like a saloon. Now nothing but ghosts of memories lived here.

Along the subsequent long, flat road, I could actually see the mountains of Mexico ahead of me. But they were far, far away. Then I heard a car—no, a van—and it was speeding straight towards me.

zzzzzzzZZZZZOOOOOMMMWWWOOOOSSSHHHH

It about blew me off the road, it was going so fast. Then the hum of another van came behind me and wooshed the other way. This happened every 15 minutes and I guess it was some form of a taxi service. I was unsure. Occasionally a family from Mexico would ride by and look at me like I was nuts as I kept counting down the miles.

65...64... 63... This is going to take forever.

The sun grew to high noon. My GPS thermometer registered 111 degrees.

My second-to-last Red Bull had worn off. Now, having had very little sleep the last four days, I was starting to get extremely loopy. When I started to fall asleep on my bike, I devised a plan. I knew if I could jolt myself awake, I could ride a little farther.

I straddled my bike, crossed my arms on the handlebars and placed my head on my hands... and fell into a deep sleep. As I'd guessed, it wasn't 10 minutes before I fell over on the road with my bike flopped on top of me. Painful, but it did the job. I was now wide awake from the shock of falling. I would do this every 45 minutes to an hour to keep moving forward.

53...52...51...If I have to hear another song off my racing playlist I'm going to scream!

I pedaled on through the hot sun. All the water was sucked out of my mouth leaving it dry and begging to be wet. I had to ration out my water; I had one bottle left and a dab left in my camelback. All my food was eaten and the sun was unrelenting.

48...47....46... Are those zombie cows!?

I passed some cattle that looked emaciated. You could count their ribs; they looked at me saying, "Please, please have water." I thought any minute now they'd keel over dead from the heat.

43...42...41... Hey look at that, I'm almost to a mile for every year now!

I knew if I could get the remaining mileage below 40 I'd feel like I had hit a big milestone. I took the last slurp left in my Camelbak and as soon as the water hit my mouth, it was gone, dry, and I was having trouble swallowing. I saw a house in the distance, maybe they had water. The house was abandoned and falling in on itself, no water.

38...37...36... What I'd do for a four-gallon jug of beer.

I was starting to feel loopy again, so I did the sleeping-astride-a-stationary-bike thing again and fell asleep. When I did, and started to fall, I caught myself and jolted back awake, but that sent the last full water bottle I had flying off my bike. It smacked the ground, knocking off the lid and spilling all of my precious water.

"OH, GOD!" I screamed. "OH NO NO NO!"

In my sleep-deprived state, I did not screw the lid on tight, so it busted right off when it smacked the ground. I tried to not pay it any mind and continued to pedal.

34...33...32... I probably shouldn't panic.

I started to panic. I stopped and sat on the side of the road thinking what I was to do. I had no water, I was in the middle of the desert and it was 111 degrees.

C'mon, think, think, think.

I thought about grabbing a forked stick and doing the "Water Witch" thing for a chuckle. I put my head in my hands trying to think. I heard a car pull up.

"Hey!" a guy said in a thick Spanish Accent. "Hey, Amigo, HEY! You okay, bro?"

"I'm out of water," I said.

I heard the wife say something in Spanish. He looked back at me.

"Man, all I got is this half-dranked Slurpee," He offered. "You wanna it?"

I said yes and he handed it to me.

"Man, be careful out here in this heat, it's muy caliente!" He cautioned.

I gulped down the Slurpee. The sugar, cold ice, and water was divine.

I heard the roaring of one of those shuttle vans firing down the road at lightning speeds. I started to move my bike off the road but then I realized it was quickly coming and coming directly towards me.

Oh no...

I braced for impact, but instead the shuttle van only slowed down and the tinted window rolled down. I didn't see anything but a hand extend out and offer me a water bottle. It was cold, cold as ice, and I quickly stuffed it in my bag to keep it that way. The van never even stopped, just slowed down enough to hand me water.

Trail magic, right to the end.

31...30...29... How big can a desert be!?

This was it, 29 miles to go and 39th place was mine. I started pedaling and then I looked back just to see if anyone was chasing me down on their bike. No one. I tried to sit on my seat, but it stung so badly. When I looked down on my saddle there was a mixture of sweat and blood. The only thing I could do was reposition my butt on the saddle where it drove into the fatty tissue but didn't hurt half as bad as straddling it.

27...26...25... Apparently deserts go on for forever.

I had a sinking feeling that either Eric or Mike were catching up to me. I looked back again, and nothing. I kept pedaling on, nursing the water bottle the stranger had given me and trying to keep at some pace and speed.

13...12...11... I'm pretty sure I'm in hell.

I was almost there, I was almost at the 10-mile mark, victory was going to be mine and... and I looked back and saw a figure on a bike.

No, no no no! I thought and I pedaled as fast as I could.

9...Who is that?

8... NO! I can't have Taylor, Joseph, Kristen, Ty, Eric AND Mike come blazing past me! I've worked so hard to keep ahead of them!

7... Okay, when they pass me, I'll throw a stick through their spokes so I can...

"Mister Thigpen!" a gruffy male voice said on my left. "Not who I thought I'd see here at the end of the race. Helluva work there man."

I looked back. It was Rob Orr from Montana.

"Uh... ah... he... heeey," I said, surprised who it was. "Hey, hey, HEY! You're not Eric or Mike or the rest of the gang!"

"Nope, but I know they are some fast folks, so we better get pedaling if you want to hang on to your 39th spot," Rob said.

"Oh, I think you're about to clobber me, man," I said as I struggled to keep up with him.

"Naw, man. You've earned this. But I'm going to make you work for it. So get up on that bike and pedal."

I heard him click a few gears and I started to ride next to him hearing nothing but the whooom whooom whooom of his tires as he ramped up the speed. We accelerated to 12, 13, 14 miles per hour, then 15, 16 and that was where I was doing good to just hold that keeping up with him.

6... I've ridden my bike almost 3,000 miles.

Eric and Mike could definitely catch us if they were close, as they were infinitely faster than I was. I struggled to keep up with Rob. I wanted to back off, but he was unrelenting. I also wanted my 39th place, so I continued to keep up the hard pedaling.

August 2012, The Last Day of the TNGA

I woke up to the sound of a car passing by. It was cold, and I'd been sleeping on a pile of rocks in a parking lot. I looked over and Scott McConnell was still completely knocked out after the brutal two-day trek from South Carolina to Snake Creek Gap in Dawson, Georgia. We'd gone nonstop through the night, getting over the technically hard rocky trails of Snake Creek Gap, and we were only halfway. The sun was peeking over the mountains and we were on the last leg of the TNGA.

I was in the middle of the pack in the race, and I knew if we could keep up the pace we'd been holding we could secure the middle.

I nudged McConnell awake.

"Hey man, you ready to finish Snake Creek Gap?"

He jumped up immediately as if he'd not been sleeping at all and had to shake the cobwebs out of his head, laughing.

"Yeah! Let's finish this thing!"

We rode. Hard and fast, for hours. With a bike broken in three different places, waterlogged feet, and my body about in the same shape, we finished the meanest mountain bike race in the South to secure midpack.

5... I really wish Rob would slow down, keeping up with him is killing me. I mean we've got like 80 million more miles to go.

4... Rob just said something about his wife having some colas at the finish line. Colas? Psh... Lightweight. Give me something stronger, like a chair to set my carcass down into.

3... Who is that odd dude in the car cheering at us? He looks like Santa Claus! Crap, am I hallucinating? Did I just see Santa in a four-door sedan?"

April 2013, The Last Hour of the Cohutta 100

In 2012 I was disqualified from the Cohutta 100, my body was just not prepared for such a horribly hard race. 100 miles through the Tennessee and North Georgia Mountains is anything but easy. In 2013 I went back to settle what needed to be settled. It was the last hour of the race; I could barely stay on my bike and was, by far, the last rider bringing up the rear. Over half the racers that year threw in the towel and gave up, but I never relented and I never let off—I aimed to finished that damned hard race known as the Cohutta 100. I did. I finished last, and I had never been happier.

July 10th, The Final Stretch

2... Holy cow! I can see the Antelope Wells guard station! I... wait, where are the cheerleaders? The people throwing confetti? I just rode 3,000 miles, at least someone here has some confetti. There's that odd Santa dude cheering at us again, and he has no confetti.

1...I'm about to bawl like a chick watching "The Notebook" for the first time ever.

Like the start of the race, everything went quiet. There was only the beating of my heart.

In July of 2009, I couldn't button my pants because I'd gained so much weight. I told Kate, "Hey, I think I'm going to go around the block on this old bike if the tires are still pumped up."

A year later I bought my first mountain bike and promptly managed to break both collar bones, not to mention that I'd give out on any given trail after about two miles. Two years later I entered the Trans North Georgia, tying Scott McConnell for 15th to secure "mid-pack" in the hardest race in the Southeast. The year after that, I rolled in dead last on the Cohutta 100, 2013 and could not have been happier. In the two years of training for the Tour Divide Race, I lost 55 pounds, learned how to navigate harsh terrains and tough out long and grueling rides to arrive at Antelope Wells, New Mexico.

It was 4 p.m. July 10, 2013. I heard the faint whooomp whooomp whooomp of Rob's tires ebb as I powered on ahead and it happened: I crossed into Mexico. I finished the Tour Divide, the hardest mountain bike race in the world.

While I was ahead of Rob, his spot tracker registered before mine, thus pushing me to 40. I thought it was very fortuitous number, though, because for the Tour Divide 2013 I just placed 4th in singlespeed, 40th overall at the age of 40.

The Finish

I crossed the border into Mexico. I was so wild-eyed I kept riding until I saw the Mexican guards grab their guns and draw them out of their holsters. I slammed on my brakes and screamed, "Lo Siento!" Then I turned around and rode back into America. Rob was hugging his wife. Santa Claus was laughing and taking pictures.

"As ambassador to New Mexico, I welcome you to Antelope Wells," Santa said.

"Uh... okay, thanks. I'm waiting on a guy named Fred to pick me up."

He laughed; he had a pleasant Jolly St. Nick thing going on. He cleared his throat.

"Son, I am Fred!" Santa is an IronMan?! I smiled.

"Well, hey, Fred!" I said. "I cannot thank you enough."

"I've got some clothes for you, some shoes," Fred said. "Go on and get changed in the bathroom and then we'll get you a hotel room."

I grabbed the sweat shorts and T-shirt Fred provided, walked into the bathroom, and collapsed on the floor. Tears were streaming down my face, and I sobbed uncontrollably. I rocked back and forth on the floor, hugging myself—not out of self-congratulation, but because I'd just done the hardest thing in my life. I took off my shoes, socks, and kit. My feet were blistered; my chamois a bloody nightmare. Even putting on the fresh, soft sweat shorts was painful. I could hardly get my feet in the shoes Fred brought because they were so torn up. I winced as I slid one foot in and grunted with the other. There was a banging at the door

"Son, they are closing, lets get you on in the car."

I tried to walk and could barely get out without stumbling over.

Fred loaded up my bike in his car and then we hopped in. He turned it on and the cold air conditioner hit me.

"There's some sandwiches and drinks in the cooler, my friend."

"Uh, Fred, wow, I...uh, gosh," I said, fumbling for words. "Uh, thank you. Wow."

I could not form complete sentences. Fred's car tore off like a bullet out of Antelope Wells and went barreling down the same route

I'd just biked for 65 miles. No sign of any bikers, just a lonely road. As we were getting off the dirt road and about to start onto the main road, I looked to my left where I'd just biked.

I peered as far as I could, looking in the direction of Banff, British Columbia, Montana, Idaho, Wyoming, Colorado and New Mexico. My mileage showed I'd biked 2,853 miles, including the reroute. I was still taking it in when all of the sudden a huge storm of wind, dirt and what looked like tiny tornados all over the place were coming towards us from the right.

"What are those?" I said.

"Oh just dust storms," Fred said. "We get 'em all the time."

I spotted some riders in front of the dust storms going as fast as they could to avoid them. Taylor, Ty, Kristen, and Joseph. They had apparently gone in search for supplies to make the last 65 miles of the race and met up with this storm. "Stop! STOP!" I yelled.

As Taylor rode by, I tried to wave. He didn't see me. Ty and Kristen flew by too without seeing me, but then there was Joseph. I hopped out of the car and screamed:

"SOFT PEDAL... YEEEEAAAAHOOOOWWWWW!"

And promptly I fell over in the dirt. My legs had been pushing so long and hard that the cold air conditioner and rest had made them seize up and freeze.

Fred laughed. "You okay?"

I nodded and crawled back into the car. Fred took me to a hotel, paid the bill, and bought me pizza.

"Stay as long as you'd like."

"Why are you doing this?" I said, grateful but perplexed.

"Because people paid it forward to me when I was training for an Ironman many moons ago," He said. "Now I want to do the same, paying it forward to you. Maybe one day you can do the same for someone."

I got in my room and called Kate. We had a few celebratory moments and tears. Then I took a shower, ate an entire pizza pie, and promptly fell asleep. I read up on news updates of other riders. Scott McConnell had claimed first place in the single speed division. I messaged him and told him congrats, and he promptly sent back a message saying how happy he was for me.

"I was always looking over my shoulder, seeing if you were going to appear," he wrote.

Friendship knows no distance.

The next morning Fred picked me up, took me to his house, dismantled my bike, and took it to a bike store to ship it. This shop was pristine—not like the bike shops I'd been in where the employees had beers in hands and were fixing my bike up with a Nascar pit crew like speed.

"Hey." I said to the employees. "I just got finished with the Tour Divide and I need to ship this bike back to Birmingham."

"The... Tour...de what?" said the employee.

"You know, the big bike race across the United Sta... uh, it was a big mountain bike race." He had no idea what I was talking about.

Fred took me to the airport, still wearing the sweat shorts, sneakers, and T-shirt he had loaned me. I felt awkward boarding the plane with all the nicely dressed people.

The flight back to Birmingham was a series of layovers and delays. In Dallas, I stood in a food-court line behind a guy who was test-driving the new Google Glasses eyewear, taking pictures with his eyes. I watched him photograph his coffee and muffin and post it on the Internet.

Drinking coffee and trying not look like a homeless person, I got in the boarding line and felt very closed in—almost claustrophobic—and tried not to panic as I squeezed into the tiny plane. The flight back was an adjustment. I enjoyed the air blowing on my face, which only slightly helped quell the claustrophobia. I kept flashing back to various memories of the Divide. I wondered about Eddie, and if he'd finished. I wished I'd gotten to cheer for Ty, Joseph, Kristen and Taylor on as they crossed the border. I missed Kate.

When I exited the big bird, I could feel the Alabama humidity surround my body and enter my lungs. It was really difficult to process at first, since I'd been dealing with the arid dry air for so long now. I went down the escalator towards the baggage claim.

"There he is!" I heard a familiar voice say.

And I looked out into a sea of friends cheering and clapping. They had all made makeshift blue dots—my "avatar" from the online leaderboard, which they had all followed across their screens. The blue dots bounced up and down before me now.

I frantically looked for Kate, but I couldn't seem to find her in the sea of people clapping and cheering for me. Finally she emerged from the crowd to greet me.

I remembered our first date, when I noticed one of her most striking features, her soft brown eyes. I spent most of our first date just staring into those eyes. Today they are still just as beautiful.

Now, in baggage claim, we locked eyes again. I've never run so fast or hugged someone so hard. I grabbed her and squeezed her as tight as possible, and she kissed me. Only now, back with Kate, was the Tour Divide officially complete.

Bucket list: *check!*

--

Epilogue

April 2014

"Billy!" I yelled and shook his hand followed by a big bear hug.

"So good to see you man!" I was in Austin for the convention known as South By Southwest and Billy Rice was on his way up to Salida to consider what to do for his next big adventure.

Billy knew Austin well and said he was going to take me to an old steakhouse that actually used to be Austin's courthouse.

"Gonna get you to some real Texan places and not around these freaks here in Austin."

At the steakhouse we sat in a booth sponsored by Texas' Rick Perry (I think this booth seating was deliberately ironic; Billy knows darn well that my political leanings do not include Rick Perry.

I ordered chicken fried steak and Billy caught me up with his Tour Divide finish and how fired up he was to do this new race, the Trans America: a race from Oregon to Virginia.

"You're nuts," I said.

"Well, man, you should come with me," he said with a Texas-sized grin. "Or are you going to do the Tour Divide again?"

Time froze when he said that. I was instantly thrown back five years, to the time when, as an adult, I re-learned how to ride a bike. I couldn't even get up the driveway (a bunny slope) without pushing the bike, panting and sweating profusely, and feeling close to death. The next day I went back out and tried again. I failed.

Within a week I was able to pedal up the driveway. Two months after that, I decided to take the old rusty bike out to Oak Mountain State Park and attempt to ride on the road there. I pushed my bike on all the hills, startled when real mountain bikers barked, "ON YOUR LEFT!" More than once, people asked me, "Are you okay?"

Within six months I'd purchased my first real mountain bike and started riding the trails at Oak Mountain, one by one. Within a year I entered my first race and did my first century. Within three years I'd tackled the Trans North Georgia Race, survived the Cohutta 100, and finished the Tour Divide. I consider the TNGA, the Cohutta, and the Tour Divide Race the three toughest things I've ever done in my life. For me, these three races are my Triple Crown.

The long hours of training, time away from my family, the sacrifices I made in my job and the unbelievable amount of stress I experienced was a level I had never before endured, and never hope to again. Sure, I loved every minute of the Tour Divide, but once was enough for me. And: I promised my wife that I would be an ever-present husband and father after the TDR, and would not go back for round two.

I looked at Billy and smiled. "I think I'm going to give my feet and gills a whirl for a while..."

And that's where you can find me these days: running 5ks with my family or entering in sprint triathlons around the southeast while still enjoying the occasional mountain bike ride, for fun. I've gotten heavily into nutrition, fitness and health both from a performance and practical aspect.

For those of you who may possibly have a perception that I'm this wonder-cyclist that's all Billy-Badass, let me clear that up for you. I started from zero. I was overweight, sedentary, barely had done any exercise my adult life. I could not even ride up my own driveway. But I kept at it. And, finally, I could. That driveway was my first mountain I'd ever climbed, a suburban Everest with a menacing 2% grade (if that). I built off of that. My mountains got bigger. And one day I found before my front wheel the Tour Divide's 200,000 feet of vertical elevation. That's the vertical-gain equivalent to climbing Mount Everest—seven times. (Minus all that High Altitude Pulmonary Edema stuff.)

I'm living proof that you can do anything you want if you put your mind to it and don't give up. When you fail, you get back up and try again. But the biggest secret to getting over a mountain, whether a real or metaphorical one, is love and passion. Love what you're doing, and you'll do it one way or another.

Notes

Currently upon the writing of this book I am the only Alabamian to have completed the Trans North Georgia Adventure race and the Tour Divide*. I not only hope for that to not be a reality anymore, but I'd love for someone to come in and smash my record to pieces (I finished the TNGA in three and a half days and the Tour Divide in twenty two and a half days).

*There is some discrepancy to the Tour Divide claim. John Foster, who is originally from Decatur, Alabama (mere miles from where I grew up, but never knew him) has also completed the Tour Divide (and finished days before I did). He finished as a resident of Wyoming but he was born and raised in Alabama. I state this because it would be unfair to claim that title as the only finisher of the race from Alabama and not give John credit.

When I got back home things were a blur and I got a lot of attention as being the only Alabamian to finish. I of course liked the attention and never publicly said, "No there were two riders from Alabama, John was from Decatur and I was from Guntersville."

My apologies to you, John.

Contact Info

I'm rather chatty and love to meet and talk to new people. I also will do my best to answer any questions you have about the Tour Divide, mountain biking or gear recommendation for endurance biking. I answer to all these places:

Twitter: https://twitter.com/sthig

Facebook: https://www.facebook.com/sthig

Driven2divide.com

Softpedaling.com

References

Mike Dion and Hunter Week's "Ride The Divide" movie. This is what started me on my crazy journey to conquer the Tour Divide. The movie gives a nice overview of what it's like to race across the country.

Jill Homer's Book "Be Brave Be Strong" is a must read. She did the Tour Divide before me and was very much the inspiration for me to go out and do my own race across the Continental Divide.

Paul Howard's "Eat Sleep Ride" book portrays another viewpoint of what it's like to race the Tour Divide.if there are long website addresses that would make it difficult to justify the text without leaving big spaces between words.

Made in the USA
Lexington, KY
20 September 2016